CHRISTIAN PAIDEIA, VOL. II

CHRISTIAN PAIDEIA

VOLUME II:
A HISTORY OF CHRISTIAN EDUCATION FROM 500 TO 1050 AD

BRIAN WELTER

AROUCA
PRESS

Arouca Press, Waterloo N2J 0A5
© 2025 by Brian Welter
www.aroucapress.com

ISBN: 978-1-998492-62-6 (pbk)
ISBN: 978-1-998492-63-3 (hc)

CONTENTS

THIS IS THE SECOND OF TWO VOLUMES
on how the Church appropriated Greek and Roman paideia,
and developed it into Christian paideia. Christianity's unique
molding of pre-Christian paideia to fit its own needs brought
the seven liberal arts to their apogee.

While volume one reveals a basic unity within Christianity,
despite all the heresies and the Latin, Greek, and Syriac cultures — to name only three — the years 500 to 1050 AD saw
West and East grow increasingly apart, due in large part to the
lack of Latin in the East and Greek in the West.

Did these liturgical, spiritual, and doctrinal divisions affect
education? In some important areas, they did, although much
was still shared. The West was perhaps culturally richer because
it fully embraced the Latin authors, while the Greek-speaking
areas of the empire were indifferent to Cicero, Quintilian,
Augustine, and Boethius. However, the Greeks were richer
than the Latin-speaking world because they had the full heritage of ancient Greece and the Greek Church Fathers, which
the West had to read in Latin translations, when such texts
were even available.

Then there was Byzantine unity, and the domination of
Constantinople over intellectual life for all but the earliest
centuries of the empire, versus the disunity of the West, and
the shift of dominant centers of learning from Spain in the
south to the Irish at the northern edge of Europe and multiple
points in between.

This second volume tries to capture the common themes
that remained between West and East even while alienation
grew as each half of the former Roman Empire developed
separate identities.

While some of the more general chapters, such as the first
five, include both Latin and Greek writers, with greater focus
on the Latins, the last three chapters are entirely devoted to

developments in the East because they were so unique compared to those in the West.

Hopefully this book will appeal to readers from both sides of that unfortunate divide.

CHAPTER I

Early Medieval Teaching and Learning

Listen carefully, my son, to the master's instructions, and attend to them with the ear of your heart. This is advice from a father who loves you; welcome it, and faithfully put it into practice. The labor of obedience will bring you back to him from whom you had drifted through the sloth of disobedience. This message of mine is for you, then, if you are ready to give up your own will, once and for all, and armed with the strong and noble weapons of obedience to do battle for the true King, Christ the Lord.

— The Rule of St. Benedict[1]

Therefore we intend to establish a school for the Lord's service.

— The Rule of St. Benedict[2]

1.1 THE CHRISTIANIZATION AND MEDIEVALIZATION OF ANCIENT PAIDEIA

STRETCHING FROM ROUGHLY 500 TO 1050 AD, education in this second Christian era continued the process of the canonization of the curriculum that the Church Fathers had begun in the first five hundred years of the religion. The Fathers did this in the ultimate service of Biblical exegesis, which they wanted to be as faithful as possible to the author's intended meaning. Education therefore had to include an appreciation of the figurative language that fills Scripture. Church leaders had to turn texts from a non-Christian society, with very different and even contrasting beliefs and ethics from those of Christian society, into sources of their own culture. They had to achieve this without altering or misreading those texts.

---

[1] Benedict, *The Rule of Saint Benedict* (The Liturgical Press, 1981), Prologue 1–3.
[2] Ibid., 45.

Pagan texts often spoke powerfully to Christians. The ancient Greeks had promoted many of the same values that early medieval Christendom did. Plato's *Allegory of the Cave*, for example, provides an ideal of people's liberation from the walls of ignorance through education. True education does not enable a better comprehension of the shadows on the cave's wall, but a turning away from these shadows and towards the light. The educated can see things as they truly are, in themselves, and not merely as shadows inside the cave. This movement towards the truth that brings people out of the cave and into the light begins with the imagination before moving on to trust, and then further upwards to knowledge. Afterwards comes thought, and finally intellection. At this point, the soul knows the good and the true.[3]

This turning towards the light echoes the Christian ideal of *metanoia*, the total change that Christianity demands of the person. Ultimately, the ancient Greeks saw education as freeing humans by transforming the soul and thus guiding them towards truth and virtue.[4] The Christian, too, can claim liberty. Paul often spoke of Christian freedom: "For whereas I was free as to all, I made myself the servant of all, that I might gain the more" (1 Corinthians 9:19–23); "For you, brethren, have been called unto liberty." (Galatians 5:13)

The Christian appropriation of Greco-Roman *paideia* necessitated a close Christian analysis of the canon that had already been long established by the Greek and Roman schoolmasters. Canonization is a collective work of a society, not the achievement of individual and isolated scholars. With canonization, society gives the highest value and meaning to specific texts. This act confers on those texts a certain status. They are foundational to that society and act as exemplars for artists, craftsmen, and writers. The individual does have a role in this

---

[3] Ioannis A. Pottakis, "Socrates, Plato, Aristotle. Three Mentors in Ancient Greece," in *De l'Antiquite a nos jours: histoire et methodes de l'enseignement* (Albi: Presses du Centre universitaire Champollion, 2007), 37–44, 41. The Greek words for the steps are *eikasia, pistis, gnosis, dianoia*, and *noeisis*.
[4] Ibid., 43.

in the sense that canonization turns the visions, dreams, and aspirations of a person with a transcendent perspective, such as Socrates or Jesus, into the matter of the foundational texts that have specific cultural meaning. Such texts are deemed worthy of transmission to the next generation, typically through educational institutions and exegetical analysis.[5]

The essential decisions made by Church Fathers, such as Clement of Alexandria, Origen, and Augustine, profoundly impacted the development of Christian education in the Early Middle Ages, largely in their work of canonizing the pre-Christian texts. As antiquity and the Roman Empire became more and more distant to the dawning medieval age, what emerged in the Latin West was a contemplative, liturgical, ascetic, yet extremely imaginative and even at times jovial and playful culture. In the Latin West, early medieval education was an ecclesiastical undertaking that mostly concerned the training of boys and young men for church office. Education and religious vocation went hand in hand. Although medieval education was in complete service to the Church, its content was far from entirely Christian. The pagan classics continued to be a mainstay of Christian learning. Aside from the fact that education in the Greek-speaking part of Christendom was centered in one city, Constantinople, the content of education in the two parts of the former Roman Empire did not differ dramatically in the liberal arts and philosophy, with shared epistemological, metaphysical, cosmological, and psychological concerns and perspectives.[6]

The setting and social circumstances of this learning changed drastically from what it had been in the pagan cities of ancient Greece and then the Roman Empire. Early medieval Church life in the West was dominated by the monasteries, which

---

[5] Jan Assmann,"Cultural Memory and the Myth of the Axial Age." In *The Axial Age and its Consequences.* eds. Robert Bellah and Hans Joas (Harvard University Press, 2012), 399.
[6] Basil Tatakis, *Byzantine Philosophy*, trans. Nicholas J. Moutafakis (Hackett, 2003), 178.

over these centuries slowly came under the Benedictine Rule. The ideal of the contemplative monastic life heavily impacted education. Theology was dominated by a focus on the spiritual life, the Bible, liturgy, and the Church Fathers. While the essential reading was religious in nature, the love of the classic pagan authors persisted in classrooms and monasteries, at least where such places were blessed to have the necessary texts. Being focused on eternity, religious life emphasized the awareness of sin, penance, and asceticism. Yet this was a time of tremendous missionary activity that would not be seen again until the Portuguese and Spanish empires of the Age of Exploration. Irish and Anglo-Saxon missionary monks worked ceaselessly on the Continent, both among pagan Germanic tribes, in Gaul and in Italy through their teaching, writing, and personal culture. They enriched the Church's culture in monastic centers in already-Christian areas, including the establishment and improvement of libraries.

The knowledge of Greek declined in the West. It had likely never been deep to begin with outside of centers in the West such as Rome. Boethius and Cassiodorus were the last great scholars to include the language in their scholarship until the ninth century's John Scotus Eriugena, who translated some writings of Dionysius the Areopagite and Maximus the Confessor. The lack of Greek signified a widened cultural divide between the Latin and Greek worlds. This increasing estrangement had enormous consequences for Christian education and higher culture. By 600, many Greek Fathers were no longer read in the Latin West — at least not in the original Greek. Even Pope Gregory the Great (pope from 590 to 604 AD) could not read the language.[7] While Isidore of Seville had access to the Latin translations of a few Greek fathers, such as Origen and John Chrysostom, he too could not read them in the Greek originals. Bede, however, claims in his *History of the English Peoples* that

---

[7] Paul Lemerle, *Le premier humanisme byzantine* (Paris: Presses Universitaires France, 1971), 8.

the Anglo-Saxons read religious and secular texts in both Latin and Greek. This testimony is questionable given that the Anglo-Saxon, himself hardly familiar with Greek, would not have been a very trustworthy judge of the level of Greek of other scholars.[8]

Latin was preeminent as the language of the classroom and the western Church's liturgical, legal, and bureaucratic language. A linguistic gap arose between the educated and uneducated, the latter comprising the vast majority of the population. Commoners no longer spoke the language and received no formal education. Their familiarity with Latin, other than the colloquial versions of the language that would develop into French, Portuguese, Catalan, and so on, was limited to the liturgy. In the era's increasingly manor-centered and feudal society, much education took place in rural monasteries. Society was famously composed of *those who prayed, those who fought, and those who worked.* Formal education, such as it existed, was reserved for the nobility and others with sufficient resources who hoped their sons could become churchmen or perhaps lawyers or doctors.

Medieval education was a reflection of medieval society. Educational institutions retained the hierarchical order, as evidenced by the master-student relationship. Hierarchy established a sacred order, as the root Greek word indicates.[9] Monasteries

---

[8] Lemerle *Le premier humanisme byzantine*, 10–11.

[9] The entry for *hierarchy* in the 1911 *Encyclpaedia Britannica* (Column 13) states: "(Gr. ἱερός, holy, and ἄρχειν, to rule), the office of a steward or guardian of holy things, not a 'ruler of priests' or 'priestly ruler'. . . . The word ἱεραρχία, which does not occur in any classical Greek writer, owes its present extensive currency to the celebrated writings of Dionysius Areopagiticus. Of these the most important are the two which treat of the celestial and of the ecclesiastical hierarchy respectively. Defining hierarchy as the 'function which comprises all sacred things,' or, more fully, as 'a sacred order and science and activity, assimilated as far as possible to the godlike, and elevated to the imitation of God proportionately to the Divine illuminations conceded to it,' the author proceeds to enumerate the nine orders of the heavenly host, which are subdivided again into hierarchies or triads, in descending order, thus: Seraphim, Cherubim, Thrones; Dominations, Virtues, Powers; Principalities, Archangels, Angels. These all exist for the common object of raising men through ascending stages of purification and illumination to perfection. The ecclesiastical or earthly hierarchy is the counterpart of the other." Dionysius' definition of hierarchy is important to the thinking of the ninth-century Irish and Carolingian scholar John Scotus Eriugena.

took in boarders and also welcomed day students who lived with their families or boarded with locals. Luxury was scarce. In Ireland, most students built huts near the school. Larger schools would attract so many huts that roads would develop to connect these. Poorer students sometimes found room and board in the house of a wealthier classmate, and would pay his way by serving the family and classroom peer.[10] Medieval hierarchy impacted education just as it did everything else.

One sharp difference between medieval education and medieval society was that while the individuals comprising the vast majority of the population were tied to the land and lived their entire lives in the same place, students and masters were itinerant in search of learning and teaching opportunities. This itinerancy encouraged a common culture throughout Western Europe that only declined in some countries with the Hundred Years War (1337–1453), at which time the number of English students in Paris fell sharply. Latin as the *lingua franca* played a key role in itinerancy, as masters and students were able to discuss and read texts in the same classroom language, regardless of their regional and linguistic origins. As has always been the case, the most renowned masters were much sought-after.

John Henry Newman in *The Benedictine Schools* reflects on the extremely wide range of subjects that were studied, and how these did not substantially differ in content from what ancient pagan students learned:

> History furnishes us with specimens of the subjects taught in this higher education. We read of Gerbert lecturing in Aristotle's Categories and the Isagogæ of Porphyry; St. Theodore taught the Anglo-Saxon youths Greek and mathematics; Alcuin, all seven sciences at York; and at some German monasteries there were lectures in Greek, Hebrew, and Arabic. The monks of St. Benignus at Dijon gave lectures in medicine; the abbey of St. Gall had a school of painting and engraving; the blessed Tubilo of that abbey was mathematician, painter, and musician. We read of another monk of the

---

[10] Hugh Graham, *The Early Irish Monastic Schools* (Dublin: The Talbot Press, 1923), 94–95.

same monastery, who was ever at his carpentry when he was not at the altar; and of another, who worked in stone. Hence Vitruvius was in repute with them. Another accomplishment was that of copying manuscripts, which they did with a per-fection unknown to the scholastic age which followed them.[11]

Despite this wide range of disciplines, education in the Early Middle Ages (from roughly 500 AD to 1000 AD) was far less institutionalized than in the High Middle Ages (from 1000 AD to roughly the mid fourteenth century). It was intensely personal, with the tutor serving, most prominently, as spiritual father. Michel Lemoine divides early medieval education into three parts, the first dominated by the British Isles and lone individuals, the second by Charlemagne and the needs of the state, and the third by Charles the Bald, which sowed the seeds of a whole new culture.[12]

1.2 GREGORY THE GREAT'S *REGULA PASTORALIS*

The highest minds of the Church were keenly interested in raising the intellectual level of priests. Pope Gregory the Great's *Regula pastoralis* was tremendously influential in the Early Middle Ages, especially among Carolingian scholars such as Rabanus Maurus, because it addressed this need. Pope Gregory begins his treatise by asserting the requirement for the proper spiritual training of priests and expressing frustration over the failure of this training:

> No one presumes to teach an art till he has first, with intent meditation, learned it. What rashness is it, then, for the unskilful to assume pastoral authority, since the government of souls is the art of arts![13] For who can be ignorant that the sores of the thoughts of men are more

---

[11] Newman, *The Benedictine Schools* in *A Benedictine Education* (Providence: Cluny, 2020), 81.
[12] Michel Lemoine, "Les auteurs classiques dans l'enseignement médiéval : l'état de la question," *Histoire de l'éducation*, no. 74 (1997): 39–58, 46.
[13] The term "art of arts" was often used by Christian educational authorities to refer either to dialect or philosophy.

occult than the sores of the bowels? And yet how often do men who have no knowledge whatever of spiritual precepts fearlessly profess themselves physicians of the heart, though those who are ignorant of the effect of drugs blush to appear as physicians of the flesh![14]

Pope Gregory castigates phony teachers who prize the social status and care nothing for the responsibilities that come with teaching. They care about the outward appearance of a teacher so as to act superior over others, as described in Matthew 23:6–7. Yet all the while they are not able to carry out the pastoral duties required of their office. He notes the confusion of language itself "when one thing is learned and another taught."[15] While many Church Fathers associate poor education with lack of reason, and lack of reason with heresy, Gregory is more direct. Uneducated Church leaders leave the faithful burdened by their own sins.[16]

Yet surprisingly, education cannot solve all problems, it seems. In the second chapter, Gregory reports on a harsh reality in the Church. Not all clergymen, it turns out, have a pure heart and the heart of a pastor. They have studied, but for the wrong reasons, and even if they have studied, they do not truly know what they teach because they fail to practice it: "There are some also who investigate spiritual precepts with cunning care, but what they penetrate with their understanding they trample on in their lives: all at once they teach the things which not by practice but by study they have learned; and what in words they preach by their manners they impugn. Whence it comes to pass that when the shepherd walks through steep places, the flock follows to the precipice."[17] Education, in other words, does not always guarantee

---

[14] Gregory the Great, *The Book of Pastoral Rule*, trans. George Democopoulos (Crestwood, NY: St. Vladimir's Seminary Press, 2007), Book 1, Chapter 1, 29.
[15] Ibid., 29. The reference to Matthew 23:6–7 is: "And they love the first places at feasts, and the first chairs in the synagogues, and salutations in the market place, and to be called by men, Rabbi."
[16] Ibid., 30.
[17] Ibid., 31.

a virtuous and genuine leader. And intellectual knowledge does not guarantee that what has been learned has actually affected the deepest parts of a person.

Gregory pursues this issue with strong imagery and then a Biblical reference. The failure of education to live up to the necessary standards causes terrible harm to the faithful:

> For indeed the shepherds drink most pure water, when with a right understanding they imbibe the streams of truth. But to foul the same water with their feet is to corrupt the studies of holy meditation by evil living. And verily the sheep drink the water fouled by their feet, when any of those subject to them follow not the words which they hear, but only imitate the bad examples which they see. Thirsting for the things said, but perverted by the works observed, they take in mud with their draughts, as from polluted fountains. Hence also it is written through the prophet, *A snare for the downfall of my people are evil priests* (Hosea 5:1; 9:8).[18]

The priesthood, in other words, is a heavy weight, and its members need to be not only well-educated, but also virtuous. Many people will suffer spiritually if priests fall short. Gregory warns that the most harmful individuals for the Church are those who hold clerical office, and therefore have "the name and rank of sanctity," but who act perversely.[19]

In Book III, Gregory instructs the reader how the well-instructed, by which he means Church leaders, ought to be admonished. They have to be reminded that they have the duty of living up to the ideals that they preach:

> Those who understand indeed aright the words of the Law, but speak them not humbly, are to be admonished that, in divine discourses, before they put them forth to others, they should examine themselves; lest, in following up the deeds of others, they leave themselves behind; and lest, while thinking rightly of all the rest of Holy Scripture, this only thing they attend not to, what is said in it against the proud. For he is indeed a poor and unskilful physician, who would fain heal another's disease while ignorant of that from

---

[18] Gregory the Great, *The Book of Pastoral Rule*, Book I, Chapter 2, 31.
[19] Ibid.

> which he himself is suffering. Those, then, who speak not
> the words of God humbly should certainly be admonished,
> that, when they apply medicines to the sick, they see to the
> poison of their own infection, lest in healing others they
> die themselves. They ought to be admonished to take heed,
> lest their manner of saying things be at variance with the
> excellence of what is said, and lest they preach one thing
> in their speaking and another in their outward bearing.[20]

Early medieval education was ultimately virtue education. Education was successful if it developed saintly Church leaders, and a failure if it produced hypocrites. Gregory has little concern here for masters of dialectic, Greek and Latin poetry, or rhetoric.

1.3 THE RELIGIOUS NATURE OF EDUCATION

Church leaders strived to live up to Gregory's message throughout the Early Middle Ages while also bringing Greek paideia to its fullest potential. The ancients had long developed and possessed a culture of reading, but the Early Middle Ages developed a refreshed and distinctly *medieval* culture of the book that was built on a Christian foundation, with Augustinian and Benedictine pillars. Monks were called to lead a life of contemplation, of *ora et labora* (prayer and work), as outlined in the most important *Rule* of the Middle Ages. In establishing manual labor as a central feature of monastic life, Benedict did not aim to make monks into great scholars, teachers, or other socially-beneficial workers. He aimed to get them to perform penance. Out of this penitential life emerged scholars, teachers, and others who aided society.[21] This book culture, which was based much more on grammar than on dialectic or rhetoric, was itself contemplative. It was part of a larger spiritual and liturgical landscape.

Given the Benedictine contribution to society, the economy, and educational development, one author rightfully observes that "the long and distinguished history of Benedictinism has

---

[20] Gregory the Great, *The Book of Pastoral Rule*, Book 3, Chapter 24, 160.
[21] Newman, *The Mission of St. Benedict in A Benedictine Education*, 30.

at times been almost coterminous with the history of Europe."[22] In 2008, at the Collège de Bernadines in Paris, another author, Pope Benedict XVI, reflected on this centuries-long contribution to education and to Europe's very identity. He notes that, during the anarchy caused by the movements of peoples throughout the old Roman Empire that led to new political realities, the monasteries became storehouses of Greco-Roman culture. In this way, they enabled a new culture to germinate and take root, based in large part on past achievements.[23] The Church succeeded at creating a wholly Christian educational culture from the pagan legacy.

The Pope notes the special relationship between education and Benedictine spirituality. It was a Christian education, but one that remained faithful to the pagan ideals while fully developing them for Christendom. The Benedictines reinvigorated these ideals and gave them a Christian sense. The whole process took on a life of its own, The Pope echoes John Henry Newman in arguing that they had not deliberately set out to build this new culture, either through preservation of the old or the establishment of something new. They only sought God.[24]

Pope Benedict identifies the precise gift that the Benedictines and Christianity gave to Greco-Roman paideia, the new thing about which the Greeks and Romans had never heard:

> They [the Benedictines] wanted to go from the inessential to the essential, to the only truly important and reliable thing there is. It is sometimes said that they were "eschatologically" oriented. But this is not to be understood in a temporal sense, as if they were looking ahead to the end of the world or to their own death, but in an existential sense: they were seeking the definitive behind the provisional. *Quaerere Deum*: because they were Christians, this was not an expedition into a trackless wilderness, a search leading them into total darkness.[25]

---

[22] Habiger Institute. *The Heart of Culture* (Providence, R. I.: Cluny, 2020), 40.
[23] Benedict XVI, *Address of His Holiness Benedict XVI. Friday, 12 September 2008* (Rome: Editrice Libreria Vaticana, 2008).
[24] Ibid.
[25] Ibid.

Books and learning provided guidance to the monks because of the signposts that God had left in Scripture. The vital place of God's Word in their lives gave fresh significance to the study of language. Benedict XVI echoes Jean Leclercq's point that "eschatology and grammar are intimately connected with one another in Western monasticism." The Benedictine longing for God includes the love of language in its many dimensions, including grammar and rhetoric.[26] Education and reading took on far greater significance than the Greeks or Romans had ever given these. Education and reading now had an otherworldly sense.

Western Christians, led by the Benedictines, brought something previously unknown into the study of language, even if language had also been a passion for the pagan Greeks and Romans. These precursors to the Christians had nevertheless failed to take the step of creating the trivium as a coherent unit, with its particular vocation. Only Christians, with their influence on philosophy and their peculiar Trinitarian and incarnational theology, could do this. Benedict XVI noted that because God speaks to us through the Bible, we need to understand the deepest mysteries and truths of language, including word use and the construction of sentences (both of which are grammar issues), and the various ways it can express things (the domain of rhetoric). Therefore, through the Christian search for God in the Bible, the liberal arts and philosophy were given new life and significance.[27]

This passion for language spontaneously and organically developed a material learning culture that served as the backbone to the closely connected educational culture. Because those who were seeking God required a certain linguistic culture, monasteries built libraries to house the required texts, and schools to develop the relevant intellectual skills.[28] The specific nature of this education came from its specific purpose. Benedict defines *eruditio* as "the formation and education

---

[26] Benedict XVI, *Address of His Holiness Benedict XVI.*
[27] Ibid.
[28] Ibid.

of man—a formation whose ultimate aim is that man should learn how to serve God," but notes that *eruditio* also involves the development of reason. Reason aids us "to perceive, in the midst of words, the Word itself."[29]

The seven liberal arts, along with philosophy, science, and theology, all served the same Master: God. The study of these disciplines all moved towards the same end, to the greater truth and virtue of this Master. In a monastery, Greek paideia supported the Christian belief in an environment that challenged "the prideful tendencies of the human intellect." This made the monastery "the heir, even in a sense the fufillment, of Plato's Academy," even though the monastery's vocation was distinct from that of Athens' philosophical schools.[30] The ideas and methods of the ancient writers were the tools of the developing Christian educational culture. The light that they could shine on the truth made them much-loved instruments. In other words, the monks brought this ancient learning to its apogee by contemplating the truth of Revelation. Cicero's rhetoric, which had been mostly limited to the law courts, politics, and classroom rhetorical display, now served the Biblical exegesis that played a vital role in evangelization, even if the monasteries prioritized silence over oratorical flourish. Grammar was not only concerned with the right usage of language, but, more importantly, with the correct interpretation of Scripture. The Church's task of preaching eternal life depended on these intellectual tools.

1.4 THE EDUCATION OF SAINTS

According to Bede, students in Ireland received individualized instruction, often by visiting one master's cell after another. The English saint notes the generosity of the teachers, who "willingly received them all, and took care to supply them with daily food without cost, as also to furnish them with books

---

[29] Benedict XVI, *Address of His Holiness Benedict XVI.*
[30] Habiger Institute, *The Heart of Culture*, 43.

for their studies, and teaching free of charge."[31] This type of individualized education included spiritual training. The success of education, as reflected in the *Life of St. Declan of Ardmore*, was measured more by the resulting piety of the student (in the classroom and later as an adult) than by the ability to cite Latin or Greek authors from memory or to wield dialectic in a debate:

> Declan remained a long time with Dioma, the holy man we have named, and acquired science and sanctity and diversity of learning and doctrine, and he was prudent, mild, and capable so that many who knew his nobility of blood came when they had heard of the fullness of his sanctity and grace. Moreover they submitted themselves to him and accepted his religious rule. Declan judged it proper that he should visit Rome to study discipline and ecclesiastical system, to secure for himself esteem and approbation thence, and obtain authority to preach to the (Irish) people and to bring back with him the rules of Rome as these obtained in Rome itself. He set out with his followers and he tarried not till he arrived in Rome where they remained some time.[32]

The master, simultaneously confessor and spiritual father, took responsibility for the well-being of the student's soul. This fatherhood included strict discipline. The above extract also indicates the importance of Rome, as travel there from Ireland would have been no little undertaking. Yet such an education would undoubtedly have added to the status of a churchman and scholar once he was back in Ireland. Medieval scholars kept a close eye on the educational heritage of one another.

A holy tutor was prized above all else because of the ascetic training and even mystagogical education that he provided. Mystagogy refers to the teaching on the mysteries of faith and spirituality, especially the sacraments. The *Life of St. Declan of Ardmore* depicts this religious nature of education. In addition

---

[31] Bede, *Ecclesiastical History of the English Nation*, trans. A. M. Sellar (London: George Bell and Sons, 1907), Book 3, xxvii.
[32] Anonymous, *Life of St. Declan of Ardmore*, trans. P. Power (London: Irish Texts Society, 1914).

to this required holiness, the following extract, on the life of the fifth century saint (though the earliest manuscript of the *Life* is from centuries later), indicates that the scholarly years of wandering in the search for this ascetic training could begin at a much younger age than fourteen:

> On the completion of seven years Declan was taken from his parents and friends and fosterers to be sent to study as Colman had ordained. It was to Dioma they sent him, a certain devout man perfect in the faith, who had come at that time by God's design into Ireland having spent a long period abroad in acquiring learning. He (Dioma) built in that place a small cell wherein he might instruct Declan and dwell himself. There was given him also, to instruct, together with Declan, another child,... Cairbre Mac Colmain, who became afterwards a holy learned bishop. Both these were for a considerable period pursuing their studies together.[33]

That Cairbre Mac Colmain later rose to the episcopacy, assuming this was due to his holy life, demonstrated to the medieval mind the success of this instruction.

Boys were expected to grow in holiness. Huneberc of Heidenheim wrote in admiring terms about the young Willibald, a future saint, in the eighth century:

> This boy of unassuming manners was initiated and perfectly trained in sacred studies. He gave careful and assiduous attention to the learning of the psalms and applied his mind to the examination of the other books of Holy Writ. Young though he was in age, he was advanced in wisdom, so that in him through the divine mercy the words of the prophet were fulfilled: "Out of the mouths of babes and sucklings thou hast perfected praise." Then, as his age increased and his mental powers developed, and more so as the growth of divine grace kept pace with his increasing strength and stature, he devoted his energies to the pursuit of divine love. Long and earnest meditation filled his days. Night and day he pondered anxiously on the means of monastic perfection and the importance of community life, wondering how he

---

[33] Anonymous, *Life of St. Declan of Ardmore.*

might become a member of that chaste fellowship and share
in the joys of their common discipline.[34]

While one wonders if the future saint was really as pious as
Huneberc wants readers to believe, the ideal was significant.
Masters, students' parents, and parish priests likely looked for
increased signs of saintliness in the schoolboy. The key words
in Huneberc's letter include *unassuming manners* (denoting
humility, a much-prized virtue for all Christians of the era),
careful and assiduous attention (the meticulous study habits
that were expected, if not demanded), *wisdom* (which along
with holiness was the key virtue to be acquired in what was
really virtue education), *long and earnest meditation* (referring
to the contemplative life that was at the center of monasticism),
night and day (a recurring theme of monastic spiritual texts,
the desire to pray not only in the day, but long into the night;
monastic oblates would have received training in this holy sleep-
deprivation), and *chaste* (as the student was a future cleric, if
not one already, chastity was a basic requirement).

We also read of the master-student relationship in Alcuin's *Life of Willibrord*, which depicts the master as a spiritual
father as much as an academic tutor. The primary purpose
of education was to cultivate the virtues through training in
ascetic practices such as fasting, prayer, and Bible study. The
key vocation of the student was obedience to holy men, not
primarily bookishness or scholarly work:

> When this youth, as highly endowed with sacred learn-
> ing as he was with self-control and integrity, reached the
> twentieth year of his age he felt an urge to pursue a more
> rigorous mode of life and was stirred with a desire to travel
> abroad. And because he had heard that schools and learning
> flourished in Ireland, he was encouraged further by what
> he was told of the manner of life adopted there by certain
> holy men, particularly by the blessed bishop Ecgbert, to
> whom was given the title of Saint, and by Wachtberg, the
> venerable servant and priest of God, both of whom, for

---

[34] Huneberc of Heidenheim, *The Hopoeporican of St. Willibald*, trans. Canon
W. R. Brownlow (London, 1895).

love of Christ, forsook home, fatherland and family and retired to Ireland, where, cut off from the world though close to God, they lived as solitaries enjoying the blessings of heavenly contemplation.

In the next part, the desire to imitate holy men is noteworthy. We are repeatedly reminded by these early medieval sources that innovation, creativity, and independence were not prized. The main purpose of Christian education was training in the holy life, as outlined by Christian tradition:

> The blessed youth wished to imitate the godly life of these men and, after obtaining the consent of his abbot and brethren, hastened quickly across the sea to join the intimate circle of the said fathers, so that by contact with them he might attain the same degree of holiness and possess the same virtues, much as a bee sucks honey from the flowers and stores it up in its honeycomb. There among these masters, eminent both for sanctity and sacred learning, he who was one day to preach to many peoples was trained for twelve years, until he reached the mature age of manhood and the full age of Christ.[35]

This objective remained unchanged throughout the medieval centuries. It was vital to train children for the holy life.

Bede pays a complement to the spiritual maturity of the boy who would become Benedict Biscop, noting that as a boy he had "the heart of a man of ripe age even from the time of his boyhood, for in the ways of his life he was beyond his years."[36] Yet it seems that education was a lifelong pursuit. Bede mentions the seventh century noblewoman Hilda, Abbess of the convent in Whitby, who organized her monastery with direction from Church leaders. Ironically, it seems that these leaders came to be educated in the spiritual life by her. Churchmen such as Bishop Aidan "frequently visited and diligently instructed her, because

---

[35] Alcuin, *The Life of St. Willibrord*, trans. A. Grieve, in *Willibrord, Missionary in the Netherlands* (London, 1923).
[36] Bede, "Lives of the Abbots and Letter to Egbert," in *Historical Works*, Volume 2 (Cambridge, Massachusetts: Harvard University Press, 1963), 392–489, 393.

of her innate wisdom and inclination to the service of God."[37]
It seems they were the students, and she the master. Much
spiritual education, such as from Abbess Hilda, was informal.

As we have seen with Pope Gregory's *Regula pastoralis*,
priestly education was a serious concern for Church authorities.
The topic was repeatedly brought up at official gatherings. In
Provence, the Second Council of Vaison in 529 AD instructed
parish priests to establish schools for the development of Christian virtue and instruction in the Psalms, other books of the
Bible, and the law of the Lord so that these students would be
worthy for the priesthood.[38] This strict, goal-oriented training
did not encourage the philosophical speculation that would
become the hallmark of universities in later medieval centuries.
This type of priesthood training was closer to an apprenticeship than to the seminary or university education that would
develop from the twelfth century. It therefore paralleled in
some ways the training of Benedictine monks, which was also
largely hands-on. The training of monks included, in particular,
the socialization that turned an individual into a member of a
religious brotherhood through communal activities, imitation of
proper behavior, and correction from more experienced members.[39] Such shared activities included communal reading, as
at the dinner table, when one of the brothers would read from
the *Rule*, Scripture, or a hagiography at the reading desk, the
analogium, while the others ate in silence. Only those possessing
a strong voice and fluency in Latin could carry out this task.
Thick skin and humility also helped because a mispronounced
syllable could lead to harsh criticism.[40]

---

[37] Bede, *Ecclesiastical History of the English Nation*, Book 4, Chapter 23.
[38] Henri-Irénée Marrou, *Histoire de l'éducation dans l'Antiquité. 2. Le monde romain* (Paris: Seuil, 1948), 157.
[39] Fredrick J. Long, *Ancient Rhetoric and Paul's Apology* (Cambridge: Cambridge University Press, 2004), 534.
[40] J. M. Clark, *The Abbey of St Gall as a Centre of Literature and Art* (Cambridge: At the University Press, 1926), 80.

CHAPTER 2

A Christian Culture
of Reading

*The word does not lead to a purely individual path of
mystical immersion, but to the pilgrim fellowship of faith.
And so this word must not only be pondered, but also
correctly read.*

— Benedict XVI[1]

*With God's help and by His grace I shall expose the truth
that truth which destroys deceit and puts falsehood to flight
and which, as with golden fringes, has been embellished and
adorned by the sayings of the divinely inspired prophets, the
divinely taught fishermen, and the God-bearing shepherds
and teachers that truth, the glory of which flashes out from
within to brighten with its radiance,when they encounter
it, them that are duly purified and rid of troublesome
speculations.*

— John of Damascus[2]

Adnexique globum zephyrique kanna secabant.

— Anonymous[3]

2.1 BASICS OF TEACHING

EARLY MEDIEVAL CHRISTIANS ORGA-
nized book reading in a more communal, coherent, and
logical way than it had been under the Greeks and
Romans. A single organization, the Church, though operating in
many thousands of independently-functioning units, including
parish churches, collegiate churches, monasteries, cathedrals, and

[1] Benedict XVI, *Address of His Holiness Benedict XVI* (Rome: Editrice Libreria
Vaticana, 2008).
[2] John of Damascus, *The Fount of Knowledge* in *Saint John of Damascus: Writings*,
trans. Frederic H. Chase (New York: Fathers of the Church, Inc., 1958), 5–6.
[3] Clark, *The Abbey of St Gall as a Centre of Literature and Art*, 98.

schools, relied on a select group of texts for similar assignments and interpreted them in similar ways. In both East and West, this all took place with the same language, Greek or Latin (with Syriac, Coptic, and other local languages also used in parts of the Byzantine Empire). This Church-sponsored book culture was heavily impacted by all of Church life, not just by education, and made progress throughout the West, which had fallen into serious cultural decay, or at least a decay in cultural unity. The Benedictines played an outsized role in this culture, though other centers of influence, such as the papacy and Rome, or certain political leaders, such as Charlemagne and Edward the Confessor, contributed significantly at certain times. Under the reign of such leaders, education and book culture made notable progress.

Christians retained the Roman understanding of childhood development. The Romans had held that at the age of seven, a small child (*infans*) became a boy (*puer*), and at fourteen, a young man (*adolescens*). Whereas the *infans* was seen as innocent and naive, the *puer* was much more articulate and self-aware. Work began at fourteen, when basic schooling ended, though further education or training was available.[4] Boys were often sent away from home for this more advanced learning, which initiated their years as wandering students.

A twentieth-century writer's somewhat idealized depiction of a surprisingly modern aspect of teaching in early medieval Ireland might be applicable throughout the Middle Ages, although it would have depended on the master:

> In the earlier stages of instruction the pupil was encouraged to ask questions about the difficulties which he encountered and the tutor was expected to explain everything that was obscure to the learner. At a later stage the learner was questioned to test whether he had grasped the meaning of what he read, and to raise difficulties which he was required to explain ... It was the special merit of the tutor who

---

[4] Peter Hunter Blair, *The World of Bede* (Cambridge: Cambridge University Press, 2001), 237.

obtained the degree known as *Sruth-do-aill* that "he was able to modify his instruction to the complexion of the information in mercy to the people who were unable to follow the instruction of a teacher of higher degree. In other words he was able to make hard things easy for weak students who might get frightened in the presence of the formidable scholar." This would show that the question of "individual differences" was a live one in pedagogical circles in those days and that a genuine attempt was made to solve it.[5]

The above account leaves out the often harsh physical (and likely psychological) punishment meted out not only for undesirable behavior or rule breaking, but also for failing to learn as rapidly as expected. Although schoolboys were expected to learn to speak in Latin as well as read it, they did not necessarily read, write, and speak Latin at the same level. In fact, reading and writing were frequently taught separately, and some students could read much better than they could write.[6]

Only after learning the rudiments of reading would writing be taught. The high cost of parchment restricted writing practice to renewable materials. Young writers used a *stylus*, a metal rod with a sharp end, to form letters on a wax-covered wood tablet, called a *tabula*. The flat end of the *stylus* (or *stilus*, *pl. styli*) could smooth out the wax for more writing practice.[7] To practice writing, beginning students repeatedly copied the nonsense phrase "Adnexique globum zephyrique kanna secabant," which contained every letter except f, with "frseta" sometimes added to the end.[8]

After pupils had mastered writing on the wax tablet, they graduated to using a quillpen and parchment. Students sometimes practiced reading and writing together by writing out common Latin poems that they had memorized. The poems were often authored by the teachers, likely to reinforce the

---

[5] Graham, *The Early Irish Monastic Schools*, 100.
[6] Pierre Riché and Jacques Verger, *Maîtres et élèves au Moyen Âge* (Paris: Pluriel, 2013), 46–47.
[7] Graham, *The Early Irish Monastic Schools*, 96.
[8] Clark, *The Abbey of St Gall as a Centre of Literature and Art*, 98.

acquisition of recently-taught vocabulary and grammar structures. In addition to copying down chosen phrases such as
the one mentioned above, more advanced pupils would copy
down onto parchment the day's lesson, which the master — the
only one with a book — read aloud. The boys would learn
their lessons by heart. Boys wealthy enough to have sufficient
parchment could make their own version of the book that
the master was using.[9] Latin prose writing was developed in
three stages at St. Gall from the ninth century onwards: 1) the
dictamen prosaicum, an essay in prose; 2) the *prosimetrum,* or
rhymed prose; and 3) *dictamen metricum,* or rhymed hexameters called *carmen.* Poetry writing was also taught, based on
Biblical or hagiographical topics. On a special occasion, such as
the arrival of a distinguished guest, an ode or greeting would
be crafted by students.[10]

Some monastic schools, such as St. Gall, had both an inner
and an outer school. The former, reserved for oblates, was
cloistered off from the world and featured the best master or
masters of the monastery, such as the Irishman Moengal. For a
time at St. Gall, the inner school taught Greek, while the outer
school, typically reserved for boys of wealthy parents, did not.
While these pupils could eventually opt to join the monastery,
there was no expectation that they would do so.[11] Students at
the inner school dressed as monks, whereas boys in the outer
school dressed in the white robes of secular priests.[12] While
the inner school had more demanding academic standards,
students at both schools received the same harsh discipline.
The wardens, old monks whose eyes were constantly monitoring
for misbehavior at all hours, maintained order, discipline, and
focus. Even the older boys did not escape their attention. Any
rule breaking was noted down and discussed at the chapter
the next day. Boys frequently received physical punishment.

---

[9] Clark, *The Abbey of St Gall as a Centre of Literature and Art,* 101.
[10] Ibid., 104–105.
[11] Ibid., 94.
[12] Ibid.

Some masters, such as Ratbert and Notker the Physician, were reputed to be particularly strict.[13] More happily, game days were also held on special Church feasts, with shorter classes. Sometimes, the students were given meat and even wine on such occasions.

2.2 GENRES

Classroom genres of the Early Middle Ages included encyclopedia, riddles, hymns, poems, dialogues or colloquys, hagiographies, philosophical treatises, and books from the Bible. One recurring type of textbook in the Middle Ages was the *florilegium*, a collection of writings that had also been common in Greek and Roman classrooms. Its popularity stemmed from the wide selection of excerpts of various authors. This enabled the introduction of various genres, the inclusion of only the most edifying parts of a longer work, and, in the case of certain pagan authors, the deletion of licentious selections of a work. In an age when the material for a codice, including the vellum, would have cost enormous sums, florilegia were also economical ways to give instruction in a wide range of texts and authors. In addition to florilegia, the psalter served as a primary textbook. The Psalms were often memorized, but the surviving manuscripts, filled with annotations and glosses that indicate thorough instruction, testify to more than mere memorization and repetition of the content.[14] At St. Gall, after the Psalter had been memorized at about age ten, reading practice continued with *Aesop's Fables* (by Avianus) and maxims from a text called the *Cato Censorius*. Pupils were expected to commit all of these texts to memory.[15]

Another widespread genre in the classroom was the riddle. The answer to the following Anglo-Saxon riddle is in the footnote below:

---

[13] Clark, *The Abbey of St Gall as a Centre of Literature and Art*, 94–95.
[14] Graham, *The Early Irish Monastic Schools*, 96.
[15] Clark, *The Abbey of St Gall as a Centre of Literature and Art*, 101.

I saw four things in beautiful fashion
journeying together. Dark were their tracks,
the path very black. Swift was its moving,
faster than birds it flew through the air,
dove under the wave. Labored unresting
the fighting warrior who showed them the way,
all of the four, over plated gold.[16]

The four things that the riddler so admires are two fingers, the thumb, and the quill, which write as a unit, thus necessitating the singular "its."[17] The "fighting warrior" suggests the scholars' search for, or fight for, the truth. Early medieval education was not restricted to prayer and contemplation.

The following complex and rich riddle refers to the steps to production of a common and much-beloved tool of learning that was central to the mission of the Church. The answer is in the footnote below.

An enemy came and took away my life
and my strength also in the word; then wetted me,
dipped me in water; then took me thence;
placed me in the sun, where I lost all my hair.
The knife's edge cut me—its impurities ground away;
fingers folded me. And the bird's delight
with swift drops made frequent traces
over the brown surface; swallowed the tree-dye
with a measure of liquid; traveling across me,
left a dark track. A good man covered me
with protecting boards, which stretched skin over me;
adorned me with gold. Then the work of smiths
decorated me with strands of woven wire.
Now may the ornaments and the red dye
and the precious possessions everywhere honor
the Guardian of peoples. It were otherwise folly.
If the sons of men wish to enjoy me,
they will be the safer and surer of victory
and the stronger of heart and the happier of mind

---

[16] *Anglo-Saxon Riddles of the Exeter Book*, trans. Paull Franklin Baum (1963). https://en.wikisource.org/wiki/Anglo-Saxon_Riddles_of_the_Exeter_Book/ Annotated/40. The answer to the riddle is the quill pen.

[17] Ibid.

and the wiser of spirit. They will have more friends,
dearer and closer, truer and better,
nobler and more devoted, who will increase
their honor and wealth, with love and favors
and kindnesses surround them, and clasp them close
with loving embraces. Ask me my name.
I am a help to mortals. My name is a glory
and salvation to heroes, and myself am holy.[18]

The above riddle demonstrates why the typical library in the Early Middle Ages was much smaller than libraries would be after the printing press.

2.3 BOOKMAKING

The scarcity and cost of parchment meant that much consideration went into text-production, which was an in-house operation for any monastery of note. A *scriptorium* would be set up for the production of texts. Tablets, ink, quill pens, styli, slates, pencils, and vellum were necessities. Some schools, such as in early medieval Ireland, made their own vellum from goat-, sheep-, and calfskin. Parchment was of varying quality depending on whether it was finely polished or not, hard or soft, and well cleaned. There were also regional variations, with Irish parchment thicker than that found in France from the seventh through tenth centuries.[19]

After reporting on the general educational scene in one settlement, a story from the *Book of Aicille* of Cennfaeladh (Cinnfaela the Learned) describes the boy's study habits and use of learning tools:

---

[18] *Anglo-Saxon Riddles of the Exeter Book*, https://en.wikisource.org/wiki/Anglo-Saxon_Riddles_of_the_Exeter_Book/Annotated/43. The answer to the riddle is the Bible. The translator notes: "First the preparation of the parchment, then the writing and decoration are described; then the manifold values of what is written. 'It were otherwise folly,' l.16 (literally: not at all stupid punishment, penance), has puzzled the scholars. Proposed renderings are 'not the pains of hell' and 'let no fool find fault.'"

[19] Graham, *The Early Irish Monastic Schools*, 102.

> And he (Cennfaeladh) was brought to be cured to the house
> of Bricin of Tuam Drecain at the meeting of the three streets,
> between the houses of the three professors. And there were
> three schools in the town: a school of literature, a school of
> law, and a school of poetry. And whatever he used to hear
> rehearsed in the three schools every day, he had by heart
> every night; and he put a fine thread of poetry about them,
> and wrote them on slates, and tablets, and transcribed them
> into a paper book.[20]

Rote memorization featured prominently in medieval education,
although learning ideally did not end there. All the classroom
and study tools indicate the existence of a vibrant book culture.

Monastic schools required complex logistics. Education
was not only a matter of the master, students, and classroom.
Besides students poring over the texts that teachers presented,
a book-based environment was supported by a scriptorium, a
complex undertaking in a large monastery with specialists such
as copyists, correctors, painters, illuminators, binders, parchment
producers (itself accomplished in several steps), and someone to
supervise all of this. Texts had to be corrected, collated, and sent
back for improvement. The text to be copied had to be located,
for only the best version would do. This vital need led to the
rise of a book exchange system among various monasteries.[21]

Yet because of the religious nature of the era, even these
many steps were seen in spiritual terms and as service to God.
Abbo of Fleury noted the spiritual dimension to bookmaking,
comparing the copying of a book to prayer or fasting in its
work of taming unruly passions.[22] Copying encouraged a kind
of contemplation, a *scriptio divina*. According to Jean Leclercq,
"the task of the copyist was an authentic form of asceticism.
Deciphering from an often poorly preserved manuscript a text
which was often long and badly written and reproducing it

---

[20] *Ancient Laws and Institutes of Ireland*, vol 3 (Dublin: Alexander Thom Publisher, 1873), 89.

[21] Jean Leclercq, *The Love of Learning and the Desire for God: A Study of Monastic Culture*, trans. Catharine Misrahi (New York: Fordham University Press, 1996), 122.

[22] Ibid.

correctly constituted a task which, however noble it was, was also hard and therefore meritorious, and medieval scribes have taken pains to inform us of this fact: the whole body is concentrated on the work of the fingers and constant and precise attention must be exercised. It was work that was both manual and intellectual. Calligraphy is a difficult art as we know only too well."[23] Codex (or book) production and management in a monastic scriptorium reflected the collaborative and communal reality of the monastery itself.

Codex lending meant that this collaboration went beyond the walls of a particular monastery. Inter-monastic codex exchanges and lending added another dimension to scholarly itinerancy. Boys and scholars moving from one learning center to another were presumably requisitioned to transfer these texts from time to time. The anonymously-written *On the Life of St. Patrick* depicts the students as transporters of essential religious goods, not least of which were books: "Thereafter Patrick went to Rome for the third time, and he brought relics of Paul and Peter and Stephen and Lawrence and many martyrs besides, and reliquaries and books and a sheet with Christ's blood thereon, *and they were laid up here by Patrick in Paul and Peter's shrine*."[24] While we are told of whose relics were brought back, the books' authors or subjects are left unmentioned, as apparently no justification was needed. Their usefulness and even holiness were taken for granted, as books played a vital role in God's salvation plan.

Various elements of the same culture were closely associated with the book, and included bookmaking, reading, exegesis, liturgy, and education. Liturgy depended on a robust book culture and a demanding education. The Carolingian *renovatio* made worship even more influential over culture because it envisioned monks and clergy being educated to live well, which demanded

---

[23] Leclercq, *The Love of Learning and the Desire for God: A Study of Monastic Culture*, 122.

[24] Anonymous *On the Life of St. Patrick*. trans. Whitley Stokes. *In Lives of Saints from the Book of Lismore*. (Oxford 1890).

that they pray well. To pray well required them to read and to write well.[25] A poor reader could not fully participate in the liturgy or contribute to the bookmaking process. A poorly-educated monk could not be a copyist, as attested by the many error-filled versions of common classroom texts made by young boys at St. Gall, codices known as *puerili pollice scriptus*.[26]

2.4 BOOK MANAGEMENT

Given the central role of the written texts in the liturgy, the book became a much more familiar object in Christendom than it had been in ancient Rome when it existed in the form of papyrus scrolls.[27] For the first five-hundred years of the Middle Ages, the medieval love of books largely meant the monastic love of books. Cassiodorus's monastic retreat at Vivarium centered on his abundant library. Benedict Biscop (628–690 AD) famously built a library at his monastery in Jarrow, England, and abbots did the same for St. Gall. Monasteries competed with each other to build the largest book collection just as churches competed for saintly relics. Describing the typical setup of an Irish monastic library, Graham notes that "there were no shelves for rows of books, but there was another arrangement which was more suitable for the type of book then in use. The books were kept in satchels hung on pegs or racks round the room. Each satchel containing one or more volumes was labelled on the outside. The satchels were of embossed leather beautifully adorned with designs of interlaced ornament so common in Irish art.... These satchels were also used when carrying a book from place to place."[28] Graham's description of these beautiful books, which sometimes featured beautiful art on the cover or on individual pages, suggests their extravagant cost, but also the high esteem

---

[25] Leclercq, *The Love of Learning and the Desire for God: A Study of Monastic Culture*, 227.

[26] Clark, *The Abbey of St Gall as a Centre of Literature and Art*, 98.

[27] Bernard Flusin, "La culture écrite," in *Le monde byzantine I: L'Empire romain d'Orient (330–641)* (Paris: Presses Universitaires de France, 2012), 257–280, 260.

[28] Graham, *The Early Irish Monastic Schools*, 109–110.

in which they were held. A library was a serious investment. A large library gave a monastery or cathedral school a high status.

Despite this high status, libraries were not immune from more mundane issues. An Anglo-Saxon riddle from the *Exeter Book* describes a common problem:

> A moth ate words. To me it seemed
> a remarkable fate, when I learned of the marvel,
> that the worm had swallowed the speech of a man,
> a thief in the night, a renowned saying
> and its place itself. Though he swallowed the word
> the thieving stranger was no whit the wiser.[29]

Medieval education developed its own culture of the book, or culture of the text. Before the invention of the Gutenberg printing press, the first book-making process that used movable type, books were likely much more treasured than they were afterwards because of the painstaking work and one-of-a-kind characteristics of each text.

This rarity, and the fact that most people could not read books, gave books an otherworldly feeling. The hagiography *On the Life of St. Patrick* depicts their magical or spiritual qualities:

> *Tunc dixit rex* [Then the king said], "Put your books into water, and him of you whose books escape we will adore." "I am ready for that," saith Patrick. Said the wizard, "a god of water this man adores, and I will not submit to the ordeal of water." That was the grace of Baptism which he had perceived with Patrick. Said the king, "Put your books into the fire." "I am ready for that," saith Patrick. "I will not do thus," saith the wizard, "for this man adores a god of fire every two years," that is, it was the grace of the Holy Ghost he perceived with Patrick.[30]

On the Life of St. Patrick seems to regard books as a type of sacramental (holy objects used in the practice of the faith which today include rosaries or crucifixes), thereby reinforcing their spiritual or magical qualities.

---

[29] *Anglo-Saxon Riddles of the Exeter Book.* https://en.wikisource.org/wiki/Anglo-Saxon_Riddles_of_the_Exeter_Book/Annotated/42.
[30] Anonymous, *On the Life of St. Patrick.*

2.5 BOOKS AND LEARNING

Books meant something personal that could be shared between two book lovers. In a letter to the Holy Father, St. Columbanus requests some writings and describes his own wonderful experience of reading:

> I have read your book containing the pastoral rule, brief in style, pregnant in doctrine, replete with sacred lore; I confess that the work is sweeter than honey to the needy; wherefore in my thirst I beg you for Christ's sake to bestow on me your tracts, which, as I have heard, you have compiled with wonderful skill upon Ezekiel. I have read six books of Jerome on him; but he did not expound even half. But if you see fit, send me something from your lectures delivered in the city, I mean the final expositions of the book; send too the Song of Songs from that passage in which it says, *I will go to the mountain of myrrh and to the hill of frankincense.*[31]

Rome undoubtedly received countless such charm offenses from all over Christendom for texts. Describing his reading experience as "sweeter than honey" suggests the contemplative reading style of *lectio divina* that monasteries and hermitages prioritized over more analytical approaches. *Lectio divina* nurtured a deeper appreciation of Scripture's spiritual truths. Given the central role of spiritual training in education, *lectio divina* would have been the preferred way of reading in the classroom, at least for Christian texts, in Ireland and England, given the tutor's role as spiritual father.

Though hagiographies are often idealizations, they also reflect certain truths about everyday life, including classroom life. Rudolf of Fulda's *Life of Leoba* (836 AD) indicates that at least some women and girls received instruction, as reading figured among Leoba's primary spiritual and intellectual pursuits: "Fired by the love of Christ, [she] fixed her mind always on reading or hearing the Word of God. Whatever she heard or

---

[31] Columbanus. *First Letter* in *Letters of Columbanus*, trans. G. S. M. Walker (Dublin: Dublin Institute of Advanced Studies, 2008).

read she committed to memory, and put all that she learned into practice... She spent more time in reading and listening to Sacred Scripture than she gave to manual labour. She took great care not to forget what she had heard or read."[32] Again we see the importance of memorization and meticulous study habits. A zealous learner and book lover evoked admiration from other book lovers, in this case Rudolf of Fulda.

Apparently, not all students were as diligent as Leoba. The *Life of Burchard of Worms* gives mixed information on the educational level of Burchard's sister Mathilda. Her lack of erudition as an adult did not seem to stem from a lack of educational opportunity, but from the consequence of her involvement in other business and worldly attachments. Encouraged by the famous canonist Burchard (965–1025 AD) to turn away from the world and become the abbess of a nunnery, she laments her ignorance of certain learning. According to the hagiography, she associates the need for this learning with the demands of the religious life:

> Therefore, my dearest sister, I want you to remove the brace-lets, the earrings, and the delightful clothes and accept the holy veil and thus join yourself to the eternal king. When she heard this, she was greatly afraid and, amazed beyond words, she said: O holy lord, do you not know that I have spent all the days of my life involved in wordly affairs and therefore am utterly ignorant of this office? Indeed, I am completely ignorant of books except the psalter; I do not know how to behave in this office; and therefore how can I live in this life, my lord, without scandal?[33]

Interestingly, the only book she knows is the one that the youngest students learned, the psalter. Does that mean she had little further education?

The fact that she fears a scandal is revealing. It indicates that there were clear expectations for decent educational attainment for women who occupied certain ecclesiastical positions. She had received some education, with her claim to familiarity of

---

[32] Rudolf of Fulda, *Life of Leoba* trans. Serenus Cressy.
[33] *The Life of Burchard, Bishop of Worms*, trans. W. L. North (Hannover: Monumenta Germaniae Historica SS 4, 1841).

the psalter, and seems to blame herself and her worldly preoccupations, not a lack of educational opportunities, for her
insufficient educational background. When Mathilda agrees
to the project, Burchard sets out the training required for the
position: "He immediately ordered her to learn the canonical
rule, the computus, the lives of the fathers and the dialogue
and other books appropriate to this life." It is unclear whether
all abbesses were expected to be educated in a similar manner,
or only those of important nunneries or with well-connected
brothers. In any case, this training was typical of oblates or
boys and adolescents in training to be future priests.

2.6 GLOSSES

In addition to *lectio divina*, analytical reading was also practiced.
The gloss, a type of commentary, was a mainstay of ancient,
medieval, and early modern classrooms. Some glosses bridged
the linguistic gap in non-Latin countries. Unsurprisingly, most
of the glosses from Irish sources were one-word explanations
in Latin or Irish.[34] More generally, what Graham observes in
general about the Irish practice could be seen as a norm in
all types of medieval classrooms, from the monasteries to the
universities. The glosses prove "that the Irish monks were skilled
practical teachers as well as accomplished classical scholars. In
all these interlinear and marginal notes so abundant in the
MSS. of the old Irish period (prior to 900 A.D.) we see clear
evidence of preparation for the work of teaching."[35]

Another scholar's description of the glossing of hymnals
for singing practice likely reflects glossing styles for didactic
purposes in general. All facets of the language were brought
up for discussion, with the more complex elements reserved
for later years of study, likely in the same texts that had been
studied earlier, if for no other reason than that each school,

---

[34] Daíbhí Ó Cronínín, *Early Medieval Ireland* (London: Longman, 1995), 193.
[35] Graham, *The Early Irish Monastic Schools*, 99–100.

even in monasteries, would have had limited resources and that the liturgy required the same texts:

> Hymn glosses in eleventh-century manuscripts address several aspects of the hymns: lexicon, grammar, syntax, metre, style, doctrine and textual criticism. The simpler lexical glosses include synonyms and explanatory glosses supplying the referent of a pronoun or the subject of a verb. More complex lexical glosses include equivalents that offer interpretations of terms rather than synonyms, words and etymologies. Grammatical glosses focus on the case of nouns and syntactical glosses recast strophes in prose form in order to clarify word order. Source glosses point out scriptural references. An umbrella category of glosses most conveniently termed "encyclopaedic'" encompasses a wide variety of subjects, from customs of Roman antiquity to natural science and astronomy. Text-critical glosses evaluate variants and propose emendations. The most sophisticated glosses discuss the style and authorship of the hymns and elaborate on theological points in the hymn text; the latter category also includes statements of liturgical theology. All these gloss types appear in combination in only a few manuscripts; most of the manuscripts with hymn glosses contain primarily interlinear lexical and grammatical glosses.[36]

The various types of glosses reflect the various levels of study.[37] What the above list shows us is how the same text could be recycled for different classes. The deep familiarity for texts that was produced by such repetition allowed for the construction of a common culture throughout Europe. In other words, the use of the same texts everywhere in Christendom led to the emergence of a transnational educational elite based on the memorization of the same texts.

---

[36] Susan Boynton, "Training for the liturgy as a form of monastic education" in *Medieval Monastic Education*, eds. George Ferzoco and Carolyn Muessig (London: Leicester University Press, 2000), 7–20, 14. We can simplify Boynton's list of types of glossing. The first five belong to grammar class: 1) Identifying the antecedent of a pronoun or the subject of a verb; 2) defining words or expressions (lexical glossing); 3) glosses to parse words in sentences; 4) identifying references to Scripture; and 5) encyclopedic glosses (non-scriptural references, e.g., references to Greek mythology or Roman history). Glossing types six and seven belong to rhetoric class: 6) text-critical glosses and 7) style and authorship glossing.
[37] Ibid., 14.

The study of hymns reflects the practical, Church-oriented nature of many elements of medieval education, which went against the ideals of the liberal arts. Singing and chanting practice involved much rote memorization and repetition. This resulted in a lack of instruction in musical theory, at least according to the Carolingian Réginon of Prüm, who lamented that the majority of musicians were simply playing what they had been taught.[38] What was missing was the philosophical and numerical aspect of music. Nonetheless, advances in music theory had taken place between 800 and 1000 AD in some areas, though chant continued to be taught in the old ways until Guido of Arezzo in the eleventh century. Singers were able to learn unfamiliar melodies more quickly than before with his "innovative systems of notation and sight-singing."[39] Though a more philosophical education in music may have been lacking, other skills were developed in connection with liturgical music. Oblates honed integrated reading, writing, and musical skills in the liturgy and practice for worship.[40] This would have included the grammar and vocabulary that were required to understand the theology of hymns. Even at more advanced centers of learning, such as St. Gall, where the quadrivium was taught, pupils would have become very familiar with the practical aspects of music before they even began the theoretical study of numbers.[41]

Perhaps Réginon did not appreciate the long time it took to train oblates in the liturgical chant that was at the center of monastic life. In fact, it took up a large part of an oblate's day. Supervised study and practice of chant took place in the time between services, most often in the early morning. "The early Cluniac customaries and the Decretal of Lanfranc prescribe that the children go to the chapter house to sing with their teachers in the interval between Matins and Lauds during the

---

[38] Boynton, "Training for the liturgy as a form of monastic education," 7.
[39] Ibid.
[40] Ibid.
[41] Clark, *The Abbey of St Gall as a Centre of Literature and Art*, 121.

winter months. After Prime, they return to the chapter house to sing until the sun comes up, then go into the cloister to read aloud. In the autumn, however, they stay in the cloister with the other brothers after Prime, first reading and then singing."[42] Poor singing performances were punished.

As we have seen, glossing for hymns and other texts provided specialized teaching material, and depended on the students' levels. Much knowledge of grammar, rhetoric, and theology was picked up informally through the learning of hymns. Hymns were so central to teaching that they were included in florilegia, while grammar textbooks provided glosses on the language of hymns. Commentaries on hymns were featured in numerous theological treatises, which reflects their usefulness to teaching doctrine. "With their poetic language, rich theological content, formulaic melodies and memorable rhythms, hymns demonstrate the didactic potential of chant. Glosses on the hymns attest to the use of hymns not just in liturgical training but in several levels of grammatical education, exemplifying the multifaceted formation offered by the monastic liturgy."[43]

Texts were glossed by teachers, students, and readers for a range of purposes, such as clarifying the meaning of a text or, in the case of the teacher, making a note of what to explain or highlight. The glossing of one generation was often preserved by the following. One manuscript could have the glosses of more than one owner, over the sweep of several generations. Glossing was considered so important to conveying or grasping meaning that some users of texts would copy glosses from older versions of the same text in the *scriptorium*.[44] Glosses, in other words, sometimes began to be treated as if they were an integral part of a book.

---

[42] Boynton, "Training for the liturgy as a form of monastic education," 8.
[43] Ibid., 15.
[44] John Marenbon, *Early Medieval Philosophy (480–1150)* (London: Routledge, 2002), 72.

2.7 ROMANITAS AND SCRIPTURE

Education at this time cast a much wider net than hymns and
other aspects of liturgy. Newman lists an impressive group of
classical authors who became pivotal to medieval classrooms
in the West, and therefore to reading culture in general, in the
development of the *litteratus*, the individual who could read.
This was the acquisition of *Latinitas*: "In the monastic school,
the language of course was Latin; and in Latin literature first
came Virgil; next Lucan and Statius; Terence, Sallust, Cicero;
Horace, Persius, Juvenal; and of Christian poets, Prudentius,
Sedulius, Juvencus, Aratus. Thus we find that the monks of St.
Alban's, near Mayence, had standing lectures in Cicero, Virgil,
and other authors. In the school of Paderborne there were
lectures in Horace, Virgil, Statius, and Sallust."[45]

Despite the popularity of Roman authors, *Latinitas* was *Christian Latinitas*. While medieval learning inherited ancient terms
such as *grammaticus* or *rhetor*, it also coined new expressions,
such as *psalteratus* (someone who could read), that reflected
the Christian core of medieval learning. The psalter replaced
the *Disticha Catonis* in the Early Middle Ages as the source of
primary learning. The chanting of the Psalms was so central
to monastic life, that this change was inevitable. Village parish
schools, cathedral schools, and even lay educators emulated this
prioritization of the psalter.[46]

Leclercq's following description of medieval learning leaves
out this Christian core:

> If humanism consists in studying the classics for their own
> sake, in focusing interest on the type of ancient humanity
> whose message they transmit, then the medieval monks are
> not humanists. But if humanism is the study of the classics
> for the reader's personal good, to enable him to enrich his
> personality, the monks are in the fullest sense humanists.

---

[45] Newman, *A Benedictine Education*, 79.
[46] Robert Black, *Humanism and Education in Medieval and Renaissance Italy*
(Cambridge: Cambridge University Press, 2001), 37.

As has been said, they had in view a useful and personal end: their education. And what, in fact, did they get from the classics? They took the best these authors had to give. Through contact with them, like all who study the humanities in any period, they developed and refined their own human faculties. To begin with, they owed to the classics a certain appreciation of the beautiful; this can be seen in the choice the monks made of texts to be preserved and in the quality of the texts they wrote under this influence.[47]

The ultimate purpose of personality enrichment, refinement of the intellectual faculties, and the appreciation of the beautiful was the exaltation and worship of God.

One significant feature of Benedictine education was life-long or adult learning. Monks were famously eager to have a master teach them something about Scripture or theology. In a letter, Pope Gregory the Great gives an account of teaching his monks while he was the papal ambassador to Constantinople in response to their persistent demand that he instruct them on the book of Job.[48] Pope Gregory notes:

They begged me to give an exposition of the book of Holy Job, revealing the mystery of its riches insofar as the Truth should teach me. Moreover, to this burden that they asked me to assume, they added as well that I should not only search the literal words for the allegorical sense but that I should then bend the allegorical sense to the exercise of moral action, a more serious obligation still. I should accompany what I have learned with the support of other texts from Scripture, and after these texts I should add another exposition to tie them together, when they are difficult to understand.[49]

This sounds like the request of very educated monks, who wanted a higher level type of seminar. They sound like

[47] Jean Leclercq, *The Love of Learning and the Desire for God*, Catharine Misrahi, trans. (New York: Fordham University Press, 1982), 133–134.
[48] Micol Long, "Monastic Practices of Shared Reading as Means of Learning," in *The Annotated Book in the Early Middle Ages: Practices of Reading and Writing*, eds. M. J. Teeuwen and I. Van Renswoude, Utrecht Studies in Medieval Literacy, 38 (Turnhout: Brepols, 2017), 531–559, 535.
[49] Gregorius Magnus, *Moralia in Iob, Epistola ad Leandrum*, in Long, 536.

autonomous learners who knew what to ask for and how they wanted the content presented. These monks express a thirst for ever-greater knowledge, all in the service of spiritual growth.

Despite the medieval love of the text and its centrality to scholarship, orality also played a central role in learning: "And so the brothers straightway sat down in front of me, and I began my oral exposition of the text." As was typical of medieval learners, who believed that a master's lecture was best written down for posterity, the monks took notes on the teaching.[50] Gregory's lecturing style kept to the Platonic ideal of inter-acting with students, asking questions and letting the monks determine the classroom interaction and content.[51] In his letter, Gregory shows a great sensitivity to the needs and requests of his students: "They certainly demanded a great deal; I so tried to meet their wishes by explaining the literal sense, or the higher sense tending to contemplation, or a moral precept."[52] The reference to different levels of meaning in Scripture reflects a higher level of reading ability and the thirst for more than just memorization. The monks and their teacher seem to interact with the text in an imaginative and highly personal way. The students' zeal, and Gregory's affirmative response, also demon-strate their love for the Bible. A second, and rather famous, example of adult education concerns Thomas Aquinas. While on the way to a Church council in 1274, he spent his very last days resting at a Cistercian monastery, Fossanova, where the monks pressed him into lecturing to them. Those were to be the saint's last experiences in the classroom.

2.8 LECTIO DIVINA

The early medieval development of reading placed the Bible and *lectio divina* at the center. The honored status that the *Rule* of St. Benedict bestowed on the Bible affected reading practices

---

[50] Long, *Early Medieval Ireland*, 537.
[51] Ibid., 538.
[52] Ibid.

and therefore learning. The following evokes the sense of the book, or at least the Bible, as a sacramental: "What page, what passage of the inspired books of the Old and New Testaments is not the truest of guides for human life? What book of the holy catholic Fathers does not resoundingly summon us along the true way to reach the Creator? Then, besides the Conferences of the Fathers, their Institutes and their Lives there is also the rule of our holy father Basil. For observant and obedient monks, all these are nothing less than tools for the cultivation of virtues."[53]

Reading was not solely for knowledge or passing tests, but above all for spiritual edification. In this sense, much of medieval education centered around contemplative reading, *lectio divina*, until the emergence of the universities and scholasticism. Early medieval education itself was contemplative, as we see in the spiritual fatherhood of the Irish masters. In *lectio divina*, reading is a spiritual exercise that in which the text speaks to the heart more than to the head.[54] The practice of *lectio tacita* also emerged. Typically, texts were read aloud, with either one person reading to listeners, or a solitary scholar reading aloud to himself. With *lectio tacita*, however, monks read quietly to themselves, so as not to break the silence of the monastery. This quiet reading represented a revolution in reading habits.[55]

The contemplative search for the deeper meaning and the belief in the inexhaustible nature of the truth impacted medieval thinkers' appreciation and pursuit of the liberal arts. Reading involved not only extracting the varying levels of meaning of a text, but also depended on the reader's level of spiritual development. "The progress through lectio, meditatio, oratio to contemplatio involved elevating the whole person — body, mind, heart and will — to God. At root, holiness through wholeness

---

[53] Benedict. *Rule of St. Benedict*, 73:3–6.
[54] Pierre Riché, *Ecoles et Enseignement dans le Haut Moyen Age*, 3rd ed. (Paris: Picard, 1999), 39.
[55] Ibid.

was the ideal sought in medieval monastic education."[56] The reader could only derive from a given text the meaning that matched his intellectual ability and spiritual capacity. Growth in the spiritual understanding of Scripture or other Christian writings depended on the reader's spiritual development as much as on his intellectual level.

---

[56] Aidan Bellenger, "A Medieval Novice's Formation: Reflection on a Fifteenth-Century Manuscript at Downside Abbey," in *Medieval Monastic Education*, 35–40, 39.

CHAPTER 3

The Trivium

The mind of the student is not like a pot that has to be filled.
It is a uterus that has to give birth. It is a match that has
to be lit up.

— Iannis A. Pottakis[1]

I also smooth off the unevenness of speech with elegance
and euphony, with compounds and harmonies and with
the so-called periods or periodical forms. I have persuaded
myself that these things pose no obstacle to virtue.

— Michael Psellos[2]

3.1 A CHRISTIAN TRIVIUM

THE SO-CALLED DARK AGES WAS IN
fact lit up with learning. Religious and even political
leaders, particularly Charlemagne, Charles the Bald,
and Edward the Confessor, continued to link intellectual life
with an orthodox Christian culture combined with their own
strong leadership over their peoples.[3] The Carolingians saw
this culture as uniting their vast territories of many nations,
including the Avars, Saxons, Franks, Frisians and, eventually,
Lombards, to name but a few. Education, in other words, was a
vital pillar of the cultural unity of what became western Christendom. This reflects the full meaning of the Greek word *paideia*,
which refers to both culture and education. The Christians did
as well as the ancient Greeks ever had in fulfilling the aspirations expressed by this concept. This view of education in the

---

[1] Pottakis, "Socrates, Plato, Aristotle. Three Mentors in Ancient Greece," 43.
[2] Michel Psellos, "Letter to Ioannes Xiphilinos," in *Psellos and the Patriarchs*,
trans. Anthony Kaldellis and Ioannis Polemis (University of Notre Dame Press,
2015), 175.
[3] "Orthodox" is not capitalized in this work as, before the Great Schism of 1054,
no separate Roman Catholic and Orthodox Churches existed.

early medieval West was a much more ambitious vision than that of Clement of Alexandria and Origen, who had focused on the education of the Christian community within the empire, not the education of the empire as Christian community.

Medieval Christian writers produced their own foundational texts in the liberal arts. These texts stemmed from the same desire as the ancient Greeks for a generalist educational foundation based on correct language usage and knowledge of a range of disciplines. Ilsetraut Hadot characterizes Isidore's *Etymologies* (*Etymologiae*) as more of a lexicon than an encyclopedia, likely because of this concern over language. The *Etymologies* follows the spirit of the trivium and quadrivium in its attempt to provide "a coherent demonstration of the subject matter," with an overall unity among the disciplines. She adds that "if the Latin Middle Ages often identified the totality of the seven arts with philosophy or even with wisdom, it is that Isidore himself in his *Etymologies* had registered six of these arts in the scientific domain of philosophy, all in presenting, as did Cassiodorus, the seventh, or, rather, the first (grammar) as the origin and foundation of all the others."[4] Yet Isidore was simply attempting to revive an older grammar tradition. Grammar teaching had come to a low point much earlier than in Visigothic Spain or Merovingian Gaul. The imperial period, between 27 BC and the late fifth century AD, had already seen a decline in grammar, and in education in general.

The reaction to grammar's decline sparked a renaissance of sorts, which was given impetus by the growing linguistic alienation between the Latin West and the Greek East. This rupture resulted in each half of the empire going its own way culturally and educationally. This western independence caused Roman writers to replace the old Greek manuals with Latin ones, particularly those of Donatus and Priscian.[5] This

[4] Ilsetraut Hadot, *Arts libéraux et philosophie dans la pensée antique*, (Études Augustiniennes, 1984), 207.
[5] Jacques Lafontaine, *Isidore de Seville et la culture classique dans l'Espagne wisigothique*, deuxième edition. (Études Augustiniennes, 1983), 212.

Romanization of Greek grammar and rhetorical traditions encouraged the blossoming of a whole literary culture. These grammar and rhetoric texts enabled Rome to academically order its cultural heritage into a canon of various types of texts, including revised editions of older texts, commentaries of those texts, textbooks of theoretical grammar, lexicons, encyclopedia, and glossaries.[6] The Church took advantage of this grammar culture by appropriating these texts to train future churchmen, particularly for Biblical exegesis. Grammar had a practical yet sacred vocation based on the Church's concern to use, correct, and translate the best versions of books from Scripture and to explore the smallest details of meaning in a text. The Biblical exegete was a type of grammarian whose specialty was scriptural study, commentary, and transmission.[7]

Augustine's view in *De doctrina christiana* of traditional rhetoric as a propaedeutic to the Christian truth held enormous influence throughout the Middle Ages.[8] The Bishop of Hippo and a great many medieval thinkers saw the tremendous benefits of the study of the seven liberal arts in enhancing the study of Scripture, partly by correcting poor translations of Scripture into Latin. The Church's development of its own grammar culture carried on the grammar renaissance that had started in pagan Rome. Rhetoric complemented grammar in the Early Middle Ages, even if its prestige had waned in the West.

A holistic approach to learning was founded on the vision of tradition as a unified whole. Despite the increasingly Christian identity of education, the early medieval centuries prized the handing on of tradition, not innovation. Thus, the trivium underwent clarification and consolidation, not revolutionary change or upheaval. The holistic ideal encouraged much overlap between grammar and rhetoric, with "a difference of degree

---

[6] Lafontaine, *Isidore de Seville et la culture classique dans l'Espagne wisigothique*, 31.
[7] Ibid.
[8] Ibid., 214–215.

rather than a definite line of separation" between them.[9] Often the same authors, and even the same texts, would be examined in both grammar and rhetoric classes, but to different ends. The *grammaticus* (the teacher of grammar) focused on the basic understanding of the text, including the vocabulary, whereas the *rhetor* (the teacher of rhetoric) analyzed, often through glossing, the best applications of these structures and vocabulary for certain effects on the reader.

These disciplines built a keener appreciation of language. Roland Barthes calls the trivium "a taxonomy of the word that attests to the obstinate effort of the Middle Ages to define the place of the word in man, nature, and creation. The word was not at that time, as it has been since, a vehicle, an instrument, the mediation of *something else* (soul, thought, passion); it absorbed all of the mental world," which means, according to Barthes, that for medieval minds "the word is not expression, but immediate construction."[10] This means for Barthes that the source of greatest interest for the medieval mind was not the content of each of the three paths of the trivium, but the interaction among them. It was believed that the study of the liberal arts brought the student closer to the truth. The seven liberal arts had different purposes than these disciplines do now in our materialist and disenchanted world. For the medieval mind, the distinction between the trivium and the quadrivium did not prefigure the difference between the humanities and the sciences in more recent centuries, "but instead that of the secrets of the word and the secrets of nature."[11] The liberal arts possessed an ontological nature. They helped the student to climb the ladder of being through deeper knowledge of being as it is reflected in language and in creation. They were metaphysical.

---

[9] Gabriel Codina Mir, *Aux Sources de la Pédagogie des Jésuites* (Institutum Historicum, 1968), 78.

[10] Roland Barthes, "L'ancienne rhétorique [Aide-mémoire] Aide-mémoire," in *Communications* 16, no. 1 (1970): 172–223, https://doi.org/10.3406/comm.1970.1236, 186.

[11] Ibid., 186.

3.2 LOGOS AND RATIO

Reason, denoted in Greek as *logos* (λόγος) and in Latin as *ratio*, provided an underlying unity to the trivium.[12] The way reason functioned in the liberal arts aligned with the Christian understanding and employment of reason. Many Church Fathers associated reason with orthodoxy, and deficient reason with heresy. Unsurprisingly, many hagiographies oppose rational man to irrational animals.[13] As testified in monastic writings, ancient and medieval Christians believed that the Christian life consists in accepting reasonable norms to follow and that the heretical life or the sin-filled life is caused by a lack of reason.[14] Paul the Deacon and Benedict of Aniane are just two of many writers who connected reason to chastity.

---

[12] *Logos* and *ratio* do not cover the exact same semantic territory. *Legein* (the root of *logos*) denotes *gather*, whereas the verb *reor, rerir* signifies *count, calculate, discount.* "*Ratio* is used in two large sense families: calculation and explanation." *Logos* came to have a wider sense than *ratio* ever would. Olivier Boulnois, "Les États de la Raison: Formes et Fonctions de la Rationalité Médiévale," ed. Dominique Poirel (Vrin, 2024), 306, 307.

The University of Chicago Greek lexicon at https://logeion.uchicago.edu breaks the meaning of logos into ten main categories: "1) computation, reckoning; 2) relation, correspondence, proportion; 3) explanation; 4) debate ('inward debate of the soul'), which includes thinking, reasoning; 5) continuous statement, narrative; 6) verbal expression or utterance; 7) a particular utterance, saying; 8) thing spoken of, subject matter; 9) expression, utterance, speech; 10) the Word or Wisdom of God."

Logos is defined by Bernard Wuellner, *A Dictionary of Scholastic Philosophy*, Second Edition (The Bruce Publishing Company, 1966), 174 as "1. Greek, esp. Stoic, philosophy. reason, thought, or wisdom conceived as the controlling power or soul of the world and manifested in human knowledge and speech; reason as immanent deity in the ordered universe. 2. Christian theology, following St. John's Gospel: the Son of God, the Word, the Second Person of the Blessed Trinity, the Wisdom of God. This Wisdom is also present in the universe by divine omnipresence and dwelt among us in the human nature of Christ."

Wuellner's lengthy definition of *reason* includes, "the act of drawing conclusions from other judgments; discursive thinking; proving or attempting to prove. As the typical mode of human knowing, it is referred to as 'reason as reason.' Popular usage seems, however, to include judging, analyzing, and rationally explaining acts of reason or reasoning." On page 260.

[13] Patrick Henriet, "Hagiographie et Raison," in *La raison au Moyen Âge*, ed. Dominique Poirel, (Vrin, 2024), 230.

[14] Ibid., 240–241.

Though reason differs from logic in having a psychological dimension to it, from the ancient Greeks onward, reason also possessed a mathematical foundation, which was applied to the sphere of language to ideally provide order, precision, and flawless thinking.[15] Logic was the discipline of reason, particularly for inference and right argumentation through the analysis of causes and effects or of supporting arguments and conclusions.[16] Augustine brings both senses of *ratio* (the mathematical and the linguistic) together in *On Order* by first using it in its mathematical sense and then in its meaning as "notion, discourse, and argumentation."[17] Augustine also gives reason a spiritual sense that complements the spiritual orientation of the hagiographers: "Reason is a *motio*, a movement, shaking, an activity of the *mens*, of the spirit. This definition of reason as *mentis motio*, 'movement of the spirit,' permits us to unify the various senses of the term. Reason is not only the content of thought, nor even a faculty of the spirit. It is also its very activity. But insofar as it is an internal movement of thought, *ratio est potens*. It exercises a power. It is capable of producing certain actions."[18]

Some of these actions include division (or analysis) and synthesis. Augustine sees reason at the heart of the trivium and quadrivium because reason is focused on learning. Reason is the process in the mind that seeks knowledge, *scientia*. All knowledge is the outcome of reason, and each particular type of reason belongs to a particular science.[19] As exemplified in science, reason relies on definition, which consists of analysis (normally defined as breaking things down) and synthesis (making connections among separate elements). Reason also

---

[15] Dominique Poirel, "Introduction," in *La raison au Moyen Âge*, ed. Domique Poirel (Vrin, 2024), 18–19.

[16] Julie Brumberg-Chaumont, "Raison et Logique au Moyen Âge," in *La raison au Moyen Âge*, ed. Domique Poirel (Vrin, 2024), 39.

[17] Boulnois, "Les États de la Raison: Formes et Fonctions de la Rationalité Médiévale," 307.

[18] Ibid., 308.

[19] Ibid.

refers to metacognition in its capacity to reflect on thinking. In other words, reason applies reason to itself. This is why reason is so close to dialectic and the latter tasks of bringing order to all the sciences through the act of definition.[20]

The Byzantine scholastic John of Damascus (c. 675–749 AD) wielded reason against superstitious belief in *On Dragons and Phantasms*. He condemned superstition and erroneous thinking, and blames these on ignorance. Reason destroys superstition by, for example, explaining natural phenomena such as thunder and lightning.[21] In *The Fount of Knowledge*, Damascus opposed animistic belief alongside a negative, Manichean view of matter. That is why he succeeded at answering the criticisms of those who want to focus on the study of theology at the expense of the examination of the natural world. He accused them of laziness and inactivity, and asserts that the study of nature reveals the truths of theology because reason and faith do not oppose each other.[22] This does not mean that John strongly advocated the study of the created order; he was simply asserting his belief in the rational order of the world. The details of creation are inessential as long as the thinker accepts the divine order to everything.[23] For John, reason supports dogma while working within the boundaries of dogma.[24] Unsurprisingly, he wrote a treatise on dialectic in order to promote the correct application of logic. In the philosophical chapters in *The Fount of Knowledge*, which are collectively known as *Dialectica*, John connects reason to knowledge,

> Nothing is more estimable than knowledge, for knowledge is the light of the rational soul. The opposite, which is ignorance, is darkness. Just as the absence of light is darkness, so is the absence of knowledge a darkness of the reason. Now,

---

[20] Boulnois, "Les États de la Raison: Formes et Fonctions de la Rationalité Médiévale," 311. Dialectic is therefore called the *disciplina disciplinarum* or the *ars artium*, the "science of the sciences."
[21] Tatakis, *Byzantine Philosophy*, 85.
[22] Ibid.
[23] Ibid.
[24] Ibid., 86.

ignorance is proper to irrational beings, while knowledge is proper to those who are rational. Consequently, one who by nature has the faculty of knowing and understanding, yet does not have knowledge, such a one, although by nature rational, is by neglect and indifference inferior to rational beings. By knowledge I mean the true knowledge of things which are, because things which have being are the object of knowledge. False knowledge, in so far as it is a knowledge of that which is not, is ignorance rather than knowledge. For falsehood is nothing else but that which is not.[25]

Like Augustine, John calls Christ the inner Teacher, whose instruction we can also access through Scripture. There was little challenge to John of Damascus's assumptions in the Byzantine Empire. Centuries later, in a letter to John Xiphilinos in which he defends his own use of Plato and logic, Michael Psellos notes that reasoning is not in opposition to the Church, but an instrument that the truth employs to discover what it seeks.[26]

3.3 GRAMMAR

Early medieval grammarians were blessed with the inheritance of an already well-developed discipline, though grammar had been a relative latecomer to paideia. It emerged among the ancient Greeks after the establishment of philosophy, rhetoric, and music by differentiating itself from these others. It originally concerned instruction and practice in the rudiments of writing and reading. Grammarians eventually developed more theoretical concerns, first in the science of language and then through the analysis of literary texts, which normally meant poetry. This more theoretical version of grammar worked to establish, read, explain, and evaluate texts for the classroom.[27] Writing in the late third century BC, Marcus Terentius Varro gave four tasks to grammar in its treatment of a text: reading

---

[25] John of Damascus, *The Fount of Knowledge* in *Saint John of Damascus: Writings*, trans. Frederic H. Chase. (Fathers of the Church, Inc., 1958) Chapter 1, 7.
[26] Psellos, "Letter to Ioannes Xiphilinos," 171–172.
[27] Catherine Wolff, *L'Education dans le monde romain* (Picard, 2015), 54.

out loud (*lectio*), interpreting (*enarratio*), correcting (*emendatio*), and judging (*iudicium*).[28] In other words, grammar developed two closely-related streams, one classroom-based and practical, and the other philological and theoretical.

There was a close connection between these two sides of grammar. The philological aspect that was based on textual exegesis gradually developed into the content of grammar lessons.[29] It sought the meaning of texts from Latin classical pagan writers, such as Virgil, Horace, Juvenal, and from Christian texts, particularly the Bible. It thereby became "the *ars* before and within every other *ars*. *Grammatica* involved the study of 'literary' authors."[30] The teaching of poetry widened grammar's horizon because the proper understanding of a text required a knowledge of history, geography, and mythology. History was also important in grammar's preparatory role for rhetoric class because the orator would be expected to draw on examples (*exempla*) from history.[31] Grammar came to include the art of the interpretion of historians and poets, the former including Caesar, Sallust, and the Greek Eusebius in Latin translation.[32] Geography was examined with lists of places and the creation of *mappae mundi*. Geography was frequently confused with geometry in the Early Middle Ages, which meant that students would receive instruction in geography twice.[33] By the first century of the Christian era, grammar had become an independent discipline. Concerning language, the grammar teacher would ideally limit instruction and practice to spelling, copying, and paraphrasing model texts, pointing out barbarisms and solecisms, and obsolete words, while leaving style to the teacher of rhetoric.[34]

---

[28] Wolff, *L'Education dans le monde romain*, 55.
[29] Ibid., 54.
[30] Brian Cummings, *The Literary Culture of the Reformation* (Oxford University Press, 2007), 21.
[31] Wolff, *L'Education dans le monde romain*, 58.
[32] Riché and Verger, *Maîtres et élèves au Moyen Age*, 49.
[33] Ibid., 49.
[34] Wolff, *L'Education dans le monde romain*, 58.

Donatus' *Ars minor* provided the basis for reading and writing. In fact, Donatus' domination of grammar instruction for more than a thousand years in the Latin West sometimes prevented innovation in the subject.[35] Where he was not so dominant, such as in Ireland, innovation in grammar instruction did occur. A common means of learning was the Latin word list. In non-Romance speaking areas, such as England, Ireland, or Germany, these lists were often bilingual (which indicates students' familiarity with the written form of the vernacular language). Two other common grammar tasks were the study and practice of prosody for the readings of the daily office and working on textbooks that supplemented the *Ars minor*. These included Priscian's *Institutiones*, Phocas' and Eutyches' *Artes*, and the writings of Bede and Alcuin.[36] Grammar teaching was often carried out in the form of the dialogue, a genre that remained popular for the entire Middle Ages. The texts of Quintilian and Cicero guided the teaching of writing, which revolved around the imitation of the classical authors.[37] Grammar's practical purpose for Biblical exegesis made the discipline a significant concern for the Church. At the beginning of the *Institutions*, Cassiodorus connected errors in copying Biblical texts to ignorance of grammar.[38]

In the Byzantine Empire, Homer's *Iliad* served as the main text, with the *Odyssey* serving as a secondary source of teaching. Tragedies were also studied: three from each of Aischylus (*Persians*, *Prometheus Bound*, and *Seven against Thebes*), Sophocles (*Ajax*, *Electra*, and *Oedipus the King*), and Euripides (*Hecuba*, *Orestes*, and *Phoenician Women*). Aristophanes' comedies *Wealth*, *The Clouds*, and *The Frogs* were often added to this, along with writings by Hesiod, Pindar, Theocritas, Lucian, Demosthenes, Plato, the Psalms, and Gregory Nazianzen. Aside from the *Iliad*, the selection of texts likely depended on the availability

---

[35] Lafontaine, *Isidore de Seville et la culture classique dans l'Espagne wisigothique*, 28.
[36] Riché and Verger, *Maîtres et élèves au Moyen Age*, 49.
[37] Ibid., 50.
[38] Lafontaine, *Isidore de Seville et la culture classique dans l'Espagne wisigothique*, 33.

and cost of texts and the preferences of the master, who typically ran his own grammar school. While schoolboys in the Latin West encountered Donatus, their Byzantine counterparts learned Greek grammar from Dionysius of Thrax (170–90 BC), supplemented by the texts of Theodosios of Alexandria (third century AD) and George Choiroboskos (ninth century AD). The *progymnasmata*, a series of increasingly-difficult exercises that bridged grammar and rhetoric classes, saw much more deliberate and coherent use in the Greek world than in the Latin West. In the tenth century, the *schedographia* (σχεδογραφία), derived from the word for "composition," "short passage," "sketch" (*schedos*, σχέδος), made its entrance in Byzantine classrooms. It represented a novel instruction method for practicing and testing spelling and grammar rules through riddles and puns, with hidden errors to be corrected by students.[39] The *schede* operated at the grammar, not rhetorical level, by testing basic language usage, such as selecting the correct synonym or parsing a sentence.[40] Michael Psellos defined the *schedos* as an exercise, based on a short written composition that featured difficult-to-spell or easily-confused words.[41]

3.4 LOGICA VETUS

The second element of the trivium has been called both *dialectic* and *logic*, with many writers failing to distinguish between the two, or choosing one term and ignoring the other. Confusing this further, some medieval thinkers tended to equate dialectic with scientific logic, such as found in geometry. This ambiguity over the precise meaning of logic or dialectic existed from the beginning. Aristotle regarded dialectic as "a logic dealing with

---

[39] Athanasios Markopoulos, "Education," in *The Oxford Handbook of Byzantine Studies*, ed. by Elizabeth Jeffreys (Oxford University Press, 2008), 789.

[40] Elizabeth Jeffreys, "Rhetoric," in *The Oxford Handbook of Byzantine Studies* ed. by Elizabeth Jeffreys (Oxford University Press, 2008), 831.

[41] Timothy S. Miller, "Two Teaching Texts from the Twelfth Century Orphanotropheion," in *Byzantine Authors: Literary Activities and Preoccupations*, ed. John W. Nesbitt Brill, 2007), 9.

and terminating in probabilities, such as used in debate or in discussion of hypotheses."[42] This differed from Plato's view of dialectic as necessary for the promotions of Socrates' efforts at defining and giving discipline and reasoned coherence to the substances of things. This view, along with the popularity of Heraclitus' teachings on constant change, prompted Plato to develop his theory of Ideas.[43]

Given the decline of a unified culture and education in western society after the fourth century, early medieval thinkers were forced to make do with a restricted set of foundational texts in logic. These included Boethius's works on logic (*De topics differentiis, De divisione, De syllogismis categoricis,* and *De syllogismis hypotheticis*), Boethius's translations of Aristotle's *Categories* and Porphyry's *Isagoge* into Latin, other writers' translations of Aristotle's *Interpretations,* and Cicero's *Topics.* The Early Middle Ages saw slow development in the second discipline of the trivium, particularly when compared with the more dynamic High Middle Ages from roughly 1000 AD to the mid-fourteenth century. In *Fountain of Knowledge / Fountain of Wisdom,* John of Damascus (675–749 AD) included chapters on what he calls "dialectic." Martianus Capella's *On the Marriage of Philology and Mercury* was also available, and very popular, by the ninth century. The Carolingian scholars Martin of Laon, John Scotus Erigiuna, and Remi d'Auxerre produced commentaries on Capella's text. Erigiuna was the most outstanding western dialectician from 500 to 1050 AD, as evidenced by his discussion of the created order, *Periphyseon.* In the twelfth century, these basic works of logic became known as the *logica vetus,* in contrast to the *logica nova,* the newly-appearing translations of treatises on logic, most importantly Aristotelian. In the thirteenth century, Petrus Hispanus, in his widely-read textbook the *Summulae Logicales,* begins by noting the all-encompassing role of dialectic: "Dialectic is the art of

---

[42] Walter J. Ong, *Ramus, Method, and the Decay of Dialogue* (Harvard University Press, 1958), 44.
[43] Pottakis, "Socrates, Plato, Aristotle. Three Mentors in Ancient Greece," 40.

arts and the science of sciences, possessing the way to the principles of all curriculum subjects."[44] This was the mainstream
view of dialectic for centuries.

Dialectic had become the king of the trivium by then, but
that status would be built on the grammar centuries of the Early
Middle Ages that had raised writing and reading standards to
a point that enabled this later work on dialectic. The earlier
era had consolidated a basic and relatively uniform literary
culture across Western Europe. The Socratic-Platonic vision
of dialectic reflected the belief in the participatory nature of
knowledge acquisition wherein the thinking process is acti-
vated by dialogue.[45] Dialectic had been central to paideia for
so long that Christians had to reckon with it. In *The Fount of
Knowledge,* John of Damasus provides a brief review of logic:

> One must know that there are four dialectical or logical
> methods. That is by division which divides the genus into
> species by means of the intermediate specific differences.
> That is by the definition which defines the subject by the
> genus and the specific differences divided out by the method
> of division. That is by analysis which resolves the more
> composite thing into its simpler elements. Thus, the body
> is resolved into the humors; the humors, into the fruits;
> the fruits into four elements; the elements, into matter and
> form. That is by demonstration which proves the matter at
> hand by means of something intermediary.[46]

While Augustine and Cassiodorus saw dialectic's crucial role
in the work of evangelization, other Church Fathers were not
always so sure. Ambrose of Milan (340–397 AD) condemns
dialectic as harmful to faith and contrasts it with Revelation:
"They store up all the strength of their poisons in dialetical
disputation, which by the judgment of philosophers is defined
as having no power to establish aught, and aiming only at
destruction. But it was not by dialectic that it pleased God to

---

[44] Ong, *Ramus, Method, and the Decay of Dialogue,* p. 56.
[45] Pottakis, "Socrates, Plato, Aristotle. Three Mentors in Ancient Greece," 40.
[46] John of Damascus, *The Fount of Knowledge* in *Saint John of Damascus: Writings,* Chapter 68, 107.

save His people."[47] Ambrose seemed to oppose Greco-Roman paideia as a whole. In the following, he conflates philosophy with dialectic:

> It is of the Son, therefore, that we read, thy mind under-standeth the reading, let thy tongue make confession. Away with arguments, where faith is required; now let dialectic hold her peace, even in the midst of her schools. I ask not what it is that philosophers say, but I would know what they do. They sit desolate in their schools. See the victory of faith over argument. They who dispute subtly are forsaken daily by their fellows; they who with sim-plicity believe are daily increased. Not philosophers but fishermen, not masters of dialectic but taxi-gatherers, now find credence. The one sort, through pleasures and luxu-ries, have bound the world's burden upon themselves; the other, by fasting and mortification, have cast it off, and so doth sorrow now begin to win over more followers than pleasure.[48]

Ambrose sounds like the Egyptian monk St. Anthony the Great (251–356 AD) in this opposition to philosophy and dialectic.

Like Tertullian, the Bishop of Milan connects pagan learn-ing with heresy, and in doing so sounds anti-intellectual. One justification is his observation that the Arians rely on philoso-phy and dialectic as much as pagans do. This underscores the harmful nature of these disciplines:

> Let us now see how far Arians and pagans do differ. The latter call upon gods, who are different in sex and unequal in power; the former affirm a Trinity where there is like-wise inequality of power and diversity of Godhead. The pagans assert that their Gods began to exist once upon a time; the Arians lyingly declare that Christ began to exist in the course of time. Have they not all dyed their impiety in the vats of philosophy? But indeed the pagans do extol that which they worship, the Arians maintain that the Son of God, Who is God, is a creature.[49]

---

[47] Ambrose of Milan, "Exposition of the Christian Faith," in *The Principal Works of St. Ambrose*, trans. H. De Romestin (Wm. B. Eerdmans, 1885), 500.
[48] Ibid., 518.
[49] Ibid.

Some Church officials in the Byzantine Empire also pushed back against secular education. The author of the *Life of St. Nicephorus of Latmos* argued that "profane" education is harmful. Had more churchmen shared this disapproval, certain elements of paideia may have died out. Fortunately, this opposition was in the minority, and grammar, logic, and rhetoric thrived in Christendom.

3.5 RHETORIC

The common roots of dialectic and rhetoric have ensured their long and close relationship, with much overlap. In *De natura*, Rabanus Maurus (c. 780–856 AD) identifies the role of dialectic as separating truth from falsehood, and that of rhetoric as focusing on the study of famous authors such as Plato and Epicurus for the best language models. Some authorities saw dialectic in a supportive or propaedeutic role for rhetoric: "Rhetoric is first the art of argumentation, and the condition of argumentation is determined by dialectic," according to a modern definition.[50] In the first book of *Rhetoric*, Aristotle distinguishes dialectic from rhetoric:

> It is clear, then, that rhetorical study, in its strict sense, is concerned with the modes of persuasion. Persuasion is clearly a sort of demonstration, since we are most fully persuaded when we consider a thing to have been demonstrated. The orator's demonstration is an enthymeme, and this is, in general, the most effective of the modes of persuasion. The enthymeme is a sort of syllogism, and the consideration of syllogisms of all kinds, without distinction, is the business of dialectic, either of dialectic as a whole or of one of its branches. It follows plainly, therefore, that he who is best able to see how and from what elements a syllogism is produced will also be best skilled in the enthymeme, when he has further learnt what its subject-matter is and in what respects it differs from the syllogism of strict logic. The true

[50] Bosch Rabell, Magdalena, and Baro Queralt, Xavier, "El Nacimiento de la Retórica Moderna a través de Cipriano Suarez (1524–1593)," *Comprendre* 20, no. 2 (2018), 45–60, p. 52.

> and the approximately true are apprehended by the same
> faculty; it may also be noted that men have a sufficient
> natural instinct for what is true, and usually do arrive at
> the truth. Hence the man who makes a good guess at truth
> is likely to make a good guess at probabilities.[51]

In the *Gorgias*, Plato defines rhetoric as the capacity to persuade. The roots of rhetoric were in the courts, in the form of judicial rhetoric, and then in politics, in the form of persuasion from democracy's need to form a majority.[52] To this political and practical form of rhetoric was added the didactic side of the discipline, famously undertaken at first by the Sophists, who trained their students to be persuasive on any matter, regardless of the truth. This aroused opposition from anyone concerned about virtue, who asserted that the Sophists undermined social stability and certainty of knowledge and moral principles. Socrates combated this relativism and uncertainty with definition.[53] Definition places limits on a term, specifically on what can be said about it. Exceeding the definition of a term amounts to the same hubris that, for the Greeks, is inherent to the violation of any boundary in life.[54]

Socrates' strong reaction to the Sophists went beyond his battle against rhetoric. He demanded that education focus on the truth. This focus requires the development of virtue. Socrates prompted a major shift, "from nature to the human, from the outside world to the internal, from the Philosophy of nature to Moral Philosophy. What is of utmost importance is the proverb 'Know Thyself.' And this self is his psyche."[55] *Psyche* had originally meant what the Romans called *spiritus*, breath. Socrates redefined "psyche" as the center of virtue, knowledge, justice and injustice, and goodness and evil. He saw the psyche as the seat not only of decision-making, but also of the true self,

---

[51] Aristotle, *Rhetoric*, trans. W. Rhys Roberts (Megaphone ebooks, 2008), Book I, Part 1, 67.
[52] Pottakis, "Socrates, Plato, Aristotle. Three Mentors in Ancient Greece," 38.
[53] Ibid., 40.
[54] Ibid.
[55] Ibid., 38.

which we need to know and nurture.[56] The alignment of this perspective with the Christian viewpoint provides one more example of why the Church appropriated so much of Greek paideia. Christians wholeheartedly accepted the core of Greek paideia, including philosophy, dialectic, and rhetoric.

Early medieval thinkers saw ancient grammar and rhetoric as the handmaidens of theology. This judgment stimulated the further development of the liberal arts, even while these disciplines remained rooted in their foundations. Rhetoric continued to be based on the canons of *inventio, dispositio, elocutio, memoria,* and *pronuntiatio. Inventio* refers to the step of conceiving one or more persuasive arguments to develop.[57] *Dispositio* involves the arrangement of these arguments. *Elocutio* identifies the most appropriate words and expressions that will provide the best style for a given argument.[58] The memory, or *memoria,* was far more greatly esteemed than it is now. This is unsurprising, given that ancient Greek or Roman orators could not rely on any paper notes to jog their memories. An entire speech would have to be memorized. *Pronuntiatio,* alongside orthography, became an increasing issue for churchmen such as Isidore of Seville because of the widening gap between the Latin of the liturgy and the classroom on the one hand and the vernacular Latin that would eventually develop into Italian, Portuguese, French, and so on. Greek masters also had to reckon with such linguistic changes to their language.

Alcuin gave a boost to classical rhetoric with his "profoundly classical spirit," which Edgar de Bruyne characterizes as *"le bon goût,"* or good taste.[59] Grammar, rhetoric, and logic took on more than merely utilitarian roles, as they were esteemed for their psychological and spiritual benefits. Remi d'Auxerre argued that rhetoric and poetics possess inherent value and are

---

[56] Pottakis, "Socrates, Plato, Aristotle. Three Mentors in Ancient Greece," 39.
[57] Paul McKechnie, "St. Perpetua and Roman Education in A. D. 200," in *L'antiquité classique,* Volume 63 (1994), 283.
[58] Wolff, *L'Education dans le monde romain,* 68.
[59] Edgar de Bruyne, *Etudes d'esthétique médiévale,* Volume 1 (Albin Michel, 1998), 216, 221. De Bruyne's italics.

therefore desirable in themselves. They are a part of the human mind.[60] Such thinking expresses the microcosmic-macrocosmic relationship that possessed so much ontological meaning. This parallel between the outer world of creation, of the cosmos, and the inner world of the person, of the soul, enabled the liberal arts to provide a suitable foundation for later studies in philosophy and theology, which also deal with metaphysical questions at the micro and macro levels.

The doctrine of Adam's fall, which heavily impacted medieval psychology, influenced how some scholars approached the teaching of the ancients. Remi argued that, as one outcome of the Fall, not everyone possessed rhetoric even though it is a basic human quality. In other words, Edenic man and woman possessed the fullness of rhetoric and poetics, but the Fall contaminated all humans. Thereby deprived of the ideal state of being, humans were left in profound ignorance. Strenuous effort can, with God's grace, lift humans out of this.[61] Remi speaks of "reminiscence," by which humans can produce rhetoric and poetics through effort. There are larger implications of this reminiscence, or *anamnesis*. The basic substance of each art, such as perfect melody in music and eloquence in speech, exists deep in the unconscious nature of the artist. The artist recalls elements of a given artful substance through his memory.[62] This reflects the Carolingians' esteem for art's spiritual value, even if they did not practice the eastern veneration of icons.

A letter from Rabanus Maurus highlights the realist perspective of the trivium. In this letter, he values literature over art:

> Writing is more valuable than tricky painted form. Writing contributes more to the soul's growth towards beauty than the harmony of colors, which only shows the shadows. Scripture is the perfect and pious norm for our salvation. It is worth more regarding its contribution to our understanding of reality. It is more useful than all other things. It

---

[60] De Bruyne, *Etudes d'esthétique médiévale*, 240.
[61] Ibid., 241.
[62] Ibid., 242.

affects our artistic sensibility more immediately than painting. The signification that the written work conveys is the most perfect for the human sense of things. It is easier to retain in the memory... It places us in the presence of reality.[63]

Rabanus here seems to mix literature with Holy Writ. He later adds in the letter the more general sense: "Writing was given to us by God, who taught Adam to name things" (Genesis 2:20).[64] Despite the Christian confidence that the trivium could aid in the soul's ascent, the Church Fathers put clear limits on this ascension without the aid of grace. In *De Trinitate*, Boethius notes in reference to "the study of divinity," that "we should not of course press our inquiry further than man's wit and reason are allowed to climb the height of heavenly knowledge. In all the liberal arts we see the same limit set beyond which reason may not reach."[65] This is the way for Christian theologians to avoid the hubris from overextending their use of the liberal arts or philosophy.

Rhetoric in the early medieval West did not have the status that the Romans had given it in antiquity. This was due to practical religious reasons. The quiet, contemplative life of the monastery prioritized silence, not rhetoric. The latter was seen as potentially dangerous by some clerics. Isidore of Seville minimized the role of rhetorical display, which he regarded as unnecessary for the exposition of the Bible. A twentieth-century scholar notes: "A few generalities based on the theoretic treatises of classical writers formed the stock-in-trade of the mediaeval teacher. It was generally considered sufficient to be acquainted with the terminology of Rhetoric, to be able to distinguish the three kinds of eloquence, to have some idea what was meant by *inventio*, *dispositio*, and *elocutio*, to know the six parts of an oration, and so on. The greatest authority was Cicero, whose sway was unchallenged."[66]

---

[63] De Bruyne, *Etudes d'esthétique médiévale*, 279.

[64] Ibid., 280.

[65] Boethius, "De Trinitate, Proemium," in *The Theological Tractates*, trans. H. F. Stewart (Harvard University Press, 1968), 5.

[66] Clark, *The Abbey of St Gall as a Centre of Literature and Art*, 114.

Rhetoric mainly consisted of government-related texts. The relatively stagnant discipline changed during the ninth and tenth centuries, as it became associated with the *dictamen prosaicum* (free prose composition). This new rhetoric referred to letter writing or legal documents. These genres followed a clear plan, with writing reduced to the imitation of models. The oratorical terms *exordium, narratio,* and *conclusio* now denoted different parts of this pre-determined style. Students relied on *formulae,* which were texts that brought together model letters and charters. The scholars Iso and Ruadpert authored one collection each. Other *formulae* were produced at St. Gall, including its most complete, the *Collectio Sangallensis* or *Formelbuch Salomos,* which was produced under Abbot Salomo (890–920), probably by Notker Balbulus. The forty-seven models of this text range from various types of charters to genuine and hypothetical letters to churchmen and rulers.[67]

3.6 RHETORIC IN THE BYZANTINE EMPIRE

Rhetoric was esteemed and prioritized by the Byzantines more than it was in the Latin West in the Early Middle Ages. Rhetoric was the primary discipline and skill of the second level of Byzantine education. It was primarily taught through the *progymnasmata.* These were the series of exercises that bridged the grammar and rhetoric classes, and prepared the student for the declamation, the long speech of praise, which in the Byzantine Empire would ideally be delivered on the subject of the greatness of the emperor — often in front of the emperor himself. The *grammatikos* relied on the first few exercises from the *progymnasmata* to train the student to write brief texts on topics from ancient Greek mythology, popular sayings, or even speeches of praise of characters from mythology or history. This included the description and comparison of characteristics of

---

[67] Clark, *The Abbey of St Gall as a Centre of Literature and Art,* 115.

mythological or historical figures or events.[68] Michael Psellos's poem, *Synopsis of Rhetoric*, composed for the emperor Michael VII Doukas, summarizes the standard textbook in the empire, *On Rhetorical Exercises*, Hermogenes of Tarsus's second century AD manual of the progymnasmata.

Psellos's poem covers the rhetorical topics of *stasis*, *invention*, *style*, and *forcefulness*. The author, a famous speaker and teacher, begins with the promise of rhetoric:

> If you learn the art of rhetoric, crownbearer,
> you'll be an able speaker, and you'll have a graceful tongue,
> and you'll have the most persuasive epicheiremes.[69]

Next, Psellos notes the probability, not certainty, of rhetorical argumentation, along with the usual topic of rhetoric:

> The art surveys political questions,
> and a political question, according to the technographer,
> is a doubtful matter that is arguable and divisible on both
>   sides,
> according to the customs and laws of cities,
> concerning the just, the good, and the advantageous.
> Indeed the kinds [eidê] of rhetoric are just these three —
> judicial [dikanikon], advisory [sumboulê], and panegyric
>   [panêguris] —
> for the end of judicial rhetoric is the just,
> of panegyric the good, and of advisory the advantageous.

The polymath Psellos was keenly interested in the teaching of both philosophy and law. Instruction in rhetoric in the Byzantine Empire, which prepared students for a career in the bureaucracy, would have focused on legal rhetoric. Later in the poem Psellos provides an ideal for rhetoric:

> Let civic discourse be adorned in every way,
> and let it have these types [ideas] of style in particular:
> character, sincererity, abundance,
> rapidity, clarity, asperity, florescence,

---

[68] Markopoulos, "Education," 789.
[69] Michael Psellos, *Synopsis of Rhetoric*, trans. Jeffrey Walker (2006). Walker notes: "Epicheirêma: in rhetorical theory, an argumentative movement composed of linked sub-arguments and amplifications."

solemnity, brilliance, and forcefulness of method,
which I will overview for you, as in one heading.

The objective of Byzantine rhetoric was to emulate the past masters.[70] Though rhetoric saw development over the centuries in the empire, Maximos Planoudes in the thirteenth century cited a sixth century definition that revealed the original political foundation of rhetoric's development out of the *polis*: Rhetoric is "the art that deals with the power of the word in political matters, whose purpose is persuasive argument against the prevailing view."[71]

Education in rhetoric was closely associated with the imperial court, and included the *basilikos logos*, an *encomion* to the emperor. Eusebius of Caesarea set the example with his *Life of Constantine* and its idealization of the emperor.[72] The ninth-century *Life of the Empress Theodora* is a *basilikos logos* of a different type, as it concerns "a female ruler where deeds of piety are substituted for deeds of valour."[73] In other words, Byzantine rhetoric, used in the political arena, could often have a religious aspect because of the intertwining of Christianity with all of Byzantine society. There was no sacred-secular split. Christian belief, more than rhetoric or philosophy or another aspect of the ancient Greek heritage, was the most important source of identity for the empire's leading thinkers from the ninth century to its fall in 1453 AD. The acquisition of rhetoric and philosophy in the classroom was justified for their roles in elevating the preaching of the Gospel and the rule of the Christian emperor.[74] The Byzantines Christianized the trivium as much as the western Latin thinkers did, even if education was more independent of direct ecclesiastical oversight than it was in the West.

---

[70] Jeffreys, "Rhetoric," 827.
[71] Ibid.
[72] Ibid., 832. An encomion is the praising of a person or thing.
[73] Ibid., 833.
[74] Paul Magdalino, "From 'encyclopedism' to 'humanism': the turning point of Basil II and the millennium," in *Byzantium in the Eleventh Century*, eds. Marc D. Lauxtermann and Mark Whittow (Routledge, 2017), 4.

CHAPTER 4

The Foundations of the Quadrivium

All the ancient authorities who, under the leadership of Pythagoras, demonstrated the superior brilliance of their minds and the force of their thought are clearly of the opinion that no one can rise to the height of perfection in philosophical studies unless he inquires into such a noble wisdom through what we could call the fourfold path.
— Boethius[1]

4.I A PROPAEDEUTIC TO PHILOSOPHY

ROME'S IMPERIAL ERA (27 BC–476 AD) saw a consolidation and systematization of past intellectual achievements. Not every discipline that had been developed in Greece centuries earlier was prized equally. The Roman prioritization of grammar and rhetoric over the other disciplines contributed to the decline of the study of mathematics from the time of Euclid (flourished circa 300 BC) to Nicomachus of Gerasa (c. 60–c. 120 AD).[2] Nicomachus's *Introduction to Arithmetic* regards mathematics as a propaedeutic to philosophy.[3] This reflects the belief that mathematics itself contains philosophical and metaphysical truths. His phrase *tessares methodoi*, in reference to the four mathematical elements, may have inspired Boethius's term *quadrivium*, the "fourfold path." Keeping to the philosophically syncretic spirit of the time that produced what modern scholars call Neoplatonism, Nicomachus also employed Aristotelian logic. This included

---

[1] Boèce, *Institution Arithmétique*, trans. Jean-Yves Guillaumin (Belles Lettres, 1995), 5.
[2] Lafontaine, *Isidore de Seville et la culture classique dans l'Espagne wisigothique*, 351.
[3] Ibid.

definition and classification, as his discussion moved from simple to more complex numbers.[4] As with most writings on philosophy or the liberal arts of the era, the text contains little originality.

Boethius's scientific writings were tremendously influential throughout the entire Middle Ages.[5] This included perhaps the most important source of the quadrivium for the Middle Ages, *De Arithemtica*, which he based on Nicomachus's text. Boethius emphasizes the foundational nature of mathematics: "It is therefore certain that whoever neglects these sciences fails to acquire all philosophical knowledge. It is by this quadrivium that those with a superior spirit let themselves be led by the senses, which are created with us, to the highest certainties of intelligence."[6] He notes the different degrees to this "determined and measured" progression towards the truth and contemplation. The unity that Boethius gave to the quadrivial *disciplinae*, based on their ontological qualities, challenged the independence of music as envisioned by Aristoxenus in the fourth century BC.[7]

Despite this lack of independence, the ontological unity of the four disciplines does not erase their individual characteristics. The Pythagorean-Platonist concept of number clearly delineates the identities of the four disciplines. Arithmetic considers number in itself, geometry and astronomy examine the size of number (geometry deals with number at rest, astronomy with number in movement), and music looks at number in relationship. The ancient view, which Boethius passed along to the medieval mind, regarded mathematics as inquiring into number as non-material and unchanging. Number is always identical to what it has always been.[8] Two plus two is always

---

[4] Jean-Yves Guillaumin "Introduction," in Boèce, *Institution Arithmetique*. Translated by Jean-Yves Guillaumin. (Belles Lettres, 1995), xxxiii.

[5] Ibid., xxv.

[6] Boèce, *Institution Arithmétique*, 1,7, 8.

[7] Jean-Baptiste Guillaumin, "Introduction," in Martianus Capella, *Les Noces de Philologie et de Mercure. Livre IX. L'Harmonie*, trans. Jean-Baptiste Guillaumin (Les Belles Lettres, 2011), liii.

[8] Guillaumin, "Introduction," in Boèce, *Institution Arithmetique*, li.

four. This perspective clearly separates geometry from geodesy (land surveying), arithmetic from logistics and calculation, and the philosophical examination of the harmony of the spheres from instrumental and sung music, even if geodesy, logistics and calculation, and instrumental and sung music preceded and may even have served as the origins of the quadrivial disciplines.[9] Some writers such as Martianus Capella prefer to refer to music as the discipline of "harmony." This is consistent with the ancient Greek understanding, as exemplified by *logos*, which can mean relationship and reasoning, including mathematical reasoning.[10] This was never seriously challenged in the Middle Ages. In fact, the Middle Ages and Renaissance connected music to the soul, based on the Pythagorean tradition of the correspondence among *harmonia instrumentalis*, *harmonia humana*, and *harmonia mundana* that Boethius helped bequeath to later generations. However, the traditionally sharp distinction and hierarchy between theory and practice was not so clear in the Christian centuries, as *computus* and music in particular were needed both for determining the Church calendar and for the practice of liturgical chant and music. Training in these did not demand any knowledge of the quadrivium.

Not all Christians were accepting of the Greek investigation into the natural world, and the twin pillars of philosophy and the quadrivial disciplines. Ambrose of Milan expresses skepticism in the capacity of natural philosophy to find the truth:

> Philosophers dispute about the course of the sun and the system of the heavens, and there are those who think that these should be believed when they are ignorant of what they are talking about. For neither have they climbed up into the heavens, nor measured the sky, nor examined the

---

[9] Jean-Baptiste Guillaumin, "Introduction," in Martianus Capella, *Les Noces de Philologie et de Mercure. Livre VII. L'Arithmetique*, trans. Jean-Baptiste Guillaumin (Les Belles Lettres, 2003), lxviii.

[10] César González Ochoa, *La música del universo* (Universidad Nacional Autónoma de México, 1994), 44. In mathematics, *logos* refers to the relationship between two numbers, a-b or a:b. Arpad Szabo, *Les débuts des mathématiques grecques*, trans. M. Federspiel (Paris: Vrin, 1977), 181–182.

universe with their eyes; for none of them was with God in
the beginning, none of them has said of God: "When He
was preparing the heavens I was with Him, I was with Him
as a master workman, I was he in whom He delighted." If,
then, they are believed, is God not believed, Who says: "As
the new heavens and the new earth, which I make to remain
before Me, saith the Lord; so shall your name and your seed
abide; and month shall be after month, and sabbath after
sabbath, and all flesh shall come in My sight to worship in
Jerusalem, saith the Lord God; and they shall go forth, and
shall see the limbs of men who have transgressed against
Me. For their worm shall not die and their fire shall not be
quenched and they shall be a sight to all flesh."[11]

Despite this doubting Thomas spirit, it seems that in the end,
hardly any debate took place on this issue. Natural philosophy
and the quadrivium were well-respected in the Early Middle
Ages, even if more resources and attention went into the trivium.

The quadrivium mirrors the trivium's hierarchical nature,
with arithmetic as the foundation of the other disciplines just
as grammar provides the foundation of the trivium. Instead
of a crossroads of four paths, *quadrivium* denotes the four
successive paths that need to be studied and contemplated on
the way to philosophy. Boethius followed this perspective in
prioritizing virtue and the student's moral development. From
the time of Pythagoras and Plato, no distinction was made
between the search for knowledge and the search for wisdom,
the latter of which is intrinsic to virtue.[12] The Roman senator's
writings on music and arithmetic outlined Pythagorean, not
technical, ideas. For instance, his treatise on music emphasized
the Pythagorean teaching on cosmic harmony.[13] His thought
reflects Platonic teaching, itself inspired by two ideas. First,
numerical relationships underpin the universal harmony of the
cosmos. Second, man's happiness comes from participating in

---

[11] Ambrose of Milan, "On the Decease of his Brother Satyrus," in *The Principal
Works of St. Ambrose* (Wm. B. Eerdmanns, 1885), 468.
[12] Jean-Yves Guillaumin, "Introduction," in Boece, *Institution Arithmetique* (Paris:
Belles Lettres, 1995), liv.
[13] Ibid., xxxix.

this harmony.[14] This notion, shared by pagans and Christians, was embraced by medieval thinkers. The ontological nature of these disciplines encouraged an ascetic outlook and practice that aligned with the initially-Platonic and then Stoic virtues that the Church Fathers appropriated and called the "cardinal virtues."[15] The association of the term "quadrivium" with virtue education had wide currency among Church authorities. In fact, for some writers, such as Flodoard of Reims (died in 966 AD), *quadrivium* denoted the four cardinal virtues. In the Boethian approach, the elements of the quadrivium work together because they possess the same Pythagorean spirit of approach to the physical world.

Martianus Capella's *On the Marriage of Philology and Mercury* reflects the hierarchical orientation and the associated spiritualization of science and mathematical learning. Through allegory, he expresses the upward movement revealed and guided by the liberal arts. In the beginning of his nine-book treatise, Mercury takes the counsel of Apollo and decides to marry Philology. This is the allegorization of the "divine character of the union between erudition (that is, Philology) and eloquence (represented by Mercury) in a marriage that is approved by the laws of the gods and of number."[16] The Byzantine polymath Michael Psellos claimed to exemplify this unification of content and style. There is a spiritual aspect to the unity that Capella describes. The marriage of Mercury and Apollo represents the union of the soul with Logos. Logos is both Word and Reason. This path to heaven is the way of knowledge, which is attained by the study of the seven liberal arts. Capella's idea parallels in allegorical form Augustine's ideas in book two of *De Ordine*, whether purposely or not.[17] Even though there is nothing explicitly Christian about Capella's text, both its

---

[14] Guillaumin, "Introduction," in Boèce, *Institution Arithmetique*, xxx.

[15] Ibid., lvi.

[16] Guillaumin, "Introduction," in Martianus Capella, *Les Noces de Philologie et de Mercure. Livre VII. L'Arithmetique*, xx–xxi.

[17] Ibid., xxv.

allegory and its depiction of the liberal arts strongly appealed to the medieval mind in the West.

Coherence, discipline, and harmony are inherent to the quadrivium. *Proportio* denotes the relationship between two numbers or sizes, and reason (or *ratio*) guides the way of thinking that is at the core of the quadrivium.[18] At the core of *ratio* is the rational, predictable, and eternally-unchanging behavior of numbers. Medieval thinkers inherited the ancient fascination for the predictability, constancy, and efficiency of mathematical reasoning. Mathematical truths have a timeless quality about them. They hold true forever. Ancient and medieval thinkers connected this mathematical precision and predictability to the precision and predictability of the movements of the stars.[19] This became the model for how to see and contemplate all things in the created order. The world was a "vast domain of which reason takes stock, scrutinizes the laws, and calculates the results of its operations."[20] The quadrivium and natural philosophy were based on the idea of a rational God creating a rational universe that can be understand in a rational way by humans, who are rational. The cosmos is as rational as man himself (insofar as man is *potentially* rational) in this microcosmic-macrocosmic outlook.

4.2 NUMBER THEORY

The consideration of the ontological nature of numbers was central to the quadrivium and, in fact, to philosophy itself. Since Plato, the Greek educational tradition had made it virtually mandatory to prepare for philosophy through mathematics. The study of mathematics was a spiritual and moral preparation. Augustine followed the Neoplatonists in asserting that the study

---

[18] Clelia V. Crialesi, "Les 'Raisons' Mathématiques," in *La raison au Moyen Âge*, 80. Boethius uses *ratio* in his writings on arithmetic and geometry to denote "criterion, way, and rule," words which do not necessarily refer to science or mathematics.
[19] Dominique Poirel, "Introduction," in *La raison au Moyen Âge*, ed. Dominique Poirel (Vrin, 2024), 18.
[20] Ibid., 18.

of mathematics enabled the soul to turn away from the sensory, material world, and "rise to the spiritual world by way of the intelligible."[21] Boethius adopted this moral perspective of the study of mathematics. To take the path of the *quadrivium* was to take the right path of the more basic *biuium* (*bi-vium*, or forked road). The *quadrivium* represented the way of goodness, and the other path the way of vice.[22] Ancient and medieval Christians as a whole saw ontological significance in numbers, which they based on a mixture of Scripture, Christian tradition, and the Greeks, particularly the Pythagorean understanding of numbers.

The Byzantines shared the western fascination for the meaning of numbers. For example, Maximos the Confessor in *On Difficulties in Sacred Scripture: The Responses to Thalassios* (questions 38–41) addresses the symbolic use of numbers in the Bible, including "the seven brothers in the Gospel of Matthew (Qu. 38), the six jars of water at the wedding in Cana (Qu. 40), and the five husbands of the Samaritan woman (Qu. 41). These Neo-Pythagorean exercises in the theology of arithmetic — a mode of analysis in which the meaning of physical and literary phenomena is grasped on the level of numerical units and their combinations — rank among the most elaborate exegetical treatments of numbers in all of Greek patristic literature."[23]

Each number held unique significance. One, the *monad*, was not regarded by all authorities as a number. It represents the unity and oneness of God for Christians. It is seen as the undifferentiated first cause, as explained by the Irish scholar and translator of Denys the Areopagite, John Scotus Eriugena (800–877 AD). He notes that "in themselves these first causes are one and simple and none knows the order in which they are placed or are distinguished one from another. For this is something that happens to them in their effects, and as in the

---

[21] Lafontaine, *Isidore de Seville et la culture classique dans l'Espagne wisigothique*, 343.

[22] Boèce, *Institution Arithmétique*, 142–144.

[23] Nicholas Contas, "Introduction," in Maximos the Confessor, *On Difficulties in Sacred Scripture: The Responses to Thalassios*, trans. Maximos Constas (The Catholic University of America Press, 2018), 15–16.

monad although in the sphere of reason alone all the numbers
subsist in it, yet no number is distinguished from another
number—for they are one and a simple one and not a one
that is a composite of many, for it is from the monad that
every multiplication of numbers proceeds to infinity whereas
the monad is not composed from the multiples that issue in
progression from it as though it were made up of the collection of them into one."[24] Eriugena then ties number to order
by noting that "when they proceed into their effects that are
multiplied to infinity they acquire their numerable and ordered
plurality—not that the Cause of all things is not Order or
Ordering, or that order-through-itself is not included among
the principles of things, for every ordered thing is ordered
by participation in it; but because all order in the supreme
Cause of all things and in the first participation in it [is] one
and simple and is distinguished by no differences, and in it no
order clashes with any other since they are an inseparable one
from which the multiple order of things descends."[25]

Numbers from two onwards held a range of meanings. The
number two, the first number (in the case that *one* is not a
number), denotes the two natures of Jesus. The Pythagorean
number of completion, three, holds the obvious significance
for Christians of the Trinity of Divine Persons. More philosophically, Isidore calls three the perfect number because "it
has a beginning, a middle, and an end, with each digit having
the same relationship to unity."[26] The Biblical significance of
three also includes the three wise men coming to visit the
infant Jesus just as three angels had visited Abraham; Jonas
spending three nights in the belly of the whale and Jesus (like
Lazarus) spending three nights in the tomb; Jesus asking three
times that He be spared the Passion; and Peter denying Jesus
three times. As for the number four, it held a special place for

the Greeks, due to the *tetraktys* (τετρακτύς), 1,2,3,4. The sum of these four numbers is ten, the perfect number: $1 + 2 + 3 + 4 = 10$. There are four gospels, four cardinal virtues, and four rivers of Eden. The fourfold path of mathematics, the *quadrivium*, added another dimension to the number-ontology of the Old and New Testaments. Five was considered a perfect number that refers to the *quintessence*. It is also the number of Jesus' wounds. Sir Gawain's shield in *Sir Gawain and the Green Knight* featured a pentangle (also called pentagram) for this reason.

As we can see, the ancient Greek and the Christian traditions enjoyed a harmony with their philosophical understanding of numbers. The initially-Biblical significance of the number six is expanded to encompass philosophy. In the Biblical view, Genesis recounts the act of creation as occurring in six days, as Isidore reminds us: "The [number] that contains six units (*senarius*),which is perfect in its own parts, declares the completion of the world by a certain signification of its number."[27] Eriugena expands on Isidore's Christian conception of this number: "If, therefore, that perfect number, namely the number six, is constituted in the unity of the numbers, let him take care who says that it is not eternal, for in it the Creator of all things perfected His works. But here it must be noted that the number six is not perfect because in it God concluded all things which He wished to create, but He created His works in it because by the perfection of the number the perfection of His works should be revealed."[28] Numbers reveal the connection of the Creator with creation. Yet Eriugena waxes more philosophically about six. His following observation would have been recognized by the pre-Christian Greeks: "The number six is not excluded from the unity and multiplication of the other numbers, especially as, alone among the cardinals, that is, among the first series of numbers from one to ten, it is perfect. For it is perfected by its parts, namely, the sixth and the third

---

[27] Isidore of Seville, *The Etymologies of Isidore of Seville*, ed. Stephen A. Barney, et al (Cambridge University Press, 2006), 3.iv.2.
[28] Eriugena, *Periphyseon*, Book 2, 656A–656B, 277–278.

and the half. For the sixth is one, the third is two, the half is three, and these added together perfect the quantity of six. For one and two and three make six."[29] Christian thought often seems to make the journey from an initial Biblical significance to deeper metaphysical speculation that the Greeks would have recognized. Churchmen went from Jerusalem to Athens, but with a Christian sensibility of ancient Hellenic thought that far surpassed the late ancient mimickry of the past.

Numbers provided a way of expressing certain truths about the Christian life. Christians developed the seven cardinal virtues and the seven deadly sins. Concerning the seven gifts of the Holy Spirit, the *Catechism of the Catholic Church* teaches:

> The moral life of Christians is sustained by the gifts of the Holy Spirit. These are permanent dispositions which make man docile in following the promptings of the Holy Spirit. The seven *gifts* of the Holy Spirit are wisdom, understanding, counsel, fortitude, knowledge, piety, and fear of the Lord. They belong in their fullness to Christ, Son of David. They complete and perfect the virtues of those who receive them. They make the faithful docile in readily obeying divine inspirations.[30]

Baptismal fonts were often eight sided, as the number signifies a new beginning. Boys from the culture of the first Covenant (including the Savior, Jesus of Nazareth) were circumcised on the eighth day. The Resurrection occurred on the eighth day. There are nine choirs of angels. Ten, as the perfect number, is symbolized by the Ten Commandments. Twelve was significant because of the twelve tribes of Israel and the twelve apostles. There are twelve fruits of the Holy Spirit. The *Catechism* explains: "The fruits of the Spirit are perfections that the Holy Spirit forms in us as the first fruits of eternal glory. The tradition of the Church lists twelve of them: 'charity, joy, peace, patience, kindness, goodness, generosity, gentleness, faithfulness,

---

[29] Eriugena, *Periphyseon*, Book 2, 656C–656D, 277.
[30] *Catechism of the Catholic Church*, 2nd ed. (Washington, DC: United States Conference of Catholic Bishops, 2000), 1830–1831, part 3, §3, chap. 1, art. 7, iii, 450, https://www.usccb.org/sites/default/files/flipbooks/catechism/452/.

modesty, self-control, chastity.'"[31] Forty is an oft-repeated number in the Bible, and symbolizes perseverance, exemplified by
the Israelites' wandering in the desert and Jesus' retreat into
the desert to face temptation. As we can see, the philosophical
and theological consideration of numbers already had a long
and rich pedigree by the Early Middle Ages.

Numbers held aesthetic meaning as well. This reflects the
foundation of the cosmos on the metaphysical significance of
numbers. The association of numbers with beauty reflects the
ontological significance of beauty. Proportion, symmetry, and
harmony produce beauty because they arise out of the human
participation in God's creation and creativity. Humans are
positively impacted psychologically by beauty because of the
microcosmic-macrocosmic correspondence according to which
outer beauty has a profound effect on the human soul. Proportion, symmetry, harmony, and allegory featured as prominently
in painting as in the other creative domains. These four elements
took on a contemplative role. Musical proportions strongly
influenced medieval artistic techniques.[32] Aesthetic truths held
across all of the creative arts, including architecture, the plastic
arts, and human-produced music. Particular numbers, such as
three, six, seven, eight, nine, ten, achieved particular prominence
in depicting the human body. It was believed that numbers
help determine the right proportion, with proportion being
"an intelligible reality and thought that predetermines relations
through the senses; it is a law to which form must submit."[33]
The failure to submit to this leads to ugliness, which is harmful
to human psychological and spiritual health.

4.3 ARITHMETIC

The philosophical, and specifically metaphysical, spirit of Boethius' *De Arithmetica* is clear from his own observations. At the

---

[31] *The Catechism of the Catholic Church*, 1832, Part 3, §3, ch. 1, art. 7, iii.
[32] De Bruyne, *Etudes d'esthétique médiévale*, 292.
[33] Ibid., 297.

very beginning of the text, he associates the unchanging nature of numbers with ontology, which is familiar to readers by now, but that bears repeating because of the centrality of this notion to the quadrivium: "Wisdom is the understanding of the truth of the things that are and that have their own immutable substance. We speak of things that know neither development by extension nor diminution by reduction, nor change by variations, but which always remain in the character of their nature."[34]

This ontological nature gives numbers a key role in creation, as Boethius continues:

> Everything that was built by nature in its first age appeared formed according to the system of numbers because it was the first principle in the spirit of the creator. It is the system that is the origin of the plurality of the four elements, the origin of the succession of time, the movement of the heavenly bodies and the revolutions of the sky. Because it is so, and that the stability of the universe is founded on numerical connections, it is necessary that number always remains equally in its own substance and that it not be composed of diverse elements.[35]

He notes that numbers are united through their first principles, and that these unchanging principles are a part of the substance of numbers. This is so "because it is impossible that anything be created from things that do not exist, and the principles from which something is created must be dissimilar, but also possess the possibility of being combined."[36] The ontological nature of these uncreated things indicates their non-material natures.

In the same treatise, Boethius examines pure number and its unique participation in creation. Pure number is "the first being and that which possesses the greatest power of creativity, even, one can say, fecundity. This is why Boethius follows Nicomachus in so frequently using the terms 'mother' (*mater*), 'root' (*radix*), or origin (*principium*...)"; Boethius regards mathematics as the "principle of unity [and] the mother of the other mathematical

---

[34] Boèce, *Institution Arithmetique*, I, 5.
[35] Ibid., 1,2,1–2, 11.
[36] Ibid.

sciences."[37] A recurring theme of *De Arithemtica* is "the idea of 'birth' (*nasci*) and 'generation' (*generare*) of numbers by the coupling (*copulare*) with other numbers."[38] This is reminiscent of the demiurge that creates the universe on behalf of God, but is itself created by God.[39] In any case, none of this calls for creativity on the part of the mathematician or young student of the quadrivium, but instead passive acceptance in the form of the contemplation "in number and in possible combinations of a purely objective reality that owes nothing to the human spirit. One 'finds' or 'discovers' (*inuenire*) something that preexists the intellectual operation of the mathematician."[40] This investigation into metaphysical reality not only aligned with the medieval Christian prioritization of the spiritual over the physical, but also helped to explain from a philosophical perspective why the spiritual surpassed the physical: "The ideality of mathematical beings, far from depriving them of all real existence, on the contrary gives them an order that is superior to that of the sensory."[41] This ontological view of numbers is what assigned the quadrivium its propaedeutic role in ancient and medieval education. It was a spiritual as much as intellectual propaedeutic. Boethius's inclusion of philosophical statements within the text of *De Arithemtica* reveals the double philosophical role of mathematics, as it is not only a propaedeutic for philosophy, but as itself philosophy.[42]

---

[37] Guillaumin, "Introduction," in Boèce, *Institution Arithmetique*, li–lii.

[38] Ibid., lii.

[39] John P. Arendzen in the *Catholic Encyclopedia* of 1913 (volume 4) notes: "The word means literally a public worker, *demioergós, demiourgós*, and was originally used to designate any craftsman plying his craft or trade for the use of the public. Soon, however, *technítes* and other words began to be used to designate the common artisan while demiurge was set aside for the Great Artificer or Fabricator, the Architect of the universe. At first the words *toû kósmou* were added to distinguish the great Workman from others, but gradually *demiourgós* became the technical term for the Maker of heaven and earth. In this sense it is used frequently by Plato in his 'Timæus.'" The notion of a demiurge was important for both the Gnostics and Neoplatonists.

[40] Guillaumin, "Introduction," in Boèce, *Institution Arithmetique*, lii.

[41] Ibid.

[42] Ibid., lii–liii

Martianus Capella's observations on arithmetic frequently paralleled those of Boethius. Capella differed in placing arithmetic after geometry, though he did note "the ontological primacy of number with regards to all that exists, and the priority of arithmetic with regards to the other mathematical sciences."[43] He followed Nicomachus of Gerasa and Boethius in noting the "maternity" of arithmetic that arises from the power of number as "the first being and also that which possesses the greatest power of creativity, even fertility."[44] As we have seen, this generativity of number did not mean that the study of arithmetic encourages creativity. Like Boethius, Capella believed that mathematical concepts are not to be exploited, but to be contemplated. In fact, the real object of contemplation was the purely objective reality that number provides and that "owes nothing to the human spirit, to whom it simply gives itself to be seen."[45] In their writings on the quadrivium, Boethius and Capella described philosophy as the study of wisdom.

Other early medieval thinkers added little to the quadrivium, and acted more as encyclopedists. In the *Etymologies*, Isidore followed Cassiorodus (c. 485–c. 585 AD), Lactantius (c. 250–c. 325 AD), and Theon of Smyrna (first century AD) in classifying the quadrivium as arithmetic, geometry, music, and astronomy.[46] The Bishop of Seville discussed numbers in the third book of his encyclopedia. He followed Augustine in noting their religious symbolism.[47] This lack of development in the understanding of the disciplines of the quadrivium did not undermine their high status. Charlemagne's *Admonitio generalis* (from 789 AD) called for every cleric to be trained

---

[43] Guillaumin, "Introduction," in Martianus Capella, *Les Noces de Philologie et de Mercure. Livre VII. L'Arithmetique*, lxv.

[44] Ibid.

[45] Ibid., lxix.

[46] Cassiodorus was the author of the *Institutiones divinarum et saecularum litterarum*, Lactantius of the *Divine Institutions*, and Theon of *On Mathematics Useful for the Understanding of Plato*.

[47] Lafontaine, *Isidore de Seville et la culture classique dans l'Espagne wisigothique*, 348.

in arithmetic, mostly because of the need to calculate Easter, but also based on the Carolingian esteem for the liberal arts. Capella's *On the Marriage of Philology and Mercury* was loved by the Carolingians, particularly among the third generation of scholars. Such esteem for mathematics was widespread and deeply-rooted. In the eleventh century, the Byzantine scholar Michael Psellos argued that the universe cannot be known without numbers, and that arithmetic and geometry inquire into the created order from two different perspectives, the discontinuous and the continuous respectively. In other words, for Psellos the universe was simultaneously continuous and discontinuous.[48]

---

[48] Tatakis, *Byzantine Philosophy*, 158.

CHAPTER 5

The Advanced Quadrivium

Remove numbers from all things, and everything perishes.[1]
—Isidore of Seville

Great God! Who can deny that You are the orderly ruler of all? Everything is related to everything else, each thing impelled to its appointed effects by a series of fixed laws. They are so many and act in so many fashions as to force us to speak of them endlessly. In so doing, we find You.
— Augustine.[2]

5.1 GEOMETRY

CHRISTIAN THINKERS INHERITED A rich tradition in geometry. The discipline had been tepid for centuries, largely due to the Romans' lack of enthusiasm. Euclid (circa 300 BC), whose treatise was only one in a long line of texts called the *Elements*, personified the period of tremendous advances in geometry and other scientific and mathematical domains, from Thales of Miletus (c. 629–548 BC) to the fourth century BC. By the Roman imperial period of the first through fifth centuries AD, stagnation had set in, and systematization and consolidation of previous gains became the norm. This was exemplified by the Pythagorean-Platonist Theon of Smyrna (late first century AD) and the Alexandrine mathematicians, including Theon of Alexandria (c. 335–405 AD). His version of Euclid's *Elements* became the standard for centuries.

Later thinkers contributed by passing on these gains to the Middle Ages. The most general attitude was supplied by Augustine, who, in his foundational Christian document on

---

[1] Isidore of Seville, *The Etymologies of Isidore of Seville*, 3.iv.4.
[2] Augustine, *On Order [De Ordine]*, trans. Silvano Borruso (St. Augustine's Press, 2007), 1.5.14, 19.

the quadrivium, *On Order*, argues that the world, despite its seeming chaos, is not only founded on order, but founded on God's order, which "proceeds from Him and is to be found in Him."[3] More specific to geometry, Boethius defines the second through fourth quadrivial disciplines through proportion. The study of proportion underpins inquiry into these three disciplines.[4] He defines proportion as "the association, the gathering of two, of three, or of whatever number of relations in a single relation. . . . It is the reunion of relations that makes proportion."[5] Martianus Capella's book on geometry in *On the Marriage of Philology and Mercury* borrows a few sections from Euclid's *Elements* (including numerous definitions from the first book of the *Elements*). However, Capella spends most of the discussion on geography, mostly from Pliny. This reflects the poor state of geometry under the Romans.[6] Nevertheless, Martianus followed the ancients in clearly separating the practical applications of the quadrivial disciplines from theory.

In his dialogue between a master (*nutritor*) and disciple (*alumnus*) in the *Periphyseon*, John Scotus Eriugena provides a succinct and clear picture of the role of geometry as the basis of contemplation for the Christian student or scholar. He asks the reader, "Have you not noticed how all the lines are united at the centre so that none of them can be distinguished from the others? No wonder, for all are one in it and are in no way distinct from one another so that the centre is reasonably defined not as the place where the lines come together in one but as the source and simple and indivisible principle from which either by nature or by art the multiplicity of the lines proceeds. For the centre is the common starting-point of the lines in which they are all one."[7] This is reminiscent of Augustine's image in *On Order* in which he refers to the

---

[3] Augustine, *On Order* [*De Ordine*], 1.7.17, 23.
[4] Boèce, *Institution Arithmetique*, 2,40, I, 140.
[5] Ibid., 2,40,I&3, 140.
[6] Guillaumin, "Introduction," in Martianus Capella, *Les Noces de Philologie et de Mercure. Livre VII. L'Arithmetique*, lviii.
[7] Eriugena, *Periphyseon*, Book 2, 625A–625B, 240.

correspondence between human psychology and spirituality
on the one hand, and the created order on the other hand.
Awareness of this correspondence underlies contemplation:
"However great a circumference is, there is a single point of
convergence, the *center*. The circumference can be divided and
subdivided, but not at the center. Everything in a circle refers
to the center and is ruled by it as it were. In whatever direction you move from the center, the more diversity you pursue,
the more unity you lose."[8] Eriugena also points out that this
correspondence is not primarily sense-oriented, even though
it is connected to the human sensory experience. The mind's
perception of these things surpasses the power of the senses,
whether these concern the imagination or the things of the
material world.[9] Contemplation can begin with the senses, but
tends to move up and away from the sensory experience, aided
by such theoretical disciplines as geometry.

The fact that geometric shapes or figures do not have a
beginning or an end reflects an important feature of the
nature of reason: "Do you then see that there is no law relat-
ing to figures to restrain or prevent you from starting to order
and number the whole figure from any interval or line? For
so does reason demand, and therefore as many beginnings
and endings of numbering and ordering can be made as there
are intervals and lines."[10] This truth possesses theological and
contemplative importance for Eriugena. Thus, theologians can
start their:

> contemplation of the primordial causes from any one of
> them at all and set the term of their contemplation in
> any one of them as each may wish so that as many as
> there are of the primordial causes, or rather, to speak more
> cautiously, as many as they are formed in whatever way
> they are or can be formed in the intellects of those who
> contemplate them, so many are the ways of ordering and
> numbering them that offer themselves of their own accord

---

[8] Augustine, *On Order* [*De Ordine*], Book 1, Chapter 2, 5, 7.
[9] Eriugena, *Periphyseon*, Book 2, 625B, 240.
[10] Ibid., 626A, 241.

by a wonderful dispensation of the Divine Providence to those who practise philosophy rightly in accordance with their capacity for contemplation and in accordance with the inclination of each; and although they operate in various and marvellous modes of divine science and divine theophanies in the minds of those that contemplate (the[m]).[11]

He adds that ultimately "in themselves the primordial reasons of all things that are subsist eternally as an immutable unity in the Word of God in which they are made all one and the same beyond all ways of ordering and numbering."[12]

Such a description of the microcosmic and the macrocosmic correspondence by the ninth-century Irishman demonstrates that even though early medieval thinkers had little of the innovative genius of the ancient Greeks or of the High Middle Ages, there was brilliance in the way that the thinkers of this period enriched and deepened the paideutic tradition that they inherited. It was for them a living tradition, which may explain why they did not feel the need for innovation. They experienced the rich truths of this tradition, and did not simply hand on a brittle, mostly-dead tradition. Eriugena was convinced that the philosophical heritage of the Greeks not only aligned with Revelation, but brought this Revelation to a higher or more fulfilled state. Philosophy was the handmaiden of theology in a more contemplative and ascetic sense than it would be with the Parisian scholastics of later medieval centuries.

Despite Eriugena's brilliance, on the whole geometry was relatively neglected, because of the lack of practical value for churchmen and of adequate textbooks. Gerbert of Aurillac's rediscovery of the *Geometria* of Boethius, with its extracts of Euclid's *Elements* and explanations of "the measurement of the simplest plane figures," brought about a deeper study of geometry. Before that, scholars had been forced to make due with Martianus Capella's sixth book of the *Noces*.[13] In

---

[11] Eriugena, *Periphyseon*, Book 2, 626A–626B, 241–242.
[12] Ibid., 626B, 242.
[13] Clark, *The Abbey of St Gall as a Centre of Literature and Art*, 120.

other words, just as there was in this period an imbalance in the trivium — with grammar far outweighing the other two disciplines, particularly rhetoric — so too in the quadrivium did arithmetic and the parts of astronomy relevant for the dating of Easter, as well as music, greatly surpass the status and teaching of geometry.

5.2 MUSIC

John Scotus Eriugena's attitude of overlooking or minimizing the potential tension between, in his case, philosophy and theology, is also reflected in the early medieval embrace of traditional teachings more generally. The early medieval mind tended to adopt a *both-and* attitude regarding the Greco-Roman past instead of an *either-or* posture. The never-resolved conflicts, such as between Plato and Aristotle, or Plato and the Sophists, or one perspective on music versus another, were not regarded as unbridgeable. This conciliatory attitude, as we have seen, had also been a pillar of the pre-Christian Neoplatonists. Early medieval Christian writers gave a fresh impulse to this bridge-building. This conciliatory attitude was apparent most of all within the discipline of music. The ancient Greeks bequeathed to medieval thought a foundational division between Pythagoras and Plato on the one side, and the Aristotelian Aristoxenus (mid-fourth century BC) on the other. The seemingly irreconcilable gap had arisen between those focused on number and those focused on sensory experience; in other words, between a mathematical understanding of music and an aesthetic one. Pythagoras's discovery of musical intervals within the octave — which he associated with numbers — established a science that brought together music and mathematics. This was a new dimension to mathematics that centered on the relationship among sounds and that was brought to students' attention through the plucking of the "canon," otherwise known as the monochord. This was a long, narrow piece of wood with a string for making sounds stretched its length. The monochord was used for carrying out mathematical operations on relationships of harmony.[14] Boethius' theory of music featured the monochord.

Long before Boethius, Aristoxenus, whose sole surviving text is the *Elements of Harmony*, had rejected this Pythagorean mathematization and asserted that musical sounds ought to be evaluated by sensation. He applied a geometrical schema to musical intervals by cutting each segment into equal parts, and each of these parts into more equal parts, and so on, until he arrived at twelve half-tones and twenty-four quarter tones. This separation of music from numbers was a "true epistemological revolution."[15] Nicomachus of Gerasa and Boethius favored the Pythagorean perspective, but other writers in the imperial period, such as Claudius Ptolemy, tried to downplay the tension and reconcile the two approaches.[16] Early medieval churchmen applied their *both-and* approach to the issue of music. The ancient division of music into sung or played music, called *cantus*, and music theory, called *musica*, encouraged a multifaceted approach to music by medieval scholars, some of whom saw music as a science that envisioned the true musician as a philosopher, not a musical virtuoso.[17] Others took a much more practical view. Overall, of the four mathematical disciplines, early medieval Christians reworked music more than the others, molding it into a truly Christian discipline that served the Church's practical needs.

Christian writers did not attempt to resolve the Pythagorean-Aristoxenus split, but established their own understanding of music, which contained elements from Pythagoras, Plato, and Aristoxenus. As part of their wider efforts at encyclopedic knowledge, Augustine, Boethius, Cassiodorus, Martianus Capella, and Isidore of Seville contributed to the medieval

---

[14] Guillaumin, "Introduction," in Martianus Capella, *Les Noces de Philologie et de Mercure. Livre IX. L'Harmonie*, xxiv–xxvii.

[15] Ibid., xxviii.

[16] Ibid., xxix.

[17] De Bruyne, *Etudes d'esthétique médiévale*, 331–332.

understanding of cosmic, vocal, and instrumental music. Keeping to the Greek tradition, none considered music in itself, but within their encyclopedic or philosophical systems. Christians made notable changes to music. In *De Ordine*, Augustine positioned music as the first quadrivial discipline because, in his view, the listening faculty is less pure than sight. Augustine also referred to music as a science, not an art. In the medieval view, an art was something practical, and therefore a part of experience, whereas science implied the capacity for explanation through reason.[18] Capella, in contrast to the Bishop of Hippo, placed 'harmony,' his term for music, as the last quadrivial discipline because his story ends with the harmonious union of Philology and Mercury.[19]

Influenced by Pythagoras, Augustine in *De musica* argued that one can rise towards God through numbers. He closely linked numbers with rhythm, harmony, and proportion. Harmony is a central strand in the microcosmic-macrocosmic vision of man and creation. Augustine identified harmony as a major characteristic of the soul, particularly in the memory, senses, and reason. The Carolingians placed music alongside physics, ethics, logic, and 'the science of numbers' as building blocks of philosophy. Augustine, Rabanus Maurus, and Eriugena all agreed that the immutable laws of numbers and proportions elevate the soul to God because they come from God, not man, and therefore reflect a metaphysical reality.[20] Cassiodorus had already observed the spiritual qualities and powers of music. Music works in the service of God through its creation of harmony. Humans regulate all of their acts through harmony, which is music.[21] Harmony had wider significance than denoting music. Humans participate in harmony by following God's law and choosing right from wrong,

---

[18] César González Ochoa, *La música del universo*, 49.
[19] Guillaumin, "Introduction," in Martianus Capella, *Les Noces de Philologie et de Mercure. Livre IX. L'Harmonie*, lvii, xix–xxx.
[20] De Bruyne, *Etudes d'esthétique médiévale*, 332.
[21] Ibid., 311.

according to Cassiodorus. This lead him to connect music with wisdom and assert that "only the sage is a musician."[22]

While Boethius would agree with this close relationship between music and harmony, the Carolingian scholar Réginon de Prüm (842–915 AD) rejected it. In *Musica enchiriadis*, he divided music into natural and artificial music. He asserted that humans could come to an understanding of these divinely-ordained laws of music through man-made, that is, artificial, music.[23] Human-made music possesses a spiritual or meta-physical dimension and elevates us away from the material. In the second chapter of the *Epistola de harmonica institutione*, Réginon discusses the Pythagorean outlook on music after recounting the famous story of Pythagoras discovering musical tunes by hearing blacksmith hammers. Starting from the ancient, pre-Christian Pythagorean view of music, Réginon believed that the human ears and mind naturally know the consonances that, through God's will, Pythagoras had discovered. Réginon further argued that this discovery allowed scholars to register the melodies of the Church's plain chant in mathematical terms because of their grounding in the consonances. It is in this way that Pythagorean music theory, as transmitted by Boethius, became "the theoretical foundation of a concrete musical repertory. This transformation was an extraordinary achievement in the Carolingian age."[24] There is a seamlessness from the Pythagorean to the Christian outlook because of the centrality of God in the workings of music, as in the universe as a totality.

A century earlier, Aurelian of Réôme mentioned the same story of Pythagoras's discovery at the blacksmith's in *Musica disciplina*. He showed a practical and seamless connection between Pythagoreanism and Christianity by associating "each of the

---

[22] De Bruyne, *Etudes d'esthétique médiévale*, 311.

[23] Ibid., 314. Also spelled Regino.

[24] Cecilia Panti, "Pythagoras and the Quadrivium from late Antiquity to the Middle Ages," pp. 47–81 in *Brill's Companion to the Reception of Pythagoras and Pythagoreanism in the Middle Ages and Renaissance*, Irene Caiazzo, Constantinos Macris, and Aurélien Robert, editors (Leiden: Brill, 2022), 68.

consonances produced by the four hammers to a specific *Introi-tus* of the plain chant in its own *tonus* . . . *Aurelian associates antiphons and toni* of the plain chant, so that the octave-based Pythagorean scale is exemplified by means of the liturgical chant, with the outstanding consequence that church music becomes the *sounding representation of the harmony of the spheres and of human beings.*"[25] Here we see how the Church's appropriation of Greco-Roman paideia led to the further development of these disciplines, even to their fulfillment, as if they had been created by the pre-Christian world for Christendom.

In Capella's *On the Marriage of Philology and Mercury*, the character Harmony provides a summary of the quadrivial dis-cipline, first stating that from the time of her creation by God "as the twin sister of heaven, I have not forsaken numbers; I followed the courses of the sidereal spheres and the whirling motion of the entire mass, assigning tones to the swift-moving celestial bodies. But when the Monad and the first hypostasis of intellectual light was conveying to earthly habitations souls that emanated from their original source, I was ordered to descend with them to be their governess. It was I who designated the numerical ratios of perceptible motions and the impulses of perfect will, introducing restraint and harmony into all things."[26] Interestingly, restraint is closely associated with harmony. This speaks to the micro-macro relationship, as the harmony of the spheres helps, in the human form of decent music, to order the soul, which includes bringing restraint to the passions. Music and virtue were closely associated. The early medieval perspective followed the ancient teachings in the belief that music provides insight into the connection between man and the cosmos. In addition to virtue, this type of musical education aimed to foster contemplation of the cosmos.

---

[25] Cecilia Panti, "Pythagoras and the Quadrivium from late Antiquity to the Middle Ages," 68–69.

[26] Martianus Capella, *The Marriage of Philology and Mercury*, trans. William Harris Stahl, Richard Johnson, and E. L. Burge (Columbia University Press, 1977), Book 9, § 922, 356–357.

Yet, the quadrivial disciplines did not inquire solely into heavenly matters. They connected the higher world — the metaphysical reality — with the lower and physical world. While evoking these elevated things, Boethius also viewed music through the anthropological perspective of man as the microcosm. It follows that "the *musica humana* is nothing but a concretization of the *musica mundana.*"[27] Human psychology is continually influenced by this micro-macro correspondence. The resulting intimate relationship between music and the human spirit is what causes music's effect on man. Music's rhythm "corresponds with the rhythm of our own body, with the organism's rhythm expressing the rhythm of our passions."[28] Capella notes music's stimulating effect on animals and humans, observing that "trumpets rouse the spirits of prancing steeds and battle and also sharpen the keen edge of wrestlers and other competitors in public games."[29] He even participated in the healing effects of music: "I have frequently recited chants that have had a therapeutic effect upon deranged minds and ailing bodies. I have restored the mad to health through consonance."[30] This concern for the ethical and psychological impact of music had been taken up earlier by the Stoics. Certain music possesses physically and spiritually calming effects. The effect also flows in the inverse direction, as the soul influences music production. Boethius noted that the kind of music that an individual produces expresses the state of the soul. For instance, wild music or chanting is produced by an unruly soul, and the wild sounds further unleash the passions in the soul.[31]

In keeping with the spirit of the times, Carolingian treatises on music favored continuity with the ancients even if these encyclopedic writings also prioritized music's technical

---

[27] De Bruyne, *Etudes d'esthétique médiévale*, 26–27.

[28] Ibid., 27.

[29] Martianus Capella, *The Marriage of Philology and Mercury*, Book 9. Harmony. §925, 358.

[30] Ibid., §926, 358.

[31] De Bruyne, *Etudes d'esthétique médiévale*, 27.

aspects arising from liturgical practices. Authorities were more concerned with advancing the quality of chanting than in providing structured arguments on aesthetics. More practically, the music-related training of young oblates was a case of learning by doing. This music education played a major role in the larger apprenticeship in liturgy. Liturgical training, the most basic monastic education, "initiated children into both ritual and monastic discipline, including the hierarchical organization of the monastery. The redactors of the Cluniac customaries took pains to specify the order in which readings and chants should be performed, teaching the *pueri* [the boys] the structures of seniority in the community. The *Liber tramitis*, for instance, prescribes that children should read lessons according to the hierarchies of age and seniority."[32] Despite all this practicality, progress was made in connecting music theory to aesthetics. Alcuin, for example, discussed "for the first time in the West the eight ecclesiastical tones and their division."[33] The Irish monks took their talent for music wherever they went on the European continent, including St. Gall, where Moengal became headmaster of the choir school in 870 AD. St. Gall became famous for copying music manuscripts.[34] Moengal's student and fellow Irishman Tuathal (Latinized as Tuotilo/Tutilo) succeeded him.

In 2008, in Paris, at the Collège de Bernardins, Pope Benedict XVI spoke of the central role of music for the Benedictines and for Christians as a whole. Music took on a new sense and purpose from its foundation in classical Greece. As with the early medieval view of numbers, this had a decidedly Biblical, not Greek, sense: "For Benedict, the words of the *Psalm: coram angelis psallam Tibi, Domine* — in the presence of the angels, I will sing your praise (cf. 138:1) — are the decisive rule governing the prayer and chant of the monks."[35] While retaining the

---

[32] Boynton, "Training for the liturgy as a form of monastic education," p. 16.
[33] De Bruyne, *Etudes d'esthétique médiévale*, 306.
[34] Graham, *The Early Irish Monastic Schools*, 152.
[35] *Address of His Holiness Benedict XVI* (Rome: Editrice Libreria Vaticana, 2008).

basic Greek framework to music (or, at least, not challenging it directly), Christians added to this framework with their own practices and the awareness of certain theological truths, particularly "that in communal prayer one is singing in the presence of the entire heavenly court, and is thereby measured according to the very highest standards: that one is praying and singing in such a way as to harmonize with the music of the noble spirits who were considered the originators of the harmony of the cosmos, the music of the spheres."[36] Practice, mostly liturgy-related, preceded theory, but the theory was not forgotten. The Greek understanding of the harmony of the spheres was given a Christian sense with this perspective.

Here we see why so much Greek paideia aligned with Christian beliefs and practices. No less a heavyweight than the greatest holy man of his century, Bernard of Clairvaux, practiced this fusioning, according to Benedict XVI:

> From this perspective one can understand the seriousness of a remark by Saint Bernard of Clairvaux, who used an expression from the Platonic tradition handed down by Augustine, to pass judgement on the poor singing of monks, which for him was evidently very far from being a mishap of only minor importance. He describes the confusion resulting from a poorly executed chant as a falling into the 'zone of dissimilarity' — the *regio dissimilitudinis*. Augustine had borrowed this phrase from Platonic philosophy, in order to designate his condition prior to conversion (cf. *Confessions*, VII, 10.16): man, who is created in God's likeness, falls in his godforsakenness into the 'zone of dissimilarity' — into a remoteness from God, in which he no longer reflects him, and so has become dissimilar not only to God, but to himself, to what being human truly is. Bernard is certainly putting it strongly when he uses this phrase, which indicates man's falling away from himself, to describe bad singing by monks. But it shows how seriously he viewed the matter.[37]

As the pope has it, Christians did not separate the production of music from the theory and philosophy of music, as had

---

[36] *Address of His Holiness Benedict XVI* (2008).
[37] Ibid.

occurred with the Aristoxenus-Pythagoras split. Perhaps the reason for the continued unity was that the Christian practice of music had a very real theological sense.

It bears repeating that the Christians took what was already there and developed it for their own needs. They appropriated the Greek understanding of beauty in their own contemplative practice. Benedict XVI describes the Christian renewal of music through the religion's theological understanding of beauty: "It shows that the culture of singing is also the culture of being, and that the monks have to pray and sing in a manner commensurate with the grandeur of the word handed down to them, with its claim on true beauty."[38] Christian theology and practice took the Hellenic seed and developed it in a way that the ancient Greeks, who had not known the Gospel, could not have foreseen and were therefore incapable of accomplishing:

> This intrinsic requirement of speaking with God and singing of him with words he himself has given, is what gave rise to the great tradition of Western music. It was not a form of private "creativity," in which the individual leaves a memorial to himself and makes self-representation his essential criterion. Rather it is about vigilantly recognizing with the "ears of the heart" the inner laws of the music of creation, the archetypes of music that the Creator built into his world and into men, and thus discovering music that is worthy of God, and at the same time truly worthy of man, music whose worthiness resounds in purity.[39]

The early medieval appropriation of music shows that the liberal arts and philosophy did not stagnate in Christendom. While the Roman imperial and early medieval periods saw few advances in the theory of music, musical practice was profoundly altered by Christianity. Christians gave a certain elan to these disciplines, and none more so than to music.

---

[38] *Address of His Holiness Benedict XVI* (2008).
[39] Ibid.

5.3 ASTRONOMY

Quadrivial astronomy cannot be understood without its musical aspects. Astronomy was a close counterpart of music. Pythagoras's discovery and explication of "the ratios of the music of the spheres" held wide currency in the Middle Ages, inspired in part by Pliny's entry on astronomy in his *Historia naturalis*.[40] Pliny writes:

> But occasionally Pythagoras draws on the theory of music, and designates the distance between the earth and the moon as a whole tone, that between the moon and Mercury a semitone, between Mercury and Venus the same, between her and the sun a tone and a half, between the sun and Mars a tone (the same as the distance between the earth and the moon), between Mars and Jupiter half a tone, between Jupiter and Saturn half a tone, between Saturn and the zodiac a tone and a half: the seven tones thus producing the so-called diapason, a universal harmony; in this Saturn moves in the Dorian mode, Jupiter in the Phrygian, and similarly with the other planets — a refinement more entertaining than convincing.[41]

This close association between music and astronomy stems from their shared basis in numbers. The Pythagorean assertion that the physical expression of symbolic numbers (such as the dyad) could accomplish the harmony of humans and of the cosmos gained acceptance in the Middle Ages.[42] Not many treatises were written in the Roman imperial period. Claudius Ptolemy's *Almageste* in the second century AD was the last major advance by ancient thinkers in astronomy. This work followed Greek tradition by offering a theory of the movements of the objects of the heavens. Plato had theorized on this.[43] Book 8

---

[40] Cecilia Panti, "Pythagoras and the Quadrivium from late Antiquity to the Middle Ages," 48.

[41] Pliny, *The Natural History of Pliny*, volume 1, trans. John Bostock and H. T. Riley (London: Taylor and Francis, 1855), 2.20.

[42] Cecilia Panti, "Pythagoras and the Quadrivium from late Antiquity to the Middle Ages," 49.

[43] M. Joseph Moreau, "L'essor de l'astronomie scientifique chez les Grecs," in *Revue d'histoire des sciences*, tome 29, no. 3, 1976, pp. 193–212, 194.

of *On the Marriage of Philology and Mercury*, with regard to astronomy, offered an original perspective on the subject, first discussing cosmography before turning to the planets, without mentioning mythological legends related to the constellations.[44]

5.4 NATURAL PHILOSOPHY

The quadrivial disciplines provide a foundation to further studies in science because all of these studies are based on reason. In *De Trinitate*, Boethius divides these further science studies into physics, mathematics, and theology:

> Physics deals with motion and is not abstract or separable…; for it is concerned with the forms of bodies together with their constituent matter, which forms cannot be separated in reality from their bodies…

> Mathematics does not deal with motion and is not abstract, for it investigates forms of bodies apart from matter, and therefore apart from movement, which forms, however, being connected with matter cannot be really separated from bodies.

> Theology does not deal with motion and is abstract and separable, for the Divine Substance is without either matter or motion. In Physics, then, we are bound to use scientific, in Mathematics, systematical, in Theology, intellectual concepts; and in Theology we will not let ourselves be diverted to play with imaginations, but will simply apprehend that Form which is pure form and no image, which is very Being and the source of Being.[45]

Contemplation was the goal of the study of natural philosophy because of the central position in the Early Middle Ages of Augustine's "interior, reflexive, and soliloquial reason," which had not yet lost its place of privilege to an exterior, physics-based reason oriented to natural phenomena.[46] Aristotle's syllogistic logic had not yet taken over from Neoplatonism.

---

[44] Guillaumin, "Introduction," in Martianus Capella, *Les Noces de Philologie et de Mercure. Livre VII. L'Arithmetique*, lxi.

[45] Boethius, "De Trinitate Proemium," ii, 9. This was discussed in the first volume.

[46] Poirel, "Introduction," 22.

Such was also the case further east. Neoplatonism would guide scientific thought in the Byzantine Empire throughout its history. In *Brief Solutions to Questions in Physics*, Michael Psellos adopted an "inverted inquiry" that begins down below and moves towards heaven. Starting with physical phenomena, through demonstration, he takes the inquirer upward to the origin of everything. He starts with the earth, then the sky above the earth, which includes the observable facts of water, meteors, planets, and stars. The inquiry becomes more abstract and beyond the capacity of the senses, with matter, form, and nature. These topics are followed by analysis of the soul, intelligence, and, finally, the primary cause.[47] This entire outline is an expression of the Neoplatonist hierarchy of knowledge, with its foundation in the liberal arts, and its revelation of how all knowledge is interconnected.[48]

Over the centuries, and in both West and East, Neoplatonism was the glue that held the various disciplines together. What ran through Neoplatonism's steerage of these disciplines, as we have already seen, is the emergence of the reasoning faculty in the developing student. Although the Neoplatonist spirit, as represented here by Psellos, is religious, and even mystical, it envisions philosophy as the increasing emergence or development of reason because the study of transcendent issues requires the best and fullest of the human mind and understanding.[49] Psellos notes: "All that came into existence subsequent to the mysterious first principle of all beings, became a principle for other substances."[50] Psellos's definition of *physis* was likely acceptable to nearly all Christian thinkers of the period: "The regular order of nature is a force which is invisible to sight though known by intelligence; it is disseminated by God in all bodies as a principle of movement and rest."[51] God

---

[47] Tatakis, *Byzantine Philosophy*, 154.
[48] Ibid., 154.
[49] Ibid.
[50] Ibid., 156.
[51] Ibid.

is at the apex of this hierarchy, which descends to intelligence, then the soul, and finally nature. With Psellos we have the fusion of the Neoplatonic and the Christian worldview, from God to the created order.

CHAPTER 6

Isidore of Seville:
The Love of Learning

*I believe that after so many years of decline in Spain, God,
as if he had set before us a certain goal, raised this man
up in these latest times so that we should not altogether
grow old in our boorishness.*[1]

—Braulio of Zaragoza

6.1 THE CHRISTIAN INHERITANCE
OF GRECO-ROMAN PAIDEIA

EVEN AS CHRISTIAN EDUCATION developed and began to take on its own identity, tradition, and characteristics, it did not cut itself off from paideia's pagan, Greco-Roman roots. Instead, the strong connection and accord between Christian and pre-Christian education developed the original paideia much further. In the West, this *translatio studii*, the shifting of the center of scholarship from one region to another over the centuries, started in Spain, moved on to the Irish and Anglo-Saxons, and reached its early medieval zenith with the Carolingians. Advances in education were not only based on the Good News of Jesus Christ, but also on the writings and practices of the foundational western thinkers on education. This interaction between Christian and pagan writings continually rejuvenated Christian education. Isidore of Seville (560–636 AD), bishop of the southern Spanish city from 601 to 636 AD—later declared a doctor of the Church in 1722 and Patron Saint of the Internet in 1997—exemplifies this interaction between Christian and Greco-Roman paideia.

---

[1] "Introduction" in *A Companion to Isidore of Seville*, eds. Andrew Fear and Jamie Wood, (Leiden: Brill, 2020), 11, the editors cite *Renotatio librorum domini Isidori* by Braulio of Zaragoza.

He was, at first glance, a compiler of ancient culture, similar to Cassiodorus, and was best known as an encylopedist. *Compiler* and *encyclopedist* are not misnomers, as he was keen to conserve much of ancient knowledge and culture for Christendom.

In attempting to make this knowledge and culture suitable for Christian students, the author of the *Etymologies* did not simply hand on the old culture. Instead, he followed a long line of Church Fathers, such as Clement of Alexandria, Origen, and Augustine, in Christianizing ancient Greco-Roman paideia: "Like Virgil taking Dante by the hand, Isidore can seem like a tour guide to a vast museum of antiquities. But open the *Etymologies* to any page and its author will stare out at you in a different mask. He lives in Christian time... He distills Christian knowledge: the Bible and ecclesiastical offices; God, angels, and the saints; the Church and deviant sects."[2] Isidore was faithful to the call of the Second Council of Toledo in 527 AD to continue to provide traditional Roman education in Spain. One of its articles directed the bishops to supervise the education of oblates until they were 18.[3] Education was still a concern a century later, at the Fourth Council of Toledo in 633 AD. Presided over by Isidore himself, it called on Church leaders to improve the situation of uneducated clergy by establishing a school in each cathedral city.[4] It had been only a few decades since the conversion of the Visigothic King Reccared I to the Catholic faith in 587 AD. Even after the Council of Toledo in 589 AD called for the conversion of the people, orthodox Roman Christianity was still putting down its roots in Spain in the face of rebellions by local Arian leaders.

Isidore carried on Augustine's vision of reworking classical civilization, including paideia, to create an "epistemology of God."[5] He was the right man for this mission. As a Hispano-Roman

---

[2] Graham Barrett, "God's Librarian: Isidore of Seville and His Literacy Agenda," in *A Companion to Isidore of Seville*, eds. Andrew Fear and Jamie Wood (Brill, 2020), 43–44.

[3] Ibid., 45.

[4] Ibid.

[5] Ibid., 46.

and member of the aristocracy in Visigothic Spain, he had received the well-rounded education that the Greco-Roman world had idealized and that Visigothic Spain still cultivated. Pope Benedict XVI notes, "The wealth of cultural knowledge that Isidore had assimilated enabled him to constantly compare the Christian newness with the Greco-Roman cultural heritage, however, rather than the precious gift of synthesis it would seem that he possessed the gift of *collatio*, that is, of collecting, which he expressed in an extraordinary personal erudition, although it was not always ordered as might have been desired."[6]

Isidore's older brother, counselor to Reccared I, likely played a central role in his intellectual and spiritual development. In fact, Pope Benedict XVI notes that Leander, who preceded Isidore as Bishop of Seville, not only educated his younger sibling, but gave him his whole purpose:

> He [Isidore] was a younger brother of Leander, Archbishop of Seville, and a great friend of Pope Gregory the Great. Pointing this out is important because it enables us to bear in mind a cultural and spiritual approach that is indispensable for understanding Isidore's personality. Indeed, he owed much to Leander, an exacting, studious and austere person who created around his younger brother a family context marked by the ascetic requirements proper to a monk, and from the work pace demanded by a serious dedication to study. Furthermore, Leander was concerned to have the wherewithal to confront the political and social situation of that time: in those decades in fact, the Visigoths, barbarians and Arians, had invaded the Iberian Peninsula and taken possession of territories that belonged to the Roman Empire. It was essential to regain them for the Roman world and for Catholicism. Leander and Isidore's home was furnished with a library richly endowed with classical, pagan and Christian works. Isidore, who felt simultaneously attracted to both, was therefore taught under the responsibility of his elder brother to develop a very strong discipline, in devoting himself to study with discretion and discernment.[7]

---

[6] Pope Benedict XVI, *General Audience*.
[7] Ibid.

The "Isidorian renaissance" creatively fused the foundations of Greco-Roman paideia with Church teaching and monastic spirituality, and was continued by bishops in Zaragoza and Toledo in the seventh century.[8] Isidore fulfilled the teaching office of the bishop in an exemplary fashion.

A prolific writer, Isidore saw himself as handing on the entire body of Christian knowledge in a way that his readers would be able to handle.[9] The impressive list of his writings, recorded by his companion and editor, Bishop Braulio of Zaragoza, includes two two-book texts, the *Differences* (*Differentiae*) and the *Synonyms* (*Synonyma*), plus *On Numbers* (*De Numeris*), *On the Nature of Things* (*De natura rerum*), the three-book *Sentences* (*Sententiae*), and his tremendously influential and enduring *Etymologies* (*Etymologiae*), one of the most-read and fundamental texts of the entire Middle Ages, even if the author had left it unfinished. Drawing from the wealth of pagan civilization, Isidore intended the *Etymologies*, along with his other writings, to be a foundation for the nascent Christian civilization. Readers of the *Etymologies* have traditionally divided it into a first half, Books 1–10, with a more intellectual and spiritual theme, and a second half, Books 11–20, with a more worldly priority.[10] The sometimes eclectic and always wide-ranging content — an attempt at summarizing the culture and education of the ancients with some Christianization of contents — is much more ambitious in its range of subjects than Cassiodore's *Institutions* or the pagan Martianus Capella's *On the Marriage of Philology and Mercury.*[11]

Isidore had many admirers in his own day. Braulio described the impressive extent of Isidore's learning: "In him antiquity gained some new fame for itself, or rather our age saw in him an image of antiquity, for he was a man well trained in every

---

[8] Barrett, "God's Librarian: Isidore of Seville and His Literacy Agenda," 45.
[9] Ibid., 72.
[10] Jacques Elfassi, "Isidore of Seville and the Etymologies" in *A Companion to Isidore of Seville*, eds. Andrew Fear and Jamie Wood (Brill, 2020), 251.
[11] Lafontaine, *Isidore de Seville et la culture classique dans l'Espagne wisigothique*, 13.

kind of locution, so that the quality of his words made him adaptable for one who was learned and for one who had no knowledge, famous both for suiting his words to his subject and for his incomparable eloquence. It can now be very easy for any prudent reader to judge how great his knowledge was from his varied interests and carefully written works."[12]

Another supporter, Ildefonsus of Toledo (607–667 AD), declared that Isidore exemplified the best of Greco-Roman paideia in his capacity as a well-rounded orator: "Isidore held the bishopric of the see of Seville, in the Province of Baetica, after his brother Leander. He was a man esteemed for both his propriety and his intellect. In speaking he had acquired a supply of such pleasing eloquence that his admirable richness of speech amazed his listeners. Indeed, someone who had heard a sermon of his a second time would not approve unless it were repeated still further. He wrote not a few exceptional works."[13]

Isidore's appropriation of Greco-Roman oratory for the work of the Church parallels that of Basil of Caesarea and John Chrysostom, even if he did not have the same reputation for eloquence as the latter did. Isidore expresses his love for learning and books in what is likely his own poem. The verses apparently refer to the inventory of the Seville cathedral library and reflect his love of ancient learning and respect for the Church Fathers who had preceded him. He pays homage to four of them:[14]

> IV. Origen
> I, the celebrated Origen, at one time a Doctor most true,
> Whom famous Greece first brought to the faith:
> I was lofty in merit and famous for my abundance of speech,
> But was suddenly ruined, cut short by a malicious tongue.

---

[12] Braulio of Zaragoza, "Renotatio," in *Iberian Fathers, Volume 2: Braulio of Saragossa, Fructuosus of Braga*, trans. Claude W. Barlow (Catholic University of America, 1969), 140.
[13] Isidore of Seville, *The Etymologies of Isidore of Seville,* "On Illustrious Men," 10.
[14] Ibid., "Introduction," 16.

I toiled, if you may believe it, to compose as many thou-
  sands of books
As a legion has armed men.
No blasphemy ever touched my senses,
But I was watchful and wise, and safe from the enemy.
Only the words in my *Peri Archon* brought this misfortune
  on me.
Impious darts attacked me when I was assailed by these
  words...

VII. Augustine
He lies who says he has read you entirely.
What reader could possess your complete works?
For you, Augustine, glow with a thousand volumes.
Your own books bear witness to what I say.
However pleasing may be the wisdom of books by many
  authors,
If Augustine is there, he himself will suffice you.

VIII. Jerome
Translator Jerome, most learned in the various languages,
Bethlehem praises you, the whole world resounds with
  your name;
Our library also celebrates you through your books.

IX. John
I am John by name, called 'Chrysostom,'
Because a golden tongue makes my work glitter.
Constantinople glows with me as its teacher
And I am everywhere renowned for my books as a Doctor.
I have established morals, I have spoken of the rewards
  of virtues,
And I have taught wretched culprits to bemoan their
  crimes.[15]

The poem sheds light on Isidore's appreciation of key Church
Fathers in the establishment of Christian paideia. Isidore
was not so much an innovator as, in Pope Benedict XVI's
words, a "collector," in his attempt to support the Christian
classroom by strengthening its educational pillars by building
on tradition.

---

[15] Isidore of Seville, *The Etymologies of Isidore of Seville*, "Introduction," 16–17.

6.2 ENCYCLOPEDISM AND ETYMOLOGY

The history of Christian education until recent centuries was closely intertwined with that of the encyclopedia, which was a common type of writing in pre-Christian Greece and Rome. In its selection and arrangement of knowledge, the genre reflected the content of the liberal arts, philosophy, and theology throughout the centuries. Some encyclopedias, such as Vitruvius's *On Architecture*, were specialized, whereas others, such as the *Etymologies*, offered entries on a wide range of an era's available knowledge. The first encyclopedists, including Pliny the Elder (23–79 AD), Vitruvius (80/70–c. 15 BC), Cicero (106–43 BC), and Martianus Capella (fifth century AD), both influenced and were themselves influenced by the notion of a wide-ranging education. Central to the Roman idea of the encyclopedia — as evidenced in the works of Pliny and Varro — is a logical, easy-to-use arrangement of entries by topic for simple access.[16] As knowledge grew and matured in Christendom, primarily through translations from Greek and Arabic into Latin, or as new issues and opportunities arose, such as the growth of cities and concomitant development of the cathedral schools and universities, the content, organization, and aims of encyclopedia changed. The encyclopedia reflected the educational values, goals, and practices of the ancient Greeks and Romans, and then, later, those of Christendom. To varying degrees, the genre reflected the ideals of multidisciplinary education, exhaustive knowledge, and the systematic presentation of that knowledge. Braulio's *Renotatio* mentions the first two in relation to the *Etymologies*.[17] With the *Etymologies*, Isidore did not try to establish a new genre, but aimed to fit his Christian agenda into an already-existing one.

The encyclopedia's purpose and content were determined by educational authorities. Cicero saw a broad and virtue-based

---

[16] Isidore of Seville, *The Etymologies of Isidore of Seville*, 10.
[17] Elfassi, "Isidore of Seville and the Etymologies," 250.

education as aiding the orator. Vitruvius took a wider view
of the liberal arts than most writers did, as he saw the same
type of education that Cicero advocated as providing an intellectual foundation to the architect, a more earthy application
of this learning. For Vitruvius, the liberal arts disciplines, the
enkyklios paideia [ἐγκύκλιος παιδεία], comprised a united whole
and served as the necessary propaedeutic to the more technical,
practical, and specialized arts.[18] The enkyklios paideia, from
which the word encyclopedia originates, was the general cycle
of language and mathematical studies that made up the initial
and wide-ranging education of the schoolboy in ancient Greece
and Rome. It developed into the trivium and quadrivium in
the Middle Ages. Quintilian, Seneca, and Vitruvius agreed that
the enkyklios paideia was not an end in itself, but served higher
things. The latter noted that the architect "should be a man of
letters, a skilful draughtsman, a mathematician, familiar with
scientific inquiries, a diligent student of philosophy, acquainted
with music; not ignorant of medicine, learned in the responses
of jurisconsults, familiar with astronomy and astronomical
calculations."[19] The architect had to be a full representative
of his own culture. This general education required a parallel
genre that would provide this information in an organized way.

The Romans did not see the encyclopedia as a neutral text.
It was not a simple collection of facts. It served an ideological
purpose. For instance, with the display of knowledge from the
entire world in the Naturalis Historia, Pliny the Elder aimed
to demonstrate the empire's political and military might and
economic wealth.[20] While rooted in the enkyklios paideia, Pliny's
encyclopedia also catalogued this prosperity, as it triumphantly
showed off the most appealing and attractive trophies from
imperial expansion.[21] The Naturalis Historia also expressed

[18] Valérie Naas, Le projet encyclopédique de Pline l'Ancien, (École Française de
Rome, 2002), 21.
[19] Vitruvius, On Architecture, trans. Frank Granger (New York: Loeb, 1931), I.c.I, 9.
[20] Naas, Le projet encyclopédique de Pline l'Ancien, 9.
[21] Ibid., 9.

the spirit of the Romanized version of Greek paideia, which the Romans called *humanitas* or the *artes liberales*.[22]

Isidore's long-lasting contribution to the medieval Christian inheritance of this genre was based on the solid and consistent foundation provided by his Christian faith. This faith promoted an underlying consistency to a seemingly inconsistent text. Benedict XVI describes the unique encyclopedism that resulted: "Isidore's cultural and spiritual interests, as they emerge from his works themselves... include an encyclopaedic knowledge of pagan classical culture and a thorough knowledge of Christian culture. This explains the eclecticism characteristic of Isidore's literary opus who glided with the greatest of ease from Martial to Augustine or from Cicero to Gregory the Great."[23] His eclecticism was united by the one overriding objective, which was to seek the truth. Like other medieval encyclopedists, his wide-ranging yet detailed entries reflect his aim of presenting all necessary knowledge on each topic.[24]

The Byzantines were as enthusiastic as western Christians, as they produced scores of encyclopedia, particularly in the ninth and tenth centuries. Just as Isidore personified encyclopedism in the West, so Michael Psellos did in the East in the eleventh century with this encyclopedic mind. Psellos worked to reinvigorate ancient philosophy and science.[25] Like Isidore, Psellos was a compiler of already-established knowledge in the service of the Christian truth, not an innovator. In a letter to Patriarch Kyr Michael Keroullarios, Psellos describes his encyclopedic learning: "I thoroughly mastered some areas of philosophy;

---

[22] Naas, *Le projet encyclopédique de Pline l'Ancien*, 15, 18–19. Valérie Naas notes that despite their close association, the *enkyklios paideia* and the encyclopedia differ in some aspects. The latter, particularly Pliny's, was far more exhaustive in scope than the former, which did not aim at exhaustivity.

[23] Pope Benedict XVI, *General Audience*.

[24] Carol Muessig, "Learning and mentoring in the twelfth century: Hildegard of Bingen and Herrad of Landsberg," in *Medieval Monastic Education*, eds. George Ferzoco and Carolyn Muessig (Leicester University Press, 2000) 87–104. Bellenger, Aidan. "A medieval novice's formation: reflection on a fifteenth-century manuscript at Downside Abbey," 96.

[25] Tatakis, *Byzantine Philosophy*, 154.

I purified my speech through the sophistic arts; I taught my students geometry, and was the first to institute it as a subject; I also discovered some of the principles of musical theory; I set straight not a few accounts of the motions that surround the sphere; I also made the science of our beliefs [Christianity] far more accurate; I expounded the teachings of theology; I disclosed the depth of allegory, and finally — though may the bolt of malicious envy not strike me! — I made every science exact."[26] Much of this could be said about Isidore as well. The Early Middle Ages was the era of polymaths, not specialists.

One key to the Bishop of Seville's eclectic love for the truth was etymology, which accorded with the wider Christian search for the truth. "The idea that knowledge of the origins of words can yield up the words' 'true sense' (ἔτυμον), and indeed something of the intrinsic character of the thing named by the word, is very ancient. The oldest Greek and Hebrew writings take for granted that proper names can conceal and reveal the characters and fates of their bearers," Isidore notes.[27] Interest in etymology dated back to the Greeks, as exemplified with Plato's *Cratylus*. While Plato and Aristotle were lukewarm towards etymology,[28] the Stoics extensively investigated word origins. However, in the belief in the purity of the Greek language, some writers did not give enough consideration to words from other languages. The many resulting errors caused some to question certain etymological writings. Cicero mocked the Greek Chrysippus for the latter's far-fetched etymological sketches. Etymology was a well-known yet controversial topic among the ancients.

---

[26] Michael Psellos, "Letter to the Patriarch Kyr Michael Keroullarios" in *Psellos and the Patriarchs*, trans. Anthony Kaldellis and Ioannis Polemis (University of Notre Dame Press, 2015), 40. Keroullarios, patriarch of Constantinople from 1043 to 59 AD, angered the pope's delegates in 1054, leading Cardinal Humbert to excommunicate him, and he to do the same to the Cardinal. Keroullarios also had disagreements with the Byzantine emperors.

[27] Isidore of Seville, *The Etymologies of Isidore of Seville*, 11. The Greek word ἔτυμον (etymon) is the root of *etymology*.

[28] Lafontaine, *Isidore de Seville et la culture classique dans l'Espagne wisigothique*, 40–41.

This controversy did not discourage Isidore. His aim in establishing a word's precise meaning reflects the typical concern of the Church Fathers for precision when expressing ideas. They feared imprecision. They saw heresy as arising from ambiguity which, by failing to express the truth, misleads the listening or reading audience. The other common name for the *Etymologies*, the *Origins*, explains much of the author's intention, which was to find the original, even ontological, sense of a word as a way to express the truth. Isidore's thinking revolved in large part around this notion of origin, which he applied in more of a philosophical than a scientific way. This application was derived in turn from the bishop's concern for the metaphysical and theological *why* rather than for the empirical *how*.[29] In addition to the Greek roots to this, Isidore was inspired by the Old Testament belief that the name of something denotes its ontological essence. Beginning with the name of God, this was most true for proper names. The knowledge of a proper name revealed the secret of that being.[30] This Hebrew orientation provided a mystical element to etymology.[31] Ultimately, Isidore's belief that language could express and convey knowledge was the foundation of his belief that basing knowledge on etymological research could shed light on the truth. For Isidore, the act of naming, as Adam did the animals of creation, is the first step in coming to understand the nature of something.[32]

Isidore's etymological and encyclopedic projects are closely related. He provides a significant insight into his entire encyclopedic work with his justification for his etymological method: "The knowledge of a word's etymology often has an indispensable usefulness for interpreting the word, for when you have seen whence a word has originated, you understand its force more quickly. Indeed, one's insight into anything is clearer

---

[29] Lafontaine, *Isidore de Seville et la culture classique dans l'Espagne wisigothique*, 43.
[30] Ibid., 43–44.
[31] Ibid., 44.
[32] Ibid., 50.

when its etymology is known."[33] He does admit to limitations
to his method: "However, not all words were established by
the ancients from nature; some were established by whim, just
as we sometimes give names to our slaves and possessions
according to what tickles our fancy. Hence it is the case that
etymologies are not to be found for all words, because some
things received names not according to their innate qualities, but
by the caprice of human will."[34] The notion of a word's 'innate
qualities' reveals Isidore's primary motivation in his etymological
investigations. Language's special relationship with the truth
gives words ontological properties. This special relationship
between a word and the thing it signifies can be known in
the clearest and most powerful way through the etymological
revelation of a word. Uncovering a word's deepest and original
sense comes close to discovering the essence of something about
God's creation, or what the Greeks called the *logos* of creation,
because this original meaning is typically not arbitrary or man-
made.[35] In other words, Isidore's understanding of etymology
is closely related to his understanding of grammar. They both
deal with the essence of reality.

Isidore's *Etymologies* was simultaneously rooted in the Greco-
Roman and Christian worlds. It belonged to the first of two
major eras of medieval encyclopedism, the first extending from
the sixth through roughly twelfth centuries, which was marked
by the influence of the Church Fathers and the confidence in
the supremacy of Revelation over human knowledge.[36] These
encyclopedia attempted to hand on Greco-Roman knowledge to
a Christian readership. Cassiodorus's *Institutions*, Rabanus Maurus's *De rerum naturalis*, and even Augustine's *De doctrina christiana* were other key texts for the Middle Ages from this genre.[37]

---

[33] Isidore of Seville, *The Etymologies of Isidore of Seville*, 1.xxix.2.
[34] Ibid., 2–3.
[35] Elfassi, "Isidore of Seville and the Etymologies," 260.
[36] "Enciclopedia," *Enciclopedia Europea*, volume IV (Milano: Garzanti, 1977),
496–497, 496.
[37] Benoît Beyer de Ryke, "Encyclopédisme," in *Dictionnaire du Moyen Age*, eds.
Claude Gauvard et al (Presses Universitaires de France, 2004), 475.

The second period of medieval encyclopedism, from the twelfth to fourteenth centuries, was influenced by both the scholastic method and the flood of translated works, many from Aristotle's corpus. Encyclopedists had to organize and assimilate the ceaselessly-growing knowledge, and to do so in the spirit of the schoolmen of the universities. The most famous encyclopedia of this era was Vincent of Beauvais's mid-thirteenth century *Speculum Maius*, though the earlier encyclopedia were still widely consulted and esteemed. The tenth century was the high point of encyclopedism in the Byzantine Empire.

One pillar of medieval encyclopedism that Isidore helped to solidify was the appeal to authority. Etymology and reference to authorities from the past, including abundant references to pagan writers such as Cicero and Virgil, formed the basis of the *Etymologies* and would be central to other encyclopedias produced in Christendom. This reverence for tradition idealized both Greco-Roman and Christian sources of knowledge, including the Bible. The reference to Revelation replaced Pliny's ideology of Roman greatness. Isidore and other Christian encyclopedists added a distinct element to the pagan-originating encyclopedic genre. They had no interest in the natural world for its own sake, but so that they could uncover and contemplate the trace of God in created beings.[38] To this key to knowledge, Isidore added etymology, because knowing the name of something helped to more clearly understand its nature.[39] Some ancient pre-Christian thinkers would have agreed with this.

---

[38] Beyer de Ryke, "Encyclopédisme," 475.
[39] Ibid., 476.

CHAPTER 7

Isidore and the Liberal Arts

Thou hast ordered all things in measure, and number (numerus), and weight.

—Wisdom 11:21

DESPITE THE HIGH ESTEEM FOR THE liberal arts, they were traditionally not pursued for themselves, as Seneca famously noted in *Letter* 88 to Lucilius. Instead, they were foundational for all future educational endeavors. Sounding like Vitruvius on the role of the liberal arts for the future architect, Isidore notes the high practical value of the seven subjects for the professions in book four of the *Etymologies* when he discusses medicine:

> 1. Some people ask why the art of medicine is not included in the other liberal disciplines. It is for this reason: the liberal disciplines treat individual topics, but medicine treats the topics of all. Thus the physician ought to know grammar, so that he can understand and explain what he reads. 2. Similarly he must know rhetoric, so that he is capable of summing up the cases he treats with true arguments. He must also know dialectic in order to scrutinize and cure the causes of disease with the application of reason. So also arithmetic, to reckon the number of hours in the onsets of illness, and their periods of days. 3. Likewise with geometry, so that from his knowledge of the qualities of regions and the location of places, he may teach what a person should attend to there. Then, music will not be unknown to him, for we read of many things that have been accomplished for sick people by way of this discipline—as we read of David who rescued Saul from an unclean spirit with the art of melody. The physician Asclepiades also restored a certain victim of frenzy to perfect health through harmonious sounds. 4. Finally, he will be acquainted with astronomy, through which he may observe the logic of the stars and the change of seasons. For, as a certain physician says, according to their mutations our bodies are also changed.

5. Thus medicine is called the Second Philosophy, for each discipline claims for itself the entire human: by philosophy the soul is cured; by medicine, the body.[1]

The professional disciplines cannot be studied without the generalist foundation of the liberal arts. In fact, as Isidore's above thoughts assert, success in the professions requires this foundation.

7.1 GRAMMAR

The first two books of the *Etymologies* discuss the trivium. The author begins by differentiating between a discipline and an art and by associating key Latin words with these two terms. He follows the Platonic notion that a discipline investigates the truth whereas an art, because it is not restricted to one possibility alone, deals with the probable:[2] "A discipline (*disciplina*) takes its name from 'learning' (*discere*), whence it can also be called 'knowledge' (*scientia*). Now 'know' (*scire*) is named from 'learn' (*discere*), because none of us knows unless we have learned. A discipline is so named in another way, because 'the full thing is learned' (*discitur plena*)."[3] On the other hand,

> an art (*ars*, gen. *Artis*) is so called because it consists of strict (*artus*) precepts and rules. Others say this word is derived by the Greeks from the word, that is, "virtue," as they termed knowledge. Plato and Aristotle would speak of this distinction between an art and a discipline: an art consists of matters that can turn out in different ways, while a discipline is concerned with things that have only one possible outcome. Thus, when something is expounded with true arguments, it will be a discipline; when something merely resembling the truth and based on opinion is treated, it will have the name of an art.[4]

Isidore defines the liberal arts as comprised of the trivium and

---

[1] Isidore of Seville, *The Etymologies of Isidore of Seville*, 4.xiv.1–5.
[2] Lafontaine, *Isidore de Seville et la culture classique dans l'Espagne wisigothique*, 52.
[3] Ibid., 1.i.1.
[4] Ibid., 1.i.2–3.

quadrivium before turning to the most basic aspect of grammar, which is the Greek and Latin letters, and their origins in Hebrew. He reasons that the similar pronunciation of the Greek "alpha" indicates that the letter came from the Hebrew "aleph." Latin in turn took A from the Greek "alpha." Even the forms of these three letters reveal this borrowing. Therefore, Isidore concludes, Hebrew is "the mother of all languages and letters."[5] This passage reflects the theological spirit of the *Etymologies*. Just as Christians are the spiritual heirs of the ancient Hebrews, so the two major languages of the new Israel, Greek and Latin, are derived from the Hebrew language.

After this discussion of letters, Isidore turns at length to grammar, which he defines as "the knowledge of speaking correctly" and "the origin and foundation of liberal letters."[6] Isidore classifies the subject as an art and then turns to etymology: "It is truly called an art, because it consists of strict (*artus*) rules and precepts. Others say that the word 'art' is derived by the Greeks from ἀρετή, that is, 'virtue,' which they called knowledge."[7] Given the esteem that Isidore has for grammar, it is unsurprising that he would link it to virtue. He then goes into considerable detail on the parts of speech before turning to the syllable and, from that, meter and accent. Punctuation, shorthand writing, legal and military signs, and finger signals follow, before there begins a lengthy discussion on orthography. This is followed by a paragraph on analogy. While Isidore borrows much from Aelius Donatus for his grammar section in the *Etymologies*,[8] he goes well beyond the text of the famous pagan Roman grammarian. Writing in an era of severe decline in cultural unity, Isidore evidently felt the need to re-establish the basics of culture. The concern with grammar would continue throughout the Early Middle Ages, particularly with the

---

[5] Isidore of Seville, *The Etymologies of Isidore of Seville*, 1.iii.4. The alphabets of these three languages are in fact adaptations of the Phoenician alphabet.

[6] Ibid., 1.v.1.

[7] Ibid., 1.v.2.

[8] Lafontaine, *Isidore de Seville et la culture classique dans l'Espagne wisigothique*, 188.

Irish and the Carolingians. The Early Middle Ages was clearly the Age of Grammar, and it was Isidore more than any other individual who established it as such.

Isidore includes more than simply the basics in his grammar. One scholar describes several strands found in the *Etymologiae* that would play central roles in education, particularly in the cathedral schools and universities of later medieval centuries:

> The *analogia* ("analogy") is a systematization principle in ancient grammar based on the similarity between elements, in the knowledge of an element from its similarities to another known element. Isidore mainly associates analogy with the precise identification of vocabulary. The *etymologia* ("etymology") allows us to know the exact meaning of a word on the basis of its origin and its natural association with what the word denotes. The *glossa* ("gloss") refers to the explanation of a word through another having the same or an analogous meaning; it is therefore directly linked to analogy and synonymy. The *differentia* ("difference") is the specific element distinguishing a word from another very similar in meaning and form. Isidore uses these four grammatical categories as a methodological basis for research and literary creation. Not only do they appear with great frequency in Isidore's writings, but they also serve as a specific outline providing the title to some of his works.[9]

Isidore borrows his concept of analogy from Quintilian and applies it in various ways. First, analogy consists of revealing

---

[9] Jose Carrededo Fraga, "Isidore of Seville as a Grammarian," in *A Companion to Isidore of Seville*, eds. by Andrew Fear and Jamie Wood (Brill, 2020), 226. In the *Etymologies*, Isidore notes that "'Gloss' (*glossa*) receives its name from Greek, with the meaning 'tongue.' Philosophers call it *adverbum*, because it defines the utterance in question by means of one single word (*verbum*): in one word it declares what a given thing is, as *contiscere est tacere* ('to fall still' is 'to be silent')." I.xxx.I. In the next section he defines differentia: "A differentiation (*differentia*) is a type of definition, which writers on the liberal arts call 'concerning the same and the different.' Thus two things, of the kind that are confused with each other because of a certain quality that they have in common, are distinguished by an inferred difference, through which it is understood what each of the two is. For instance, one asks what is the difference between a 'king' and a 'tyrant': we define what each is by applying a differentiation, so that 'a king is restrained and temperate, but a tyrant is cruel.' Thus when the differentiation between these two has been given, then one knows what each of them is. And so on in the same way." I. xxxi.I.

an unknown or obscure element by comparing it to a known element; the uncertain is made clear by the certain. Second, analogy can be applied to numbers, though this covers the qualitative, not quantitative, nature of numbers.[10] Third, analogy involves the Greek belief in correspondence between the macrocosmos and the microcosmos. In practical terms, this is the correspondence between the physical universe and the individual man, and reveals the place of man in this world.

Like many Church Fathers, Isidore applies such correspondence-oriented thinking to Biblical exegesis, through typological, allegorical, moral, and mystical readings of the Bible. Like analogy, such readings sought parallels from seemingly unassociated elements in order to reveal the real meaning of a text in the light of Christian revelation.[11] Many Church Fathers and medieval minds practiced such multilayered reading. The "bottom-up" interpretation provided by etymology balances this "top-down" hermeneutic. In other words, etymology and analogy operate like analysis and synthesis: the former breaks down and isolates a text to the simplest unit possible, whereas the latter takes a more holistic view and identifies connections between small and large units to reveal how a text is woven together and how one text relates to other texts.[12] The latter operation is 'top-down' because it takes a much wider view of a given passage than the bottom-up operation, and integrates knowledge of history, geography, poetics, and Scripture into Biblical exegesis.

The next three sections of Book I reflect Isidore's preoccupation with the falling standards of Latin grammar in his own day, as he discusses barbarisms, solecisms, and faults. He observes:

> A barbarism (*barbarismus*) is a word pronounced with a corrupted letter or sound: a corrupted letter, as in *floriet* (i.e. the incorrect future form of *florere*, "bloom"), when one ought to say *florebit* ("will bloom"); a corrupted sound, if the

---

[10] Lafontaine, *Isidore de Seville et la culture classique dans l'Espagne wisigothique*, 45–46.

[11] Ibid., 46.

[12] Ibid., 46–47.

first syllable is lengthened and the middle syllable omitted in words like *latebrae* ("hiding places"), *tenebrae* ("shadows"). It is called "barbarism" from barbarian (*barbarus*) peoples, since they were ignorant of the purity of the Latin language, for some groups of people, once they had been made Romans, brought to Rome their mistakes in language and customs as well as their wealth. [13]

He elaborates on this with a fairly detailed discussion of various types of barbarisms. His clear examples of common faults in the next section on solecisms likely came from his many years in the classroom observing such mistakes: "A solecism is a group of words that are not joined by the correct rule, as if someone were to say *inter nobis* ('between us,' with *nobis* in the wrong case) instead of *inter nos*, or *date veniam sceleratorum* ('grant forgiveness of sinners') instead of *sceleratis* ('to sinners')." [14] Isidore goes into detail in the section on faults, and repeats some of what he has said about barbarisms and solecisms. Such a lengthy and meticulous section raises the issue of why Isidore cared so much about grammar, and about eliminating common errors. As already mentioned, it is because such errors resulted in errors when copying Bibles and other Christian writings. Errors of this type posed as great a threat to the faith as certain pagan writings did because erroneous Biblical passages would lead to heretical theology. [15] Correct language usage was a theological concern. This worry would motivate Charlemagne centuries later to put education and Christian civilization at the heart of his empire-building. Taking the reader to the very boundary of grammar — which is literary studies — Isidore also discusses figures of speech at length. Perhaps somewhat surprisingly, he relies on pagan authors while largely ignoring Biblical figures of speech. He repeatedly cites Virgil's *Aeneid*, *Eclogues*, and *Georgics* and Ovid's *Metamorphosis*. Latin Christendom would have to wait until Bede for a Christianization of much of this.

---

[13] Isidore of Seville, *The Etymologies of Isidore of Seville*, I.xxxii.1.
[14] Ibid., I.xxxiii.1.
[15] Lafontaine, *Isidore de Seville et la culture classique dans l'Espagne wisigothique*, 126.

As we have seen, Isidore's etymological work was the key to his grammar. He aimed to establish "a universal method of knowledge. *Rerum cognoscere causas* [to know the causes of things] could be the epitaph of the *Origines* [the *Etymologies*]," particularly for the first book, which reflects the bishop's belief that language is the tool of knowledge and grammar is a propaedeutic for more advanced disciplines.[16] Isidore saw etymology as the sharpest of the four grammatical tools (which also include, as we have seen, analogy, glosses, and differentia). It is the best method of differentiation, the key to discovering the original sense of each thing or being.[17] Grammar provides the required foundation to the encyclopedic education in all disciplines. Wishing to present and analyze all of the disciplines of education in the *Etymologies*, Isidore did so as a grammarian.[18] This caused him to organize his thought around grammatical categories (whereas the scholastics from the thirteenth century onward thought in logical categories). Grammar became for Isidore a way of thinking, a totalizing science, which we see most clearly in the *Etymologies*.[19]

But this perspective of the *grammaticus* also meant something much more for the Bishop of Seville. He was the full exponent of an ancient grammar culture that, despite the overall cultural decline of the era, still flourished in certain places, including southern France and parts of Spain. Isidore's attitude to grammar can be summed up with the following:

> To the extent that language was considered to be an entirely natural phenomenon, previously granted by its very nature to that of things, it could not longer be considered as the object of a special knowledge, but as a privileged instrument of metaphysical research: the knowledge of the true sense and origin of words led straight to the heart of things and their beings, to the intelligence of their essence. By that,

---

[16] Lafontaine, *Isidore de Seville et la culture classique dans l'Espagne wisigothique*, 202. The *Origines* is an alternative title for the *Etymologies*.
[17] Ibid., 203.
[18] Fraga, "Isidore of Seville as a Grammarian," 240.
[19] Lafontaine, *Isidore de Seville et la culture classique dans l'Espagne wisigothique*, 37.

the prestige of the grammarian tended to equal that of the
philosopher. Between the rhetor and the philosopher...,
the grammarian had thereby become one of the essential
representatives of Hellenistic culture.[20]

Isidore saw grammar as representing much more than simply
the foundational years of education. As the primary tool for
research into knowledge, it was responsible for creating an
entire grammar-type of culture, just as the scholastics were
responsible for creating another type of culture, and the
humanists, returning to rhetoric, in turn.[21] In all of this, he
was once again simply following tradition. It was Augustine
in *De doctrina christiana* who had authorized grammar "as an
indispensable elementary knowledge, as a rational discipline
permitting through the meditation on the nature of language
the access to the metaphysical sense of the notion of sign, and
finally as an auxiliary science of a basic importance for the
transmission, conservation, and exegesis of scriptural texts.
This authorization was decisive for the future of grammar in
the intellectual training of Christians, particularly that of the
clergy."[22] As we have seen with the definitions of *ratio* and
logos in Chapter 3, reason is the backbone of the liberal arts,
philosophy, and theology, which requires that grammar also be
a rational discipline in its foundational role.

Isidore's ambition to establish an encyclopedia-based universal learning program starts with the foundation of universal
knowledge. He relied heavily on Cassiodorus for the first three
books of the *Etymologies*.[23] In this, he was no more an innovator
than Cassiodorus was. He did not attempt to create anything
new. The material he provided encouraged efficient reading
and organized thought. This mental organization, based on

---

[20] Lafontaine, *Isidore de Seville et la culture classique dans l'Espagne wisigothique*,
28–29.

[21] Ibid., 29.

[22] Ibid., 32.

[23] Elfassi, "Isidore of Seville and the Etymologies," 245. The traditional division
of the *Etymologies* into twenty books has been called into question by recent
scholarship.

etymology, aimed to increase the understanding of Scripture. This etymological knowledge includes the meaning of the names of the Hebrew patriarchs and prophets, which illuminate their nature, teachings, and deeds. Even knowledge of the original meaning of geographical locations improved Biblical exegesis.[24] Isidore meticulously outlined a very clear and organized vision of education. If the liberal arts provided the foundation of universal knowledge, grammar provided the foundation of the liberal arts. Grammar itself also had a general basis. This approach was already centuries-old by the time of Isidore.

There is little in the *Etymologies* of the speculative grammar that would come to characterize scholastic grammar in the High Middle Ages. Isidore developed the old grammar of the poets that analyzes grammar not according to the logic of these later schoolmen, but according to the canonical writing masters. Isidore adhered to the traditional notion of canonicity: Proper language usage was established by canonical texts. Repeated and detailed exposure to these writings would develop this desired level of language in schoolboys. This explains the essential role of the master's glossing of a given text in the classroom, and the production by schoolmasters of countless glosses on the works of the canon in the medieval centuries. This also explains Isidore's repeated citations of Virgil, Ovid, and other well-loved Romans.

The *Etymologies* was not Isidore's only grammar-related writing. His *Sentences* and *Differences* also supported the vocation of the *grammaticus*. These were as rooted in the older tradition as the *Etymologies* was. A complementary genre to the encyclopedia was lexicography. The texts from this genre featured definitions, word etymology, and *differentia* (distinguishing between two or more closely-related or easily-confused words). Verrius Flaccus's *On the Meaning of Words* was one example for later generations.[25] The first book of Isidore's *Differences*

---

[24] Isidore of Seville, *The Etymologies of Isidore of Seville*, 18.
[25] Ibid., 12.

distinguishes between word pairs of synonyms or homonyms. The *Synonyma* followed a common teaching technique for both the grammar and rhetoric classroom by providing lists of phrases with similar meanings. Despite the traditional nature of this approach, Isidore injected a Christian orientation by relying on the Church Fathers and Bible for much of the *Synonyma*.[26] Such writings set the foundation for what would become Charlemagne's Christian civilization. Language was at the heart of this civilization. The two-book *Differences* reflected Isidore's concern for the basics of Latin, as he regarded *differentia* as central to the grammar classroom.[27] In the first book, the author distinguishes the meaning and correct usage of synonym and homonym word pairs. In the second book, he distinguishes between things, such as angels, demons, and humans.[28] The encyclopedic nature of the *Etymologies* prompted Isidore to include *differentia* in that writing. For example, he contrasts a king's restraint and temperate conduct with a tyrant's cruelty (Book 1, Chapter 31). Etymology and differentiation were often two parts of the same analysis.

7.2 RHETORIC AND DIALECTIC

For the Bishop of Seville, rhetoric was much more than simply eloquent discourse. His writings on rhetoric followed the path laid out by Augustine, particularly in *De doctrina christiana*. He embraced Augustine's vision of Christian culture. The Bishop of Hippo prioritized the moral and spiritual character of the orator over technical proficiency. This idea "brought rhetoric into the service of the Christian truth and pulled it away from the amorality of pure technique and its indifference to the true and the good."[29] Yet Augustine believed that rhetoric had a purpose in Christian culture as "a powerful instrument in the

---

[26] Fraga, "Isidore of Seville as a Grammarian," 237–238.
[27] Ibid., 231.
[28] Isidore of Seville, *The Etymologies of Isidore of Seville*, 10.
[29] Lafontaine, *Isidore de Seville et la culture classique dans l'Espagne wisigothique*, 331.

service of the scriptural Word and of spiritual progress, that is, in first place, of moral progress."[30] Rhetoric served as a "spiritual propaedeutic."[31] Also like the author of the *Confessions*, Isidore continued to hold the Greek and Latin pagan authors in high esteem in the sections on rhetoric and dialectic in the second book of the *Etymologies*. Unlike most other authors, he placed rhetoric, not dialectic, after grammar. He begins the book by noting: "1. Rhetoric is the art of speaking well in civil cases, [and eloquence (*eloquentia*) is fluency (*copia*)] for the purpose of persuading people toward the just and good. Rhetoric is named from the Greek term ῥητορίζειν, that is, fluency of speech, for Ῥῆσις in Greek means 'speech,' ῥήτωρ means 'orator.' 2. Further, rhetoric is connected with the art of grammar (*Grammatica*), for in grammar we learn the art of speaking correctly, while in rhetoric we understand how we may express what we have learned."[32]

Isidore followed the tradition, established by Plato and Cicero, in demanding that the ideal orator be a moral person, and that it was the task of education to develop this moral virtue. This demand reflected the almost universal agreement of pagan and Christian writers on paideia that education by its nature is *virtue* education. Isidore mentions something that to him and to all such educational theorists is perfectly obvious: "An orator therefore is a good man, skilled in speaking. A man's goodness is based on his nature, his behavior, his training in the arts."[33]

Instead of elaborating on this, he turns to the more technical side of oratory with Cicero's scheme: "One skilled in speaking is grounded in artful eloquence, which consists of five parts: invention, arrangement, style, memory, pronunciation (*inventio, dispositio, elocutio, memoria, pronuntiatio*), and of the goal of this office, which is to persuade of something."[34] He continues this

---

[30] Lafontaine, *Isidore de Seville et la culture classique dans l'Espagne wisigothique*, 331.

[31] Ibid., 333.

[32] Isidore of Seville, *The Etymologies of Isidore of Seville*, 2.i.1–2. Square brackets are in the original translation.

[33] Ibid., 2.iii.1.

[34] Ibid. The anonymous *Rhetorica ad Herennium*, which for many medieval

adherence to tradition by noting the three types of rhetorical speech, which are deliberative, demonstrative, and judicial, as originally outlined by Aristotle. After going into more detail on these types, Isidore turns to the syllogism, defining its three parts as "proposition (*propositio*, i.e. the major premise), the additional proposition (*assumptio*, i.e. the minor premise), and the conclusion (*conclusio*)."[35] He follows the Stagirite in noting the applicability of syllogisms to both rhetoric and logic.

After this long and detailed section on rhetoric, Isidore analyzes dialectic, which he defines as "the discipline devised for investigating the causes of things." He is far from Ambrose of Milan (c. 340–397 AD), who associates logic with heterodoxy: "But see how wild is their blasphemy, how their philosophers' logic confutes itself."[36] Isidore defines logic as a branch of philosophy, as it is "the rational (*rationalis*) power of defining, questioning, and discussing. Dialectic teaches, with regard to many types of questions, how the true and the false may be distinguished by disputation."[37] He makes a crucial distinction by repeating a well-known image: "Varro in his nine books of *Disciplines* defines dialectic and rhetoric with this similitude: 'Dialectic and rhetoric are like the clenched fist and the open palm of a man's hand: the former pinches words, the latter extends them.'"[38] Isidore elaborates on this distinction: "While dialectic is indeed sharper for examining things, rhetoric is more fluent for those things it strives to teach. Dialectic sometimes appears in schools; rhetoric continually comes to the public forum. Dialectic reaches very few students; rhetoric often reaches the whole populace."[39] Such a definition reveals

---

centuries was credited to Cicero, also espoused this five-part division. Cassiodorus is the major source of Isidore's discussion on rhetoric. Lafontaine, *Isidore de Seville et la culture classique dans l'Espagne wisigothique*, 231.

[35] Isidore of Seville, *The Etymologies of Isidore of Seville*, 2.ix.2.

[36] Ambrose of Milan, "Exposition of the Christian Faith," in *The Principal Works of St. Ambrose*, trans. H. De Romestin (Wm. B. Eerdmans, 1885), 645.

[37] Isidore of Seville, *The Etymologies of Isidore of Seville*, 2.xxii.1.

[38] Ibid., 2.xxiii.1.

[39] Ibid., 2.xxiii.2.

why rhetoric was so central to the evangelization efforts of the Church, whereas dialectic typically remained in the classroom to sharpen intellects.

Isidore inherited the ambiguous boundaries between philosophy and dialectic. The Church Fathers not only had to sort out the relationship between rhetoric and dialectic, but also between philosophy and dialectic, as the Greeks had failed to define the precise nature of each discipline and its relationship with the other. The close association in Isidore's mind between dialectic and philosophy is reflected in his further discussion of the former discipline after a section on philosophy, which he expands with an analysis of some of Aristotle's writings on logic, the *Categories* and *On Interpretation*, and elaboration on syllogisms and definition. He then turns back to a topic that is more commonly found in treatises on rhetoric, *topoi*, which he defines as "the discipline of coming up with arguments."[40]

7.3 THE QUADRIVIUM

Isidore's quadrivium-related writings, such as *De natura rerum* and parts of the *Etymologies*, are an integral part of his encyclopedism. These writings continued a long line of Greek and Latin texts on the natural world. Such nature writing had deep roots in ancient learning. Philosophy began as an inquiry into nature with the presocratic Milesian school.[41] A long list of Greek philosophers wrote on the natural world. This included the Pythagorean Philolaus of Croton (c. 470–c. 385 BC), with his *Peri physeos* (*On Nature*). Writing his encyclopedia as an introduction to Epicurianism, Lucretius (c. 99 BC–55 BC) gave *De rerum natura* a materialist orientation. He promises nothing after death, as he claims that the soul dies with the body. Lucretius argued that inner peace comes from accepting that there is no supernatural or divine control of the world, even if

---

[40] Isidore of Seville, *The Etymologies of Isidore of Seville*, 2.xxx.1.
[41] Pierre Pellegrin, "La nature et être," in *Le Savoir Grec*, eds. Jacques Brunschwig *et al*, ed (Paris: Flammarion, 2011), 84.

the created order "obeys simple and constant physical laws."[42] This is the sort of assumption that Isidore set out to challenge in many of his writings.

Concerning the more theoretical perspective of the quadrivium, Isidore did not read Euclid directly. He gained his understanding of mathematics, as most scholars did in the Early Middle Ages, from Nicomachus of Gerasa. There was a direct filiation from Nicomachus to Boethius to Cassiodorus to Isidore.[43] "Boethius and Cassiodorus both adopted an epistemological sequence — arithmetic deals with number per se, music with number in ratio, geometry with number extended in space, and astronomy with number in motion — while Martianus placed 'Harmony' at the end of his series after astronomy, as it symbolizes the transcendent perfection of the heavenly realm. Isidore's *argumentum* or summary introduction to book 3 announces the Boethius-Cassiodorus order; but in the text, he follows his 'ratio order.'"[44]

We are once again reminded that Isidore was not aiming for originality in his writings. Yet in one passage he succinctly puts forth many key points about numbers that became widely accepted by medieval Christendom. These include the notions that numbers are a mystery, have Biblical meaning, are related to God's creation of the world, and have significance in salvation history:

> 1. The reckoning of numbers ought not to be despised, for in many passages of sacred writings it elucidates how great a mystery they hold. Not for nothing it is said in praise of God (Wisdom 11:21), "Thou hast ordered all things in measure, and number (*numerus*), and weight." 2. The [number] that contains six units (*senarius*), which is perfect in its own parts, declares the completion of the world by a certain signification of its number. 3. Likewise for the forty

---

[42] Lucrèce, *De rerum natura*, trans. Olivier Sers (Paris: Les Belles Lettres, 2012), 8–13.

[43] Lafontaine, *Isidore de Seville et la culture classique dans l'Espagne wisigothique*, 353.

[44] Faith Wallis, "Isidore of Seville and Science," in *A Companion to Isidore of Seville*, eds. Andrew Fear and Jamie Wood. (Brill, 2020), 203.

days during which Moses and Elijah and the Lord himself fasted: without an understanding of numbers, the span of days is unintelligible.[45]

Isidore followed the ancient Greeks, specifically Pythagorean metaphysics, in investigating number symbolism in his *Liber numerorum* and in asserting the numerical basis of the cosmos. The belief that "the real is mathematically rational" means that number is the force behind the physical world.[46]

Isidore points out the distinction between arithmetic and the other three quadrivial disciplines. Concerning the former, he observes that "the writers of secular literature would have this discipline be the first among the mathematical disciplines, as this discipline relies on no other for its existence. However, music, geometry, and astronomy, which follow arithmetic, require its support in order to exist and hold their place."[47] Consistent with his methodology, Isidore analyzes the etymology of the numbers one through ten before referring to Scripture to highlight the significance of numbers. After considerable analysis of types of numbers, such as odd and even numbers, the discussion moves on to the differences among arithmetic, geometry, and music.

> Isidore breaks from Augustine and the Pythagorean-Platonist tradition in outlining a practical view of music, which in the long run would prevail in the Middle Ages because of the daily musical needs of the liturgy. Isidore was on the boundary of a deep change to music theory. Augustine and Boethius still held to "the classical Pythagorean-Platonic contemplation of mathematical proportion; its goal was to raise the soul above the realm of the sensual and corporeal so that it could grasp rational truth and cosmic harmony. The true musician was the philosopher who could judge the fundamental essences of music, not the performer or composer."[48] Isidore followed Cassiodorus in placing music at

---

[45] Isidore of Seville, *The Etymologies of Isidore of Seville*, 3.iv.1–2.

[46] Lafontaine, *Isidore de Seville et la culture classique dans l'Espagne wisigothique*, 374, 376.

[47] Isidore of Seville, *The Etymologies of Isidore of Seville*, 3.i.1.

[48] Wallis, "Isidore of Seville and Science," 204.

the service of Christianity by outlining a new understanding
of music. This understanding was derived from the Bible's
high regard for performed music, and singing's central role
in worship, as exemplified with the Psalms. Isidore briefly
refers to cosmic harmony (3.1.1), but his discussion of music
is centered on his classification of musical instruments and
terminology, and ignores mathematics except for the last
chapter's treatment of musical ratios.[49]

Yet Isidore did not break from the traditions of the other
quadrivial disciplines. On the whole, according to one scholar,
the Isidorian synthesis of knowledge of the created order succeeded by Christianizing this previous knowledge and giving
it coherence: No Christian writer before him had been so
ambitious as to consider the physical cosmos in its overall
structure and also the elements that constituted it, and from
that account to integrate this knowledge with the disciplines
of the *quadrivium*. The sheer scope and methodical perseverance of his scientific writing gave medieval Europe not only a
treasury of information about the created world, but a capa-
cious and ambitious way of imagining scientific knowledge as
a conversation between mathematics, the world-system, and
the inventories of natural history."[50]

7.4 PHILOSOPHY AND THEOLOGY

The years 500 to 1050 AD are not known for philosophical
achievement in the West, aside from John Scotus Erugiuna.
This stagnation and decline was caused more by regression in
education and the paucity of educational institutions than by
attitudes like those of Ambrose of Milan, who doubted the
moral virtue of philosophers: "The comeliness of virginity never
existed amongst the heathen, neither with the vestal virgins, nor
amongst philosophers, such as Pythagoras."[51] Despite Isidore's

---

[49] Wallis, "Isidore of Seville and Science," 204.
[50] Ibid., 214.
[51] Ambrose of Milan, "Concerning Virgins," in *The Principal Works of St. Ambrose*,
trans. by H. De Romestin. Grand Rapids, (Wm. B. Eerdmans, 1885), 1,9, 851.

own acceptance of pagan philosophy, he contributed little to
its content and practice except by outlining learning that was
foundational to the study of philosophy. This is why Braulio
of Zaragoza declares that the *Etymologies* was appropriate for
all branches of philosophy and that, "whoever reads and med-
itates upon it frequently will have and deserve a reputation for
knowledge of divine and human affairs. It is packed with elegant
statements of many kinds, collected in concise manner; from it,
there is practically nothing that cannot be learned."[52] Isidore's
innovative hierarchy of knowledge situated grammar above
philosophy itself by portraying grammar as a "complete system
of explanation of the world." What this means is that he did
not outline a philosophy *per se*, but a "grammar of philosophy."[53]

In his wish to enhance Christian paideia, Isidore kept to an
already well-established tradition by finding much that was
beneficial in pagan philosophy for the Church. He outlines
the traditional Stoic tripartite definition of philosophy (physics,
ethics, and logic): 1) physics (*naturalis* in Latin and *physica* in
Greek), which inquires into nature; 2) ethics (*moralis* in Latin
and *ethica* in Greek), which looks into human behavior; and
3) reasoning (*rationalis* in Latin and *logica* in Greek), which
investigates the truth of moral behavior and the causes of
things through the practice of disputation.[54]

Isidore adds to this a more God-centered definition: "Again
some of the learned (i.e. Cassiodorus, *Institutes* 2.3.5) have
defined philosophy in name and in its parts in this way: philosophy is the provable knowledge (*probabilis scientia*) of human
and divine things, insofar as this is possible for a human."[55]
His definition of philosophy has also served as that of dialectic: "Philosophy is the art of arts and the discipline of disciplines."[56] He ends this section by connecting the discipline with

---

[52] Braulio of Zaragoza. "Renotatio," 142.
[53] Lafontaine, *Isidore de Seville et la culture classique dans l'Espagne wisigothique*, 54.
[54] Isidore of Seville. *The Etymologies of Isidore of Seville*, 2.24.3.
[55] Ibid., 2.24.9.
[56] Ibid. In the sixteenth century, Petrus Ramus said the same thing about dialectic.

Christianity: "Philosophy is a meditation on death, a definition more suitable for Christians who, with worldly ambition trod under heel, and a disciplined way of life, live out the likeness of their future homeland."[57] As with almost all else Isidorian, he provides a traditional definition of ethics: "That philosophy is called moral (*moralis*) through which we seek a decent conduct of life, and set up principles aiming toward virtue."[58]

Reflecting the eclecticism that Benedict XVI noted in Isidore's writing, he even includes the quadrivium in his under-standing of philosophy:

> Doctrinal philosophy is the science that studies abstract quantity, for that quantity is called abstract which we treat with pure reason, separating it by the intellect from matter or from other accidental qualities — as are even and odd — or from things of this kind. It has four branches: arithmetic, geometry, music, astronomy. Arithmetic is the discipline of numerable quantity in itself. Geometry is the discipline of unmoving size and of shapes. Music is the discipline that speaks of numbers that inhere in something, namely those that are found in sounds. Astronomy is the discipline that contemplates all the courses of the heavenly bodies and the figures of the constellations, and with searching reason discourses on the habitual movements of the stars around one another and around the earth.[59]

The inclusion of the quadrivial disciplines in his understanding of philosophy could also imply a certain circularity to studies for Isidore, with the recycling of texts from the quadrivium at the level of philosophy. Many Christian writers on education, most famously Augustine, stressed the vital importance of the liberal arts for later theological or professional studies. In his extended focus on the basics of language, Isidore has all the markings of a grammarian, but his work is also heavily informed by theology, more specifically, by a Christian vision of society. He endeavored to advance a Christian pedagogy, an education

---

[57] Isidore of Seville. *The Etymologies of Isidore of Seville*, 2.24.9.
[58] Ibid., 2.24.16.
[59] Ibid., 2.24.14–15

with a clear theological purpose. However, one scholar does note that his discussion of theology in Book 7 is an investigation of names, not of theological issues.[60] Thus he remained consistent in his etymological work even as a theologian.

Overall, the *Etymologies* played a central role in the emergence and flourishing of medieval Christendom, despite the author's sometimes-imaginative etymological work. Isidore was writing for a budding Christian civilization that had not yet found its own independent intellectual tradition. Like Augustine, Origen, and other Church Fathers, he was attempting to preserve the best of ancient pagan civilization for Christianity in order to create a Christian paideia, a Christian education and culture. His encyclopedia served a higher calling, just as Pliny's had in an earlier age.

7.5 ISIDORE'S IMPACT ON LATER CENTURIES

Isidore stands alongside Augustine, Boethius and Cassiodorus as a bridge between the ancient, pagan world and the medieval, Christian one. Unsurprisingly, along with many works of Augustine and Boethius, the *Etymologies* was one of the most read texts of the Middle Ages. The *Sententiae*, *Differentiae*, *Synonyma*, and *De natura rerum* were also found in numerous medieval libraries.[61] This quantity was matched by a certain quality in his establishment of the previously-mentioned "epistemology of God."[62] Etienne Gilson notes the staying power of Isidore's writings, particularly his most famous text: "True or false, often ingenious, and sometimes ridiculous, the *Etymologies* of Isidore were transmitted from generation to generation until the end of the Middle Ages."[63] They helped shape the medieval mind. Isidore's writings were at the heart of the *translatio studii* that

---

[60] Isidore of Seville, *The Etymologies of Isidore of Seville*, 21.
[61] Andrew Fear and James Wood, "Introduction," in *A Companion to Isidore of Seville*, eds. by Andrew Fear and Jamie Wood (Brill, 2020), 3.
[62] Barrett, "God's Librarian: Isidore of Seville and His Literacy Agenda," 44.
[63] Etienne Gilson, *La philosophie au Moyen Age*, deuxième édition (Payot, 1986), 152.

saw the center of intellectual life move around early medieval Europe due to the ravages of war, the Vikings, and political upheaval. The Anglo-Saxon scholar Bede relied heavily on Isidore for his own writings on physical creation and on time.[64] He directly cited the Spaniard for much of his *On the Nature of Things*. The Irish based much of their studies on computing, cosmology, and exegetical methods and content on Isidore's writings. Centuries later, Hugh of St. Victor (1096–1141 AD), cited Isidore far more than any other authority in his *Didascalicon*, thus revealing the staying power of the bishop's works.[65]

Isidore's contribution to medieval scholarly culture was not only as a grammarian and encyclopedist. "The novel combination of a useful and ascetic spiritual guide with a didactic grammatical form later termed *stilus Isidorianus* ('Isidorian style') transformed the *Synonyma* into a highly successful work throughout the Middle Ages."[66] Isidore demonstrated how a churchman could be both a scholar and a serious Christian. "The work was seen mainly as a moral and ascetic text in the Middle Ages, as Isidore had probably designed it. The great majority of manuscripts transmitting the work include it with other texts of theological and dogmatic treatises."[67] Thus Isidore's writings enjoyed not only staying power, but a notable range of meaning and applications.

---

[64] Faith Wallis, on (oyen Age, Seville and His LiteracA *Companion to Isidore of Seville*, 183.
[65] Lafontaine, *Isidore de Seville et la culture classique dans l'Espagne wisigothique*, 13.
[66] Fraga, "Isidore of Seville as a Grammarian," 239.
[67] Ibid., 240.

CHAPTER 8

The Irish

*They were instructors in every branch of science and learning
of the time, possessors and bearers of a higher culture than
was at that time to be found anywhere on the Continent,
and can surely claim to have been the pioneers, to have
laid the corner stone of western culture on the Continent.*
—H. Zimmer[1]

*A. D. 891 ... And three Scots came to King Alfred in a
boat without any oars from Ireland; whence they stole
away, because they would live in a state of pilgrimage, for
the love of God, they recked not where. The boat in which
they came was made of two hides and a half; and they
took with them provisions for seven nights; and within
seven nights they came to land in Cornwall, and soon after
went to King Alfred. They were thus named: Dubslane,
and Macbeth, and Maelinmun.*
— *The Anglo-Saxon Chronicle*[2]

8.1 IRISH CULTURE AND CHRISTIAN LEARNING

THERE IS SOMETHING VERY SPECIAL
about the Irish monks and early medieval Irish Christian culture. The mystical and ascetic monasticism
that covered the island has been described as a mix of eastern
and western Christian spirituality. The monks' extreme self-
discipline and hermit vocations parallel those of the Egyptian desert monks. Their missionary zeal advanced western
Christianity, and knowledge in general, first in Scotland and
northern England, and then on the European continent, at a

---

[1] Graham, *The Early Irish Monastic Schools*, quote by Zimmer, H., *The Irish Element in Mediaeval Culture.*
[2] The Anglo-Saxon Chronicle, trans. Rev. James Ingram (London, 1823), with additional readings from the translation of Dr. J. A. Giles (London, 1847) https://www.gutenberg.org/cache/epub/657/pg657-images.html [Accessed July 10, 2024].

most unstable and precarious time. Their wide learning kept western culture alive when it was but a flicker in many other parts. Ireland was unique at this time due in part to its non-Roman roots and high esteem for the learned professions of the lawyer and the poet, which required rigorous study. A pious Christian society emerged from this, though the esteem for intellectual activity remained. Irish scholarship, poetry, calligraphy, and craftsmanship began to contribute to Christianity.[3] The new faith did not dislodge this deeply-rooted and rich culture, but complemented it. Irish education came to reflect this bicultural reality.

The preaching of the Gospel in Ireland enriched education on the island by establishing a society with two cultures that increasingly grew closer together. The evangelization of the faith went hand in hand with Christian education because the Church could only put down roots when there was an educated clergy. The key to the success of this education was the introduction of the Latin language to a nation that had been limited in its contact with the Roman Empire to trade. A uniquely-Irish writing style emerged because Latin was learned as a foreign language, unlike in Gaul, Spain, or Italy, with their vernacular dialects of the language.[4] Given Latin's foreign nature to the Irish, innovations were made to manuscript writing to ease reading, such as punctuation and the separation of words.[5] They also developed distinct Irish bookmaking techniques. When St. Patrick established a school at Armagh, ca. 450 AD to train men for the priesthood, it naturally gave instruction in Latin. To support this teaching, scribes at Armagh produced texts, some of which were sent to parishes. This was the first known organized school of Christian learning in Ireland. Other such institutions sprang up later in the same century.

---

[3] Hunter Blair, *The World of Bede*, 21.
[4] Daíbhí Ó Cronínín, *Early Medieval Ireland* (London: Longman, 1995), 169. It is unclear how the uniquely Irish style of writing developed, according to Ó Croninín, 170–171.
[5] Ibid., 172. The Irish were the first to break with the *scriptura continua* style of not leaving spaces between words.

Many such centers of learning became closely associated with monasteries, which imbued the Irish classroom with the values and practices of the island's monasticism. This monasticism in turn had been shaped by British and Welsh monasticism.[6] In general, the Irish Church in the first centuries was heavily influenced by the Anglo-Saxon Church, most notably concerning the dating of Easter. The confidence in the truth of the Christian message included the belief that the long-established local culture and learning would not undermine it. This meant that the Church in Ireland did not attempt to replace traditional pre-Christian learning with a fully Christian curriculum. Nevertheless, in preserving the ancient Irish tradition of learning, the monks made it more ascetic and Biblical. Traditional learning maintained its strong and deep roots in this assertive and ascetic Christian soil.

Ireland's unique place in Europe from the sixth to eighth centuries stemmed largely from the relative peace it enjoyed, particularly from the Vikings. This peace and stability permitted scholarly achievement and the flourishing of educational institutions. The Bible, hagiographies, the writings of the Church Fathers, and the needs of the liturgy and monastic life in general comprised Christian content and learning. At least some level of Greek was widely taught,[7] as exemplified with the *Book of Armagh*, which contains Greek words and the *Lord's Prayer* in the language. Traditional Irish history, lore, and law were widely disseminated. Even monks and saints were commonly raised in pagan Irish history and traditions alongside their religious training. One scholar notes that, overall, this upbringing was so successful that Irish churchmen in the sixth century could debate with their counterparts from the rest of Europe on the dating of Easter. In fact, in roughly one hundred years, the Irish managed to assimilate Latin into their culture and education to the point that the level of Latin in Irish texts matched the level found in texts from Spain, France, and Italy.[8]

---

[6] Graham, *The Early Irish Monastic Schools*, 34.
[7] Ibid., 141.
[8] Ó Croinín, *Early Medieval Ireland*, 174.

8.2 IRISH ACHIEVEMENTS

In the seventh century letter of Cummian, and the related *De ratione computandi*, the detailed and nuanced treatment of the problem of the dating of Easter, and the accompanying mathematics, testifies to the high level of both Latin and science in Ireland.[9] The seventh century seems to have been a high point in learning in Ireland, based on the increasingly-sophisticated grammar texts, as scholars had discovered the ancient grammars of Priscian, Charisius, Servius, and Diomedes as well as anonymous grammar texts from Spain on figures, tropes, and grammatical errors.[10] Isidore of Seville's works also heavily impacted seventh century Irish scholarship, particularly the *Etymologies* and *On the Nature of Things*. The *Etymologies* provided information that had been totally unfamiliar to the Irish, given their disconnect from the Roman Empire.

Latin grammar had to be taught from the standpoint of teaching an entirely foreign language. A unique grammar tradition emerged. Latin culture and instruction in Ireland were based entirely on books, not on any direct historical contact with Roman and Latin culture. This brought a serious challenge. Quintilian, Donatus, and Priscian had all written for students with an already-acquired native familiarity with Latin, even if it was the increasingly colloquial Latin of the fourth or fifth centuries AD. Such texts were too advanced for Irish readers. The typical Irish student needed a grammar education that started from the very beginning and that provided ample practice of the basics.[11] By the end of the sixth century, this had prompted the Irish to develop a new type of Latin grammar book on the foundation of Donatus, particularly the *Ars minor*. The earliest such Irish textbook, which became the standard in Ireland, was the *Ars Asporii / Ars Asperi*, named after the assumed author, Asper. In addition to the innovative grammar teaching for the

---

[9] Ó Croinín, *Early Medieval Ireland*, 201.
[10] Ibid., 211.
[11] Ibid., 174–175.

Irish situation that Quintilian or Donatus had not foreseen,
the *Ars Asperi* had an ascetic Christian sense arising from the
many examples that came from Irish monasticism.[12] Christian
grammars, such as those of Isidore of Seville, were filled with
many examples from the pagans, especially from Virgil's writings.
The *Ars Asperi*, conversely, used Church-related vocabulary
as exemplars for declensions. This includes *ecclesia* (church),
ieiunium (fast), and *orare* (pray). The keen desire for the Irish
to improve their Latin and develop a culture of *Romanitas*
generated even more works on grammar.

Other Irish-produced Latin textbooks imply a continuous
attempt at improving the teaching of Latin. The *Anonymous ad
Cuimnanum* offerred a commentary on Donatus' larger work,
the *Ars maior*. Sedulius Scottus wrote commentaries on several grammars, including Donatus' *Ars minor* and *Ars maior*,
Eutyches's *Ars de verbo*, and Priscian's *Institutiones grammaticae*.
These unique achievements in Latin grammar would make Irish
scholars ideal for the civilization building of the Carolingian
Renaissance, and its improvement of literacy across the empire.[13]
Many Irish scholars went to the continent to support Charles
the Great's *renovatio*. Cadac-Andreas arrived at Charlemagne's
court in the early years of the Carolingian Renaissance to teach
grammar and Biblical studies. Clemens Scottus (also known
as Clemens Hibernicus) became master of the palace school
after Alcuin of York's departure.

8.3 A PEDIGREE OF LEARNING

Once a foundation of Christian education had been established,
a tradition of scholarly lineage took hold. A scholar, usually a
churchman, was only as great in his learning as his educational
pedigree. This lineage could include, in the case of Ireland,

---

[12] Ó Cronínín, *Early Medieval Ireland*, 175.
[13] Sven Meeder, "Irish Scholars and Carolingian Learning," in *The Irish in
Early Medieval Europe*, eds. Roy Flechner and Sven Meeder (Pagrave, 2016),
pp. 179–194, 181.

tutors in both pagan Irish learning and Christian paideia. St. Columba (521–597 AD) was educated by the bard Gemman, who taught Irish history and culture and helped him acquire a lifelong love of Irish culture.[14] Columba's next tutor was St. Finnian of Movilla (c. 495–c. 589 AD) at a monastic school at Clonard. One portrayal of Columba's interaction with his tutor reveals the student's saintliness and the role of another kind of knowledge — prophecy or prognostication — in the Irish Christian culture of the time: "On the day of his arrival at Clonard, Columba asked Abbot Finnian where he should put up his hut. 'At the door of the church' was the answer. Columba built his cell at some distance away from the door. 'You have not obeyed my directions', said the Saint. 'It is true that I have not done so', said Columba, 'but the door will hereafter be here.' And in course of time, as the monastery grew in extent and importance, the door of the church was at that spot."[15] This exchange reveals the close interpersonal teacher-student bond, in which, as master, the tutor was even involved in the setup of the students' lodgings. The tutor also expected obedience, though some leeway for student assertiveness seems to have been permitted.

As an adult, Columba supported the traditional, pre-Christian bardic schools, which eventually came to be led by lay Christians. He advocated for their reform, instead of their abolition, in 573 AD at the Convention of Drum Ceata. This reform resulted in each of Ireland's five regions receiving its own leading bard college under the leadership of Ireland's chief poet at the time, Dallan Forgaill (c. 560–640 AD).[16] Smaller, more local schools under the headship of the regional central schools offered free tuition and provided the opportunity for widespread education in smaller or more isolated locales. The healthy number of local

---

[14] Wentworth Huyshe, *The Life of St. Columba* (The Educational Company of Ireland, 1922), p. xv.

[15] Ibid., xvi. St. Finnian of Movilla should not be confused with St. Finnian of Clonard (470–539 or 549).

[16] Graham, *The Early Irish Monastic Schools*, 74.

schools led to further developments in educational institutions. Some schools began to specialize, depending on the interests of the teachers or on the traditions that took root. Teaching duties in law, history, and poetry were even handed down from one generation to the next in the same family.[17] Central to this non-monastic education was the participation of laymen as principals, teachers, and tutors, which was uncommon in the wider medieval Latin West aside from Italy.

One reason for the success of these non-religious schools was the lack of rivalry between the monastic- and lay-led institutions, and between religious and secular Irish culture in general. Religious schools did not attempt to steal pupils away from secular ones, but likely saw them as feeder institutions, and therefore as vital to their own success. Christian culture in Ireland did not seem to treat traditional Irish culture as a threat or rival. This is reflected in the practice of Irish monks writing down for posterity many poems from their land that had nothing to do with Christianity.[18] Unsurprisingly, many monasteries had lay teachers, and parents often sent their boys to receive a monastic education without any plans for a subsequent clerical career. In Ireland, as in the Byzantine Empire, the Church, despite its prominent role in society, did not totally dominate education. Education did not only serve ecclesiastical careers. The laity were much more involved in education in Ireland than they were in Francia at this time.

8.4 ASCETIC LEARNING

Given the monastic form of Irish Christianity, much schooling was closely related to asceticism, as depicted in the *Life of Brenainn*, a hagiography on one of the Twelve Apostles of Ireland, Brendan of Clonfert (484–577 AD). In this anecdote, education is entirely religious in content and aims: "Now, after Brenainn [Brendan] had learnt the canon of the Old Law and the New

---

[17] Graham, *The Early Irish Monastic Schools*, 75.
[18] Ibid., 77.

Testament, he desired to write and to learn the Rules of the saints of Ireland. So Bishop Eire consented that he should go and learn those Rules, for Eire knew that it was from God that Brenainn had that counsel. And bishop Eire said to him, 'Come again to me when thou hast those Rules, that thou mayest take (ecclesiastical) orders from me.'"

As in other Irish depictions of saints, the *Life of Brenainn* includes an element of prophecy: "After Brenainn had gone to commune with his foster-mother Ita, she said the same to him, that is, to learn the Rules of the saints of Ireland, and she (also) said to him, 'Do not study with women nor with virgins, lest some one revile thee. Go,' she saith, 'and a famous warrior of noble race will meet thee on the road.' It happened, then, that Mac Lenfn was that warrior." Echoing another common theme of education in Christendom as a whole, the hero's itinerancy stems from the desire to meet a holy man, which makes sense because the hero of this hagiography is a monk-in-training:

> After Brenainn had travelled (some distance) Mac Lenfn met him. Then said Brenainn to him "Repent, for God is calling thee, and thou shalt be His own child to Him from henceforward." Then did Colmin Mac Lenfn turn to the Lord, and a church was built by him at once, as Colman... After that Brenainn visited the province of Connaught, drawn by the fame of certain pious man who dwelt there. Even Iarlaithe, son of Lug, son of Tron, son of Fiacc, son of Mochta, son of Bresal, son of Siracht, son of Fiacha the Fair. And with him Brenainn learnt all the Rules of the Irish saints. And Brenainn said to Iarlaithe, "In no wise shall thy resurrection be here."

Learning "all the Rules of the Irish saints" was the ecclesiastical equivalent of the long ancestral lineage that this extract also mentions (son of Lug, son of Tron...), and reflects Irish biculturalism, with pre-Christian and Christian cultures existing side-by-side in the education system. Ireland did not become less "Irish" when it embraced the faith. Education exemplified this more than any other sector.

Reflecting that true learning in this monastic and eremetical culture was ultimately spiritual, the humble tutor soon learns that the student is really the spiritual master: "'My holy son,' said Iarlaithe, 'why dost thou hide from us the divine graces of the Holy Spirit which are manifestly in thee, and the innumerable powers of the mighty Lord which are secretly in thy spotless mind. Thou forsooth hast come to me to learn from me,' said Iarlaithe, 'but it is he who shall be thine henceforward only take me into thy service for ever and ever.'"[19] Once again we notice that spiritual powers, not intellectual achievements or dexterity, defined educational success.

The *Life of Kentigern* depicts the ideal student, whose spiritual maturity shone for all to see. His reputation for holiness spread, as his learning led to saintly spiritual progress:

> When the age of discernment approached him, and the time suitable and acceptable for learning, he handed him over to be instructed in letters. And he devoted much diligence and effort to him that in these things he might advance. And in this matter, he himself was not defrauded by his own desire, because the boy responded very well and fruitfully to his teaching by learning and retaining it *like a tree planted by the rivers of water, that bringeth forth his fruit in his season.* The boy made progress with the anointing of good hope and holy character instructing him in the discipline of letters, and not less in the practice of the holy virtues.[20]

This extract reveals that a specific payoff or outcome was sought for Christian education. Kentigern is the ideal student, as he came to possess the requisite virtues. God played a key role in Kentigern's academic success:

> For there were granted to him by the Father of light, from whom every good and perfect gift is given, an attentive heart, a keen nature for understanding, a firm memory to retain what had been learned, a persuasive tongue to produce what

---

[19] "Life of Brenainn," in *Lives of Saints from the Book of Lismore.*
[20] https://sourcebooks.fordham.edu/basis/Jocelyn-LifeofKentigern.asp (Chapters 4–5).

he desired, and a sublime voice–dripping with sweetness, harmonious, and as it were, never weary of singing the divine praises. Moreover all these gifts of grace gilded a life worthy of praise, and for that reason he was in the eyes of the holy old man more precious and loveable than all of his companions. And so it was his custom to call him in the language of his country Munghu, which is spoken in Latin as "Karissimus Amicus," and by this name up to this day the common people are accustomed to call him frequently, and to invoke him in their distress.[21]

The boy's gifts were the outward manifestations of his holiness. Yet not everyone was convinced of this holiness. Either Kentigern was a phony or his peers were envious. In any case, his spiritual renown caused tension: "The fellow students of Saint Kentigern, seeing that he was loved by their master and spiritual father more than all the others, hated him, and they were not able to speak anything peacefully to him either privately or publicly. Whereupon they plotted against him in many things, and insulted, envied, and slandered him. But the boy of the Lord always had the eyes of his heart towards the Lord, and suffering more for them than for himself, he was little weighed down by all the unjust tricks of men."[22] Hagiographies are replete with such challenges encountered by the heroic holy man, especially in his learning years. Such obstacles seem to be a part of the development of the future saint, as the audience of hagiographies comes to realize that saintliness is developed by confronting and opposing the ways of the world. This anecdote strongly contrasts the saint with the more worldly individuals. According to the *Life of Kentigern*, education failed to have its desired effect on the hero's peers, as they remained worldly and envious of his holy power and fame.

The *Life of St. Féchín of Fore* reports on the spiritual power of one apprentice for the priesthood, a certain Féchín, whose power gave him authority despite his status as a student. Even

---

[21] https://sourcebooks.fordham.edu/basis/Jocelyn-LifeofKentigern.asp (Chapters 4–5).
[22] Ibid.

the king himself acknowledges this holiness, and humbles himself before this authority:

> Of a time when Féchín was learning with Presbyter Nathi
> in Achad Conairi, he is set one day to keep the meadow
> lest it should be stript bare by strangers' cattle. Thereafter
> the king's horses and herds are put into it in spite of Féchín.
> Féchín cursed them, and struck his bell at them, so that
> they found death forthwith. When the king heard that, he
> comes before Féchín, and flung himself on his knees, and
> sought forgiveness of his sins. Féchín gives him absolution,
> and brought his horses and his herds (back) to life; and
> God's name and Féchín's were magnified by that miracle.
> And the king made an offering of that land to Féchín for
> ever, and Féchín gave it to his master, even Presbyter Nathi.
> Wherefore (a poet) sang the Lay:
>
> > A goodly marvel of him as an infant, etc.
>
> After that holy child was perfected in age and in wisdom and
> in holiness, his tutor told him to take holy orders (so as to
> be able) to offer the King of Heaven and Earth. So Féchín
> quitted his tutor, and after taking orders, went, by the angel's
> command, to Fore. And his mind rejoiced at that place, and
> he prayed and fasted there for three days and a night.[23]

It seems that Féchín was deemed qualified for holy orders
not by passing a standardized theological curriculum, but by
displaying Old Testament-style spiritual powers, along with
possessing wisdom and holiness. It also seems that, more practically, the boy had certain daily chores to do, in this anecdote
managing the pasture.

The *Life of St. Fintan* depicts the intensely personal and
religious natures of early medieval Irish education, along with
the almost necessary vision of the future of the saint's life. Also
typical is the prioritization of the study of the monastic rule
and of Scripture:

> Then the boy Fintán read with Comgall and studied the rule.
> After this Fintán arrived at the school of Saint Colum Cille,
> which was in Cell Mór Díthrib, and there he read the Holy

---

[23] Anonymous, *Life of St. Féchín of Fore*, trans. Whitley Stokes in *Revue Celtique*,
Volume 12 (1891), 318–353.

Scripture with Columba. One day Saint Columba, as was his custom, was filled by the grace of the Holy Spirit and sang for much of the day about all the things that the Holy Spirit dictated to him. And, when he was finished, Columba said:

"Who was nearest to me when I sang the words of the Holy Spirit?"

Baíthéne replied to him:

"That boy, the son of Tulchán, was nearest to you by your right-hand side."

Then Columba said:

"He will be a spiritual teacher and most learned, surpassing everyone from this school."

Thereafter Fintán departed to read with the wisest man in the whole of Ireland and Britain who was a strict abbot of a church by the lakes of Erne, and he stayed with him for 19 years, reading the Scripture, and there were nine other young men with him. And they were under a very strict [monastic] rule, such that they were not permitted to sieve the flour, but the flour with its chaff used to be mixed with water in a bowl and cooked over stones heated by fire, and this was their daily meal.[24]

The boy's constant movement from place to place to study was central to his education. The wandering life of the student in search of the ideal tutor, or *nutritor*, could sometimes begin early. This tradition of the tutor as teacher, guardian, and fosterer went back to ancient Rome and Greece (and likely pre-Christian Ireland), and was not particular to Christianity. Encouraging this itinerancy was the very strong tradition of child fosterage in early medieval Ireland. This included scholars fostering the sons of kings.[25] The close nutritor-disciple relationship was

---

[24] Anonymous, *Life of Saint Fintán, alias Munnu, abbot of Tech Munnu*, trans. Roy Flechner (2021).

[25] Ó Croinín, *Early Medieval Ireland*, 178. Anonymous, *Life of Saint Fintán, alias Munnu, abbot of Tech Munnu* (Taghmon, Co. Wexford). Roy Flechner, trans. (Cork, Ireland: Corpus of Electronic Texts, 2021). See: https://celt.ucc. ie/published/T201046.html. This work describes how a king of the Fotharta in Leinster placed two sons in fosterage, one with Fintan and the other with another holy man. Ó Croinín, *Early Medieval Ireland*, 181. The *Life of Ciaran of Clonmacnois* "states that a daughter of the king of Tara was placed at the monastery of Finnian at Clonard 'so that she could read the psalms and other texts with the holy man." Ó Croinín, *Early Medieval Ireland*, 181.

characterized by "solitary study, the master alone in his cell reading his text with the pupil looking over his shoulder, so to speak.
The solitary monk is a commonplace of early Irish lyric poetry."[26]

Education was foundational to the monastic life. St. Columbanus (540–615 AD) was trained in classical learning at Bangor,
County Down. In his *Regula monachorum*, he notes the four
daily duties of the monk, which were fasting, prayer, work,
and study.[27] Daily reading focused on Scripture, homilies, and
hagiographies or, for those in formal studies, memorization of
the psalter. One modern scholar expresses admiration at the
level of the learning and Latin writing style of Columbanus.
The monastic rules did not encourage the kind of learning
that resulted in "the astonishing grasp of Latin language and
style which makes his letters such striking documents . . . They
display a thorough command of Latin, which Columbanus
employs in different styles to suit the occasion, and they indicate that he was deeply versed in the Scriptures as well as in
the subjects of biblical exegesis and computus."[28] He was the
Venerable Bede of Ireland, in other words.

Monastic schools played a key role in the production of
illuminated manuscripts in Irish Christianity, most famously
with the *Book of Durrow* (c. 650 AD) and the *Book of Kells*
(c. 800 AD). The history of Christian art in Ireland paralleled
the history of learning and higher culture in general. The new
educational discipline or art was added or integrated with the
already existing and robust Irish parallel, and acquired dis-
tinctive Irish characteristics. In other words, the Irish did not
simply imitate continental European art (or education), but
instead used these new things to further develop their own
styles. Irish art advanced in this way from the fourth century
to the twelfth century Norman invasion[29]

---

[26] Ó Cronínín, *Early Medieval Ireland*, 180.

[27] "Ergo quotidie jejunandum est, sicut quotidie orandum est, quotidie laboran-
dum, quotidie est legendum." In Graham, *The Early Irish Monastic Schools*, 62.

[28] Ó Cronínín, *Early Medieval Ireland*, 176 and 177. Ó Cronínín, notes that these
letters are "the oldest personal letters of an Irishman that we have."

[29] Graham, *The Early Irish Monastic Schools*, 156.

8.5 THE IRISH IN ENGLAND
AND ON THE CONTINENT

As early as the mid-sixth century, Irish education had already become more focused on the outside world. The monastery of Clonard provided missionary training. Their most famous graduates were Columba (Colum Cille) and Brendan of Clonfert, men who became famous missionaries in many parts of western Christendom, where they founded monasteries and schools. This evangelical success demonstrates that the non-Christian native Irish component of their studies in Ireland had not 'contaminated' or compromised their Christian education or development in any way.[30]

The educational efforts of Irish missionaries went hand-in-hand with establishing new monasteries in Scotland, England, and continental Europe. St. Aidan of Lindisfarne (590–651 AD) was a missionary in Northumbria. Having established a missionary monastery in 635 AD, Irish monks converted the Northumbrians and established many more important monasteries, such as Ripon. Continental Irish monasteries were established far and wide on the Continent as well, including the Netherlands (Namur and Liège), France (Remirmont, Besançon, Fleury, Corbie, and St. Riquier) and the Germanic lands (Würzburg, Erfurt, Regensburg, and St. Gall). In 610 AD, St. Columbanus and his companions came to an old Roman settlement, Brigantia, at the eastern end of Lake Constance. Although Christian relics were to be found, the locals had returned to paganism. St. Aurelia's parish church, for example, had been turned into a pagan temple containing gilded images. The Irishman and student of Columbanus, Gall, fought this paganization with his eloquent preaching in the local language. He destroyed the local idols and threw them into the lake. When the Irish monks were ordered by the Duke of Alemannia to leave, Columbanus

---

[30] Graham, *The Early Irish Monastic Schools*, 35.

ventured further south to Italy and established a monastery at Bobbio.[31]

Gall fell sick, and had to remain behind. He established a hermitage in a secluded spot while evangelizing the people and fighting paganism. Over the following decades, the hermitage developed into an abbey under the monastic Rule of Columbanus due to the attraction of the saint's relics. Irish monks arrived to develop St. Gall into a center of Irish learning, alongside other Irish monasteries at Salzburg and Liège. St. Gall also had close relations with the Anglo-Saxon monastery at Fulda (Germany). The Rule of Columbanus established a life of work, reading, prayer, and fasting.[32] The direct Irish influence began to wane under the abbots Othmar (720–759 AD) and Johannes, particularly when the Benedictine Rule was adopted in 760 AD.[33]

Irish monastic foundations were even established in Italy itself, at Bobbio, Taranto, Lucca, and elsewhere. Unsurprisingly, the Irish played a central role in the education program of the Carolingian Renaissance. The Carolingian ruler Charles the Bald (823–877 AD), a patron of learning and culture, stimulated a wave of monk arrivals on the European Continent with his continuation of Charlemagne's pursuit of a more highly-educated clergy. This evangelical activity could not have come at a more dire time in western cultural history, as one twentieth-century writer notes:

> There was probably not a more barbarous period in the history of Western Europe than the seventh century. Classical studies had fallen into utter decay. Few laymen could write their names. The clergy were indifferently skilled in the Latin language. If barbarism was not to overrun Gaul, outside assistance was an essential. Fortunately such assistance came, and came unsolicited. A great period of religious activity dates from the time when St. Columbanus and his companions began to set up their monasteries. In the course

---

[31] Clark, *The Abbey of St Gall as a Centre of Literature and Art*, 1.
[32] Ibid., 23.
[33] Ibid., 26.

of time these religious foundations became great centers of learning. Of their literary activity we have ample objective evidence in the many manuscripts, *scottice scripta*, which are still preserved in Continental libraries.[34]

The monastic character of the Irish Church at this time heavily influenced its missionary work.[35] Education in Ireland was not only Christian in general, but more specifically, focused on missionary work. Much of this culture faced heavy setbacks and destruction at the hands of the Vikings in the ninth and tenth centuries, when the Northmen ransacked and burned libraries and monks fled to continental monasteries. Many of these monks Latinized their Irish names: Moengal to Marcellus, Cellach to Gelasius, Donal to Donatus, and Siadhal to Sedulius.[36] Testifying to this diaspora, numerous Latin manuscripts from this era written in the Irish writing style are found in continental libraries, such as at St. Gall.[37] The collection of poems by the figure known as *Hibernicus exul* (Hibernian Exile) included a piece on the liberal arts:

> Learn now, boys! The age for learning passes swiftly,
> time goes by, as the heavens revolve the days follow.
> Just as the swift charger gallops eagerly over the fields,
> so youth flies by without lingering as it passes.
> The pliant tip of the twig curves beneath an easy pressure
> but no one can bend the stiff boughs.
> While your minds happen to be receptive, my friends,
> waste no time and learn the divine commands of God.
> Do not squander the period generously granted to you,
> for without learning the life of man perishes.[38]

Some of this missionary work affected girls' education. The school founded by St. Mugint in Scotland was open to girls as well as boys. In general, Irish missionaries contributed to

---

[34] Hugh Graham, "Irish Monks and the Transmission of Learning," in *The Catholic Historical Review*, Vol. 11, No. 3, (1925), 431–442, 437.
[35] Ibid., 41.
[36] Sedulius may have been Sedulius Scottus.
[37] Graham, *The Early Irish Monastic Schools*, 43–44.
[38] Peter Godman, *Poetry of the Carolingian Renaissance*, (London: Duckworth, 1985), 179.

female education in Northumbria.[39] The vast majority of these women were destined for the enclosed life of a nun.

8.6 FOREIGN STUDENTS IN IRELAND

While the Irish monks famously went out into the world from the sixth to ninth centuries, many students also flocked to the island. This included the Briton St. Cadoc, tutored by St. Mocuda at Lismore. The Venerable Bede notes the high numbers of Anglo-Saxon scholars in Ireland and the charitable nature of the Irish masters:

> In the same year of our Lord's incarnation, 664, there happened an eclipse of the sun, on the third of May, about ten o'clock in the morning. In the same year, a sudden pestilence . . . did no less harm in the island of Ireland. Many of the nobility, and of the lower ranks of the English nation, were there at that time, who, in the days of the Bishops Finan and Colman, forsaking their native island, retired thither, either for the sake of Divine studies, or of a more continent life; and some of them presently devoted themselves to a monastical life, others chose rather to apply themselves to study, going about from one master's cell to another. The Scots willingly received them all, and took care to supply them with food, as also to furnish them with books to read, and their teaching, gratis.[40]

The above also notes the older students' itinerancy. Even "retired" scholars moved about in search of the best learning.

Irish learning attracted the highest reaches of European society. The Merovingian King Dagobert II (d. 679 AD) was educated in Ireland, as was Oswald, son of King Ethelfrid of Northumbria in the same century. Alcuin notes the international fame of Irish schools in his *Life of Willibrord*. Unsurprisingly, he emphasizes the tutors' spiritual qualities:

> When this youth, as highly endowed with sacred learning as he was with self control and integrity, reached the

---

[39] Graham, *The Early Irish Monastic Schools*, 82.
[40] Bede, *Ecclesiastical History of the English Nation*, Book III, xxvii. https://sourcebooks.fordham.edu/basis/bede-book3.asp.

twentieth year of his age he felt an urge to pursue a more rigorous mode of life and was stirred with a desire to travel abroad. And because he had heard that schools and learning flourished in Ireland, he was encouraged further by what he was told of the manner of life adopted there by certain holy men, particularly by the blessed bishop Ecgbert, to whom was given the title of Saint, and by Wichtberct, the venerable servant and priest of God, both of whom, for love of Christ, forsook home, fatherland and family and retired to Ireland, where, cut off from the world though close to God, they lived as solitaries enjoying the blessings of heavenly contemplation.[41]

The next section of the *Life of Willibrord* notes "the intimate circle" of fathers or teachers. Learning here is "sacred learning," which, the *Life* seems to indicate, with an emphasis on ascetic training. Learning also established lifelong friendships that revolved around references to the famous texts that churchmen had memorized as youngsters. These brotherhoods were also likely useful for those who aimed for higher Church offices.

As we have repeatedly seen, education meant training in ascetic practices as much, if not more, than in the *three r's* of reading, writing, and arithmetic. The tutor, as a spiritual father, oversaw the pupil's spiritual development as much as his intellectual progress. Alcuin observes the charisma of the tutors and how they formed a community:

> The blessed youth wished to imitate the godly life of these men and, after obtaining the consent of his abbot and brethren, hastened quickly across the sea to join the intimate circle of the said fathers, so that by contact with them he might attain the same degree of holiness and possess the same virtues, much as a bee sucks honey from the flowers and stores it up in its honeycomb. There among these masters, eminent both for sanctity and sacred learning, he who was one day to preach to many peoples was trained for twelve years, until he reached the mature age of manhood and the full age of Christ.[42]

---

[41] Alcuin, *Life of Willibrord*.
[42] Ibid.

This section of the *Life of Willibrord* ends by noting the need for educated preachers, something that was echoed by other Church leaders and kings, most famously by Charlemagne and then, centuries later, by the fathers of the Council of Trent.

8.7 JOHN SCOTUS ERIUGENA

The Neoplatonist John Scotus Eriugena (800–877 AD), who headed Charles the Bald's palace school in Aachen, strongly boosted the study of dialectic. He closely associated philosophy with logic or dialectic, something that would happen again centuries later with Abelard and the scholastics at Paris. The Irishman assigned the dialectical tasks of division, definition, demonstration, and analysis to philosophy and theology.[43] With Greek still taught in his homeland, Eriugena was able to translate Maximus the Confessor and the Syrian Church Father Dionysius the Areopagite from Greek into Latin. The growing cultural alienation between the Latin West and the Greek East made his Areopagitian outlook look jarring, misplaced, and even heretical to ninth-century western bishops, who accused him of pantheism. Eriugena's influence on the medieval West therefore did not match the level of his brilliance. His skill at translating texts and presenting them to the West testifies to the unique achievements of Irish education and its contribution to the wider West.

---

[43] Graham, *The Early Irish Monastic Schools*, 189.

CHAPTER 9

England and Scotland

MARIE-MADELEINE MARTIN IN *Immortal Latin* gives an overview of the British Isles at a crucial time in early medieval history. She refers to the foundational role of the Irish for later Anglo-Saxon accomplishments, which included educational work in the Carolingian empire:

> The Church of the British Isles, which was Latin, was first baptized in Ireland by the diminutive Patrick. He had been raised by the monks of Lérins in the Romans' old Provincia. Victricius, bishop of Rouen, then visited the Church in the time of Arianism. Finally, in the sixth century, Pope Gregory ordered a methodical evangelization. Preserved from the era's accumulated ruins of continental Europe, including the wars and pillaging of barbarians or Arabs, it was the domain of one of the most well-read Christians, the Venerable Bede. In the seventh century, the British Isles became the land of the great book-loving abbeys. St. Columbanus and his monks ventured out to convert Northern Europe. St. Boniface embarked on evangelizing Germany. In Charlemagne's era, the great Alcuin of the school of York came to the aid of the Frankish emperor in reviving Athens and Rome on the banks of the Rhine at Aix-la-Chapelle and on the banks of the Loire at Tours and Orleans.[1]

The work of the Irish and Anglo-Saxons on the Continent demonstrates the internationalization of Christian education.

The two sources of seventh century Anglo-Saxon education also reflect this European-wide educational system. The

---

[1] Marie-Madeleine Martin, *Immortal Latin*, trans. Brian Welter (Arouca Press, 2021), 52.

southern-based Roman source, with its center at Canterbury, was rooted in the work of the papal missionary St. Augustine. The northern-based Irish source was centered at Iona, off the Scottish coast. Aldhelm (or Ealdhelm) of Malmesbury (died 709 AD) received both the Roman and Irish strands. One of his tutors was the Irish hermit Maildubh (Maildulf). Marshall McLuhan notes, "In a letter to Eleutherius, Aldhelm described the course of studies in Canterbury, mentioning first that he had to study Roman law, just as though he were to become a *doctus orator*. Then came metrics and prosody" along with rhetoric, mathematics, and astronomy. This education trained him to apply his grammatical expertise to the exegesis of Scripture.[2] His writings, reflecting his classical education, included quotations from the Roman masters Virgil, Terence, Horace, and Juvenal. "Aldhelm's literary work, therefore, justifies the statement that the Canterbury school was but a continuation of the *puerilis institutio* of the late Roman Empire. At the same time it was a continuation of the Augustinian ideal, a *doctrina christiana*."[3]

Aldhelm wrote his treatise on education, the *Letter to Acircius*, to his former pupil, Ealdfrith, king of Northumbria and a well-known scholar in his own right.[4] After discussing the significance of the number seven, the writer spends much time examining technical terms related to poetry, such as caesura, dactylic hexameter, synaloepha, and eclipsis. Aldhelm ends the letter with a series of riddles. Riddles played a significant role in Anglo-Saxon education in the era, probably because they were intellectually challenging, and, with their many puns, entertaining and part of the wider culture. The following riddle comes from the late tenth-century *Exeter Book*:

---

[2] Marshall McLuhan, *The Classical Trivium: The Place of Thomas Nashe in the Learning of his Time* (Gingko Press, 2006), 83.

[3] Ibid., 83.

[4] The *Letter* is also known as the *Treatise on the number Seven, on Metres, Riddles and Rules of Metrical Feet*. W. B. Wildman, *Life of S. Ealdhelm* (Chapman and Hall, 1905), 72.

I know a noble guest, dear to princes,
whom grim hunger cannot harm,
nor hot thirst, nor age nor illness.
If kindly the servant always tend him,
he who must go along on the journey;
safe and certain they will find at home
food and joy and countless kin;
but sorrow if the servant obeys his lord badly,
his master on their journey; nor will brother fear brother
when unharmed they leave quickly the bosom of their kin,
mother and sister. Let whoever will
with fitting words name the guest or the servant
I speak of here.[5]

Aldhelm claims to have been the first Englishman to learn and then teach Latin meter. He argues that such training was well worth it, and points out that Emperor Theodosius studied it daily and had even himself made a copy of Priscian's entire work of grammar.[6]

9.2 BEDE AND HIS WORLD

One of the most influential and broadly-educated scholars in the period from 500 to 1050 AD was the Venerable Bede (672–735 AD), whose writings ended up in Carolingian centers of learning such as Fulda and St. Gall. He was the product of perhaps the greatest center of learning of his day in all of Europe, the twin monasteries of Wearmouth and Jarrow. From sheer willpower, the Anglo-Saxons built an outpost of *Romanitas* in this most unlikely place. The two monasteries had a close relationship with Rome, despite the very different cultures, vast distance, and challenges of travel. Yet the repeated journeys of the monasteries' leaders to Rome gave to these centers the very best of Gaul and Rome. This included chant and singing, books (including the Gospels), and uncial writing.[7]

---

[5] The answer is the soul. *Anglo-Saxon Riddles of the Exeter Book.*
[6] Wildman, *Life of S. Ealdhelm,* 91.
[7] Hunter Blair, *The World of Bede,* 180. "Uncial hand" refers to the uncial script, composed of capital letters, that was later replaced by Carolingian minuscule.

One reason for the success of the twin monasteries was the support of King Ealdfrith. With the lack of cities and bishops (aside from Canterbury and York), the life and administration of the English Church revolved around the monasteries, as it did in Ireland.[8] Gregory the Great, who asserted the need for educated clergymen, contributed to the love of books and learning at the twin monasteries.[9]

Wearmouth and Jarrow comprised the entire world that Bede would ever know. After entering as an oblate at the age of seven, he would never leave it. In the *Ecclesiastical History of the English Nation,* he famously describes his own educational itinerary: "I was born in the territory of this monastery. When I was seven years of age I was, by the care of my kinsmen, put into the charge of the reverend Abbot Benedict and then of Ceolfrith, to be educated. From then on I have spent all of my life in this monastery, applying myself entirely to the study of the Scriptures; and, amid the observance of the discipline of the Rule and the daily task of singing in the church, it has always been my delight to learn or to teach or to write."[10]

He informs us of the master-student lineage at the monasteries. Cuthbert (c. 634–687 AD) was filled with religious zeal since childhood, and studied under "Boisil, a priest of great virtue and endowed with a spirit of prophecy. Cuthbert humbly submitted himself to Boisil's instruction and received from him a knowledge of the Scriptures and the example of a life of good works."[11] With Boisil's passing, it was Cuthbert's turn to instruct others in holiness. He "was made prior of the monastery and trained many in life under a Rule, both in his capacity as teacher and by his own example." One theme that unites Bede's writings about Benedict Biscop, Ceolfrith, Cuthbert, and the abbess Hilda is his positive judgment on the active life, which represented a strikingly different ideal

---

[8] Hunter Blair, *The World of Bede,* 240.
[9] Ibid., 211.
[10] Bede, *Ecclesiastical History of the English Nation,* Book 5, Chapter 24, 567.
[11] Ibid., Book 4, Chapter 27, 433.

from that espoused by Celtic monasticism and its eremetical, ascetic, and contemplative practices.[12] Added to this, Bede also idealized education as an end in itself, and not only as a means to holiness and the ascetic life, which had been the Irish and Anglo-Saxon ideal until him.[13]

Abbots Benedict Biscop and Ceolfrith enormously impacted Bede's development as a saintly scholar, not least of all by endowing the library with the numerous books carried back from Rome and elsewhere. Aside from grammarians and Virgil, the library lacked works by ancient pagan writers, but had texts by Isidore of Seville and Gregory the Great, both of whom greatly impacted Bede. The writings of other Church Fathers, including their Biblical commentaries, were available. The scriptorium produced books, including a very rare pandect (an entire Bible in one bound volume), known today as the *Codex Amiatinus*, that was made in Bede's lifetime. This was likely a copy of another pandect, the *Codex Grandior*, originally from Cassiodorus's library and hauled up to Northumbria from Rome. The *Codex Amiatinus* required enormous quantities of vellum and man-hours in copying and illustrating.[14] This accomplishment testifies to the financial and human resources that were available at Wearmouth and Jarrow.

The monasteries' resources went beyond the scriptorium. Benedict Biscop had brought Canterbury's educational program to Wearmouth and Jarrow. This had been set up by Theodore and Hadrian, and included chant, Latin and Greek, and Roman law.[15] Benedict and Ceolfrith also brought back from Rome the pope's archcantor in 678 AD to teach liturgical chant to the monks in Wearmouth and Jarrow. The fact that Rome provided so much support to this monastery in northern England once again testifies to the international or pan-European spirit of

---

[12] Calvin B. Kendall, "Bede and education," 99–112 in *The Cambridge Companion to Bede*, ed. Scott DeGregorario (Cambridge University Press, 2010), 110.
[13] Ibid., 112.
[14] Rosalind Love, "The World of Latin Learning," in *The Cambridge Companion to Bede*, ed. Scott DeGregorario (Cambridge University Press, 2010), 40.
[15] Kendall, "Bede and education," 100.

the Church's educational program in the Latin West. There was a continual give-and-take among the various centers and outer regions of western Christendom. Rome's investment in Wearmouth and Jarrow would pay off when Anglo-Saxon missionaries flocked to Germanic lands in the Carolingian era.

If Isidore was the encyclopedist of the Middle Ages, Bede was its schoolmaster, given his much-used textbooks on grammar basics (orthography and metrics) and rhetoric, which he had written for his own students. Whereas Aldhelm was famous for the showy vocabulary of his prose, Bede wrote with the clarity of a schoolmaster trying to convey the content of a given subject in the clearest way possible.[16] His writings on music and science, which he took from the ancient authorities, provided the basis of medieval instruction in these areas. Bede also saw the importance of skills in calculation, *computus*, particularly for setting Easter's date, and to this end authored *De temporum ratione*. Bede understood science (*scientia*) in the traditional meaning of 'knowledge,' and *ratio* as 'reason' or 'reckoning.'[17] Like other early medieval churchmen, Bede did not regard the computation of the calendar or the inquiry into the created order as independent disciplines.[18] In *The Reckoning of Time*, he does express a special respect for the pagan Pliny the Elder and his *Natural History*.[19] Bede's *On the Nature of Things* shared the aim of Isidore of Seville in his book by the same name in refuting superstition and the belief that nature's forces acted with intent.[20]

Bede made unique contributions to Christian education, which means that he parted with Isidore in significant ways, such as writing a separate book on time. More significantly, he developed Christian cosmology. Whereas Isidore had been content with adding scriptural parallels to the original Greek

---

[16] Love, "The World of Latin Learning," 51.

[17] Faith Wallis, "Bede and science," in *The Cambridge Companion to Bede*, ed. Scott DeGregorario (Cambridge University Press, 2010), 114.

[18] Ibid., 114.

[19] Ibid., 115.

[20] Ibid., 116.

and Roman view of creation, Bede set out to show the coherence of the Christian understanding of science and of creation itself.[21] In this way, he also differed from most of the Church Fathers, who did not bother to give a Christian orientation to science as they had done to history. Regarding history, he is today most famous for his work the *Ecclesiastical History of the English People*, which recounts the evangelization of the country and gives a theological meaning to past events.[22] Overall, Bede's own scholarship was the result of the confluence of various strands of Christian and non-Christian cultures from Ireland, Gaul, Rome, and Canterbury.[23] Bede put his love for knowledge at the service of the Gospel.

Bede has been most famous in recent centuries as a historian, but his immediate impact may have been from his Biblical commentaries, which earned him a reputation that came to match those of the Church Fathers. This was in part due to his fourfold method of interpreting the Bible, which he received from tradition and passed on. The first level of Biblical interpretation, he notes in *The Figures of Rhetoric*, is literal, pointing to the fact that the event in question genuinely took place. The same passage could have other, spiritual meanings as well. The typological, also called the allegorical, interpreted the Bible with reference to Christ or the Church. The tropological reading involved the moral life of the individual Christian. The anagogical interpreted the Bible with a view to God's heavenly kingdom.[24] Bede was selective in applying allegory to Biblical exegesis in his own commentaries, and did not apply allegory to every passage.[25] If we keep in mind that the task of grammar in the Early Middle Ages was to support Biblical exegesis, and that from the time of the ancient Greeks and Romans, grammar class included instruction in history and geography, it is

---

[21] Wallis, "Bede and science," 116.
[22] George Hardin Brown, *A Companion to Bede*, (The Boydell Press, 2009), Brown, 13.
[23] Kendall, "Bede and education," 103.
[24] Ibid., 108.
[25] Ibid.

clear that Bede was every bit the accomplished grammarian as
Isidore of Seville. Bede, like the great Spanish bishop, was a
pillar of the age of grammar.

9.3 WINFRID / BONIFACE

Born in Devonshire into a wealthy family, the martyr Boniface
(also known as Winfrid or Wynfrith, 675–754 AD) excelled
at school. Willibald's *Life of St. Boniface* portrays him as inte-
grating the life of virtue, study, and monastic piety. His love
of education was clearly a part of his holiness:

> He was endowed with a spark of divine genius and so assid-
> uously fostered it by study that every hour and moment of
> his long and active life only served to increase the divine gifts
> that had been showered upon him. The longer he continued
> in the service of the priesthood, the more, as we are told by
> his trusted and intimate friends, did his continual studies
> and his protracted endeavors in the literary field stimulate
> him in his search for eternal bliss. This was a marvelous
> protection against the enticements and diabolical suggestions
> that beset young men in the flower of their youth and that
> cloud their minds with a kind of darkness. As a result, the
> fiery passions of youth and the fleshly lusts that at first made
> violent assaults upon him lost their power through his cease-
> less vigilance and his assiduous inquiries into the meaning of
> sacred Scripture. His studies, pursued with increasing ardor,
> led him inevitably to undertake the task of teaching others, a
> labor that after a short time and in accordance with episcopal
> and ecclesiastical ordinances he duly carried out. He spurned
> the fleeting successes of this world and continued under the
> able guidance of Abbot Wulfhard to follow faithfully and
> conscientiously the true pattern of monastic observance.[26]

Timor Christi et amor peregrinationis (fear of Christ and the
love of travelling) prompted Boniface to become a missionary to the Germans, which then came about in a roundabout
way. After his ordination to the priesthood in 710 AD, he went
on his first foreign mission, with Willibrord, to the Frisians

---

[26] Willibald, *The Life of St. Boniface*, trans. George Washington Robinson
(Cambridge, 1916).

in 716 AD. It was largely unsuccessful. After a brief return home, he left England forever in 718 AD. He first traveled to Rome where the next year he received papal approval to take the Gospel to the eastern side of the Rhine. Before going to Germany, he rejoined Willibrord in Utrecht for three more years. Afterwards, his missionary success among the Hessians prompted his consecration as a bishop in Rome in 722 or 723 AD.[27] As a product of the Anglo-Saxon educational system, he established Roman and Augustinian culture in Germany largely through the founding of monasteries at Utrecht, Fritzlar, Fulda, Ohrdruf, and elsewhere. These monasteries were to teach the arts and sciences on the Anglo-Saxon model.[28] Functioning as missionary outposts and seminaries in a land without cities, the monasteries were the primary tool of the spreading of Christian civilization, with education as a central pillar.[29]

Fulda would become a famous educational center in the Carolingian Renaissance. Boniface had gotten the Bavarian Edeling Sturmi (or Sturm) to decide on the site of the new monastery at Fulda and to serve as its first abbot even though Sturmi felt called to the hermit's life, not that of a Church leader. The monastery dates to 744 AD. It produced many learned Church leaders who later served as abbots or in other offices. Sturmi's successors Baugulf, Ratgar, and Eigil (Sturmi's biographer) contributed to the study and practice of architecture and painting. The monk Einhard, a contemporary of Baugulf and biographer of Charlemagne, built Aachen's monastery school. Rabanus Maurus, widely respected for his learning, received the title of *praeceptor Germaniae* for his achievements in education. Rabanus counted among his famous pupils the renowned poet Walafrid Strabo, the great letter writer Servatus Lupus, Haims of Heberstadt, and Otfrid of Weissenburg.[30]

---

[27] Lewis W. Spitz, "Saint Boniface," in *Concordia Theological Monthly*, Volume 25, pp. 647–655 (1954), 648.

[28] Ibid., 651.

[29] Ibid., 650.

[30] Ibid., 652.

Concerning this considerable multi-generational scholarship, Fulda was almost as central to the Carolingian Renaissance as the palace school at Aachen. While Anglo-Saxon, it also worked closely with the Irish monasteries. For example, the abbey of St. Gall sent monks to Fulda for training, who then brought back manuscripts of Bede's works. Alcuin's works, particularly on the trivium, were popular at St. Gall.[31] Fulda claimed to have the largest library in the Latin West, at around one thousand books, a sizable number compared to the personal libraries of Charlemagne or that of his grandson Charles the Bald, of no more than one hundred codices, or the monastery of Murbach, in Alsace, at four hundred.[32] Boniface did not overlook girls in this educational ministry, as he worked closely with Lioba, the well-educated abbess of Bischofsheim, to turn her monastery into a center of education, where many future abbesses and female teachers studied.[33]

Boniface's grammar works were representative of the educational concerns of the early medieval West. His *Ars Bonifacii*, a treatise on grammar, was inspired by the writings of Donatus, Priscian, Aldhelm, and Isidore of Seville. He also wrote *Caesurae versuum*, a treatise on poetry. So many early medieval masters wrote books on pagan poetry that it seems that all serious opposition to the use of pre-Christian writings for Christian education had all but vanished. While the light of learning among the Anglo-Saxons would soon be dimmed by the Vikings, through the work of Boniface, this light established a foothold among the Franks, as the *translatio studii* would pass the crown of education to the Carolingians. In fact, the Anglo-Saxon missionaries, led by Boniface, left such a deep impression on the German people that they impacted the language itself. The hundreds of Anglo-Saxon priests stationed in Germany in the

---

[31] Clark, *The Abbey of St Gall as a Centre of Literature and Art*, 63–64.
[32] Dominique Alibert, "La transmission des textes patristiques à l'époque carolingienne." in *Revue des sciences philosophiques et théologiques* 91, (2007), 7–21, 10. https://doi.org/10.3917/rspt.911.0007.
[33] Spitz, "Saint Boniface," 650.

first half of the eighth century, mostly in the still-pagan areas of Thuringia, Hessen, and East Franconia, spoke and wrote in Anglo-Saxon. Towards the end of Boniface's mission, entire areas of Germany had an Anglo-Saxon priest in every village church.[34] The informal network of itinerant scholars, preachers, and missionaries kept Anglo-Saxon education alive after the Vikings' destruction of Wearmouth and Jarrow.

9.4 ALCUIN OF YORK

The greatest scholar after Bede, Alcuin was initially posted at England's next center of learning, York. From the aristocracy of Northumbria, Alcuin (Latinized to Albinus) was given as a young oblate to the Church. He was educated at the cathedral school in York, which had been founded by the master Egbert (died in 766 AD), who had likely been Bede's student at Jarrow.[35] The school of York followed the scholastic tradition of Wearmouth and Jarrow. Having studied under Egbert's successor Æthelbert[36] (died in 780 AD), Alcuin played the key role in the establishment of the inter-generational master-student lineage first in York as master, or *scholasticus*. He assumed this position after Æthelbert became archbishop of York, an office Alcuin himself would have subsequently taken. He then became head-master of Charlemagne's palace school, where he was playfully known as Flaccus. Like Boniface, he excelled at training men for Church service. One of his students at York, Eanbald, became archbishop of York in 796 AD, and three others, Witzo, Fridugis, and Sigulf, followed him to Charlemagne's court.

While he is most remembered as the schoolmaster at Charlemagne's palace school, about two-thirds of Alcuin's writings are

---

[34] Clark, *The Abbey of St Gall as a Centre of Literature and Art*, 55. "Many Old High German glosses contain Anglo-Saxon words, others are translated from Anglo-Saxon manuscripts. The *Codex Fuldensis* of the New Testament contains Latin glosses in insular script which may have been added by St Boniface himself." Clark *The Abbey of St Gall as a Centre of Literature and Art*, 57.

[35] Kendall, "Bede and education," 110.

[36] Variously spelled Ælbert.

on theology, followed in volume by his vast correspondence.[37]
The size of this correspondence reflects his leadership role across
Europe in the *renovatio*. A central figure in the Carolingian
Renaissance, he envisioned a single truth with two dimensions:
Scripture contains nothing that counters the truths found in
nature, and nature contains nothing that counters the truths
of Scripture.[38]

Alcuin idealizes his studies in the poem "On the Saints of
the Church at York." The poem also gives us a glimpse of the
nature of Alcuin as a scholar. Like Cassiodorus, he was not
an original thinker, but handed on, restored, conserved, and
propagated learning that was in danger of being forgotten:[39]

> There the Euboric[40] scholars felt the rule
> Of Master Ælbert, teaching in the school.
> Their thirty hearts to gladden well he knew
> With doctrine's stream and learning's heavenly dew.
> To some he made the grammar understood
> And poured on others rhetoric's copious flood.
> The rules of jurisprudence[41] these rehearse,
> While those recite in high Aonian verse,
> Or play Castelia's flutes in cadence sweet
> And mount Parnassus on swift lyric feet.
> Anon the master turns their gaze on high
> To view the travailing sun and moon, the sky
> In order turning with its planets seven,
> And starry hosts that keep the law of heaven.
> The storms at sea, the earthquake's shock, the race
> Of men and beasts and flying fowl they trace;
> Or to the laws of numbers bend their mind
> And search till Easter's annual day they find.
> Then, last and best, he opened up to view
> The depths of Holy Scripture, Old and New.
> Was any youth in studies well approved,
> Then the master cherished, taught and loved;

---

[37] Andrew Fleming West, *Alcuin and the Rise of the Christian Schools* (Charles Scribner's Son, 1912), 89.
[38] De Bruyne, *Etudes d'esthétique médiévale*, 201.
[39] West, *Alcuin and the Rise of the Christian Schools*, 90.
[40] Yorkish.
[41] Likely canon law.

And thus the double knowledge he conferred
Of liberal studies and the Holy Word.[42]

When Æthelbert died, Alcuin became head of York cathedral's famous library. Naturally, he wrote a poem to catalog its offerings, which reveal to modern readers works ranging from pagan Greek and Roman grammarians and rhetoricians to Greek and Latin Church Fathers, and the more recent Aldhelm and Bede:

> There shalt thou find the volumes that contain
> All of the ancient fathers who remain;
> There all the Latin writers make their home
> With those that glorious Greece transferred to Rome, —
> The Hebrews draw from their celestial stream,
> And Africa is bright with learning's beam.
> Here shines what Jerome, Ambrose, Hilary thought,
> Or Athanasius and Augustine wrought.
> Orosius, Leo, Gregory the Great,
> Near Basil and Fugentius coruscate.
> Grace Cassiodorus and John Chrysostom
> Next Master Bede and learned Aldhelm come,
> While Victorinus and Boethius stand
> With Pliny and Pompeius close at hand.
> Wise Aristotle looks on Tully[43] near.
> Sedulius and Juvencus next appear.
> Then come Albinus, Clement, Prosper too,
> Paulinus and Arator. Next we view
> Lactantius, Fortunatus. Ranged in line
> Virgilius Maro, Statius, Lucan, shine.
> Donatus, Priscian, Probus, Phocus, start
> The roll of masters in grammatic art.
> Eutychius, Servius, Pompey, each extend
> The list. Comminian brings it to an end.
> There shalt thou find, O reader, many more
> Famed for their style, the masters of old lore,
> Whose many volumes singly to rehearse
> Were far too tedious for our present verse.[44]

The high cost of a book, which made it a treasured item, would have made any library of more than fifty codices a special place

---

[42] West, *Alcuin and the Rise of the Christian Schools*, 32.
[43] Marcus Tullius Cicero.
[44] West, *Alcuin and the Rise of the Christian Schools*, 34–35.

that would have attracted masters and students from far and wide. The higher the number of volumes a library had, the stronger its attractive power and the renown of the school or monastery.

9.5 ALFRED THE GREAT

Alfred the Great (848–899 AD), king of the West Saxons (871–886 AD) and then of the Anglo-Saxons (886–899 AD), paralleled the Carolingian desire to raise the educational level of the people. He called for primary education to be offered in the Anglo-Saxon language to make education more accessible, and to this end sponsored a series of translations into this vernacular language. These translations included Gregory the Great's *Dialogus* and Bede's *Ecclesiastical History of the English People*. Alfred himself claimed to have translated Gregory the Great's *Pastoral Care*, Augustine's *Soliloquies*, Boethius's *Consolation of Philosophy*, and Psalms 1–50. Overall, Alfred's impact on education was not nearly as great as that of Wearmouth and Jarrow, or of York. The impact of these institutions was Europe-wide and centuries-long. A king in western Europe, in contrast, did not normally have the same educational role as the Church, nor anywhere near the same international reach, from the royal courts to the smallest village. Charlemagne was able to impact European education because he used these churchmen and the power of the ecclesiastical networks, such as monasteries, to carry out his educational reforms.

9.6 ÆLFRIC OF EYNSHAM

Ælfric of Eynsham (955–1010 AD), also known as Ælfric the Grammarian, came from a distinguished scholarly lineage, as he had studied under Æthelwold of Winchester. Ælfric's translations of a Latin grammar and of Genesis into Anglo-Saxon were both firsts. He wrote a *Colloquy* to aid students in Latin. The colloquy, or dialogue, was a common educational genre in the Middle Ages, and followed the ancient Greek tradition, particularly Plato, as in the *Timaeus*. Many medieval schoolboys had to learn to speak Latin, not only read and write it, and dialogues supported this objective.

Ælfric's *Colloquy* provides an idealized example of a pupil (named *Scholar*), who is a model of eagerness to learn Latin. A less ideal aspect, common to the ancient and medieval classroom, is the master's threat of physical punishment for failing to demonstrate learning:

> *Scholar.* We boys beg you, Master, to teach us to speak Latin correctly, for we are ignorant, and we speak badly.
>
> *Master.* What do you wish to talk about?
>
> *Scholar.* We do not care what we talk about, as long as our speech is correct, and useful, and not foolish, or base.
>
> *Master.* Are you willing to be flogged while learning?
>
> *Scholar.* We would rather be flogged that we may learn, than remain ignorant, but we know that you are kindly, and that you will not lay strokes upon us, unless we oblige you to do so.[45]

The last sentence makes it clear that pupils bring physical punishment upon themselves, at least from Ælfric's perspective. The boys seem to have a grin-and-bear it attitude towards the flogging. They only need to be model students to avoid it.

The twenty-first century reader next gets a glimpse into an oblate's daily duties in the monastery, again mixed in with an idealized eagerness for Latin. The learning-through-doing aspect makes this closer to an apprenticeship than to classroom-based learning: "*Scholar.* I am preparing to be a monk, and every day I sing seven times with the brethren, and I am busy with reading and singing; yet in the meantime I wish to learn to converse in the Latin language."[46] This gives some evidence that the monks communicated in the vernacular at least some of the time, such as with students or less educated brothers. Part of education

---

[45] S. Harvey Gem, "Colloquy," in *An Anglo-Saxon Abbot: Aelfric of Eynsham* (T & T. Clark, 1912), 183.
[46] Ibid., 184.

therefore aimed to raise the level of spoken Latin, presumably to make graduates more employable or useful for the Church (if not more holy) and to build *Romanitas*, or Roman culture.

Later in the discussion, the boy provides more details of his highly-regimented, daily life, which, unsurprisingly, revolves around the monastic timetable of prayers:

> *Scholar.* I have done many things. This night, when I heard the call, I rose from my bed, and went out to the church, and sang nocturns with the brethren; then we sang of all the saints, and the matin song of praise; after that prime, and the seven psalms, with litanies, and the first mass, then terce, and we performed the mass of the day, after that we sang sext; then we ate and drank, and had our sleep, and rose up again, and sang nones, and now we are here before you, prepared to hear what you may say to us.[47]

There is no mention of officially-sanctioned leisure or play in this Spartan upbringing.

The discussion again assumes physical discipline as a given, though the boy offers a somewhat cheeky response to a question about his friends. The Master suddenly changes the topic after this:

> *Master.* Have you been flogged today?
>
> *Scholar.* I have not, for I behaved with caution.
>
> *Master.* And how was it with your companions?
>
> *Scholar.* Why do you ask me about that? I dare not reveal our secrets to you. Each one knows whether he has been flogged, or not.
>
> *Master.* What do you eat in the day?
>
> *Scholar.* I am allowed meat, because I am still a boy, living under the rod.[48]

Medieval childhood, including at school with the master's *in loco parentis* authority, was thus a time of "living under the rod." The rod was considered an indispensable tool for training in

---

[47] Gem, "Colloquy," 193–4.
[48] Ibid., 194.

discipline and encouraging learning. Children were to be sternly corrected not only for improper behavior, but also for failure to learn. Substandard learning was likely seen as a result of insufficient diligence, which in turn was seen as a moral short-coming that required correction in the form of punishment. Notably, the failure to learn is not blamed on shoddy teaching or unrealistic demands and standards placed on pupils. The master who shied away from administering discipline was likely seen as lazy and uncaring. He may have lost students, as parents would have sent their boys to a stricter tutor. It was thought that discipline was key to the development of the spiritual life due to the fact that the personality, distorted from the darkness of original sin, needed the correction of the rod. Fallen humans were not naturally predisposed towards virtuous behavior, and had to be sternly guided in this direction in childhood to set them on the right path for their entire lives.

After a long discussion with the *Scholar's* friends, an oxherd, ploughboy, and huntsman, on the daily chores required by their occupations, the master brings the conversation around to the value of education. His aim is not to encourage students to move up in life through higher earning careers. In this, Ælfric echoes many other medieval clerics, such as the eleventh century Peter Damian, who lamented students' focus on the career ladder in the bureaucracies of bishops and secular lords.[49] As presented here, education aims for something higher, although it is also associated with the baser instincts of the turncoat, deceiver, sophist, evil-thinker, and hypocrite. Education clearly has a morally dangerous side. Not every educated individual is morally virtuous:

> *Master.* I will ask you why you are so diligent in learning?
>
> *Scholar.* It is because we do not wish to be like brute animals, that know nothing but grass and water.
>
> *Master.* And what then is your wish?
>
> *Scholar.* We wish to be wise.

---

[49] Riché and Verger, *Maîtres et élèves au Moyen Age*, 79.

> *Master.* With what kind of wisdom? Do you wish to be clever turncoats, taking many shapes, cunning in lies, acute in speech; talking fairly, and thinking evil, given to using pleasant words, while cherishing guile within, like a sepulchre, painted outside, but full of foulness inside?
>
> *Scholar.* We do not wish to be wise in this way, for he is not wise who deceives his own self by pretences.
>
> *Master.* Then how do you desire to be wise?
>
> *Scholar.* We wish to be simple, without hypocrisy, and wise in avoiding the evil, and in doing what is good.[50]

The "we" implies that the oxherd, plowman, and other workers are students. In other words, perhaps even boys with more manual employment were allowed to study. Or, more likely, these occupations are included in the dialogue to introduce to young readers the Latin words for common occupations in an agrarian society. In any case, the primary focus of education, as presented here, is on boys' moral and spiritual development so that they can live upright Christian lives.

In the dialogue's next section, on gluttony, the boy is once again rather direct in contradicting his master. This implies that a certain amount of brashness and rebellion were allowed and even expected despite the boys' "living under the rod." It may also indicate that masters expected a certain amount of free- or critical-thinking in their students, by training them to challenge what the master tells them:

> *Master.* You are very voracious, to eat everything that is put before you.
>
> *Scholar.* I am not such a glutton as to be able to eat all these kinds of food at the same meal.
>
> *Master.* Then how do you manage?
>
> *Scholar.* I eat sometimes this food, and sometimes that, with moderation, as befits a monk; I do not eat voraciously, for I am not a glutton.

The boy directly corrects the master's judgment.

---

[50] Gem, "Colloquy," 193.

Consistent with the focus on spiritual growth, the *Colloquy* links discipline not only to education, but to the general training of a dutiful and pious monk (which could hardly be separated from this education anyway). The youth's development as a Christian apparently required firmness on the part of superiors. Oblates were expected to rouse immediately and easily from bed when awoken for night prayers, or *nocturns*:

> *Master.* Where do you sleep?
>
> *Scholar.* In the dormitory with the brethren.
>
> *Master.* Who rouses you up for nocturns?
>
> *Scholar.* Sometimes I hear the call, and rise, sometimes the master rouses me up sharply with a rod.
>
> *Master.* O good boys, and pleasant scholars, your instructor exhorts you to be obedient to the rules of divine discipline, and to behave yourselves decorously, wherever you may be.

The rod is associated not only with education, but with the prayer office of the Church. Yet not every medieval pedagogue was as harsh as Ælfric. Benedict in his *Rule* and Anselm of Bec (1033–1109 AD) advocated less disciplinarian approaches. Benedict believed God had a special love for children.[51]

This dialogue is not meant only to practice Latin, but to impart guidance on virtuous living. Self-restraint, learning, and unquestioning respect for authorities are the primary features of the schoolboy's life in the medieval monastery, as reflected in the master's parting advice: "Stand in good order, and sing together, ask forgiveness for your faults, and go out again, without playing the fool, into the cloister or the schoolroom."[52] While this *Colloquy* contains images of the spiritual father similar to that found in the Irish understanding of the tutor-student relationship, Ælfric also expects the tutor to be a tough disciplinarian.

Ælfric's dialog is merely one of "the endless list of *altercationes, disputationes, controversiae, collationes, colloquia, dialogi* on political,

---

[51] Riché and Verger, *Maîtres et élèves au Moyen Age*, 87.
[52] Gem, "Colloquy," 195.

theological, pastoral, pedagogical etc. subjects" that were produced in the Middle Ages for instruction purposes.[53] Four of
the five educational works of Alcuin, for example, were in the
form of dialogues. Plato's pedagogical dialogues were taken in
the Middle Ages as exemplars. The dialogue was an enduring
teaching tool. Centuries after Ælfric, Erasmus of Rotterdam
wrote many didactic dialogues, and Galileo explained some of
his scientific views and methods through dialogues.[54]

9.7 THE END OF AN ERA IN THE BRITISH ISLES?

As so often in history, decline set in when violence broke out.
The British Isles were not left out of this unhappy cycle. The
Vikings, who attacked northern Europe from roughly 800 to
1150 AD, hated Christian culture. When the Danes started
attacking Ireland in the late eighth century, the book-loving
country suffered grievously from widespread plundering and
arson. Anglo-Saxon England suffered the same fate. The *Anglo-
Saxon Chronicle* informs us of the devastation to Lindisfarne
in 793 AD: "The harrowing inroads of heathen men made
lamentable havoc in the church of God in Holy-island, by
rapine and slaughter." Lindisfarne was soon abandoned. Other
Northern England settlements and monasteries experienced
the same in later years, including in 794 AD, again according
to the *Anglo-Saxon Chronicle*: "The heathen armies spread
devastation among the Northumbrians, and plundered the
monastery of King Everth at the mouth of the Wear."[55] Some
of Iona's monks were killed in attacks in 802 and 806 AD, and
once again codices were also targeted. "The special fury of the
invaders appears to have been directed against books, monasteries, and monuments of religion. All the books they could

---

[53] Moos Peter I. "Le dialogue latin au Moyen Âge : l'exemple d'Evrard d'Ypres,"
in *Annales. Économies, sociétés, civilisations*, no. 4, (1989) 993–1028.
[54] *Dialogus cui titulus ciceronianus sive de optimo dicendi genere* and *De recta
Latini Graecique sermonis pronuntiatione dialogus.*
[55] *The Anglo-Saxon Chronicle*, trans. James Ingram. London, 1823. http://www.
mcllibrary.org/Anglo/part2.html.

lay hands upon they either burned or 'drowned' by throwing them into the nearest river, or lake. For two centuries this wanton destruction continued."[56] This reflects the negative side of the magical or sacramental power of books (depending on the point of view) that we saw in the second chapter with St. Patrick's dual with the wizard. Books represented Christian belief for the anti-Christian Vikings and were special targets of their destruction. Most of the Irish library holdings were lost forever, though some found their way to Bobbio in Italy and St. Gall in Switzerland, the former brought by Dungal of Bobbio in the early ninth century. He authored a poem on the liberal arts and may also be known to history as *Hibernicus Exul* (the Exiled Hibernian). Monasteries at Würzburg and Reichau also benefited from the influx of Irish monks and their high level of culture. The educational culture of the Irish and Anglo-Saxons survived in the Carolingian Renaissance, when Irish and Anglo-Saxon scholars were among the brightest lights of the *renovatio*.

---

[56] Graham, *The Early Irish Monastic Schools*, 110.

CHAPTER 10

The Carolingian Renaissance

From many lands scholars were drawn by that great hand
so generous in giving, so mighty to protect.[1]
— Henry Osborn Taylor

10.1 THE FIRST STEPS IN REBUILDING EDUCATION

AFTER THE ACHIEVEMENTS OF THE fourth century, the Latin West fell into political and social turmoil. This disorder affected education and the life of the Church. In the *Preface* to *The History of the Franks*, Gregory of Tours (c. 538–594 AD) observes the terrible condition of society, the Church, and education. He connects the cultural deterioration with a decline in moral virtue and laments the fact that no one was even capable of describing and taking note of this immorality and criminality:

> With liberal culture on the wane, or rather perishing in the Gallic cities there were many deeds being done both good and evil: the heathen were raging fiercely; kings were growing more cruel; the church, attacked by heretics, was defended by Catholics; while the Christian faith was in general devoutly cherished, among some it was growing cold; the churches also were enriched by the faithful or plundered by traitors-and no grammarian skilled in the dialectic art could be found to describe these matters either in prose or verse; and many were lamenting and saying: "Woe to our day, since the pursuit of letters has perished from among us and no one can be found among the people who can set forth the deeds of the present on the written page."[2]

What Gregory describes are the effects of the Merovingian failure to prioritize education. There may have been schools

---

[1] Henry Osborn Taylor, *The Mediaeval Mind*, Volume 1 (Macmillan and Co., 1911), 214.
[2] https://sourcebooks.fordham.edu/basis/gregory-hist.asp#pref1.

in the south, such as at Narbonne, Toulouse, and Marseilles, that had survived from the much more stable and culturally-advanced fourth century.

The Merovingians' legacy of decline and instability left the Church in a terrible condition. In his *Life of Charlemagne*, Einhard describes the last decades and the end of the long-haired kings:

> I. The Merovingian family, from which the Franks used to choose their kings, is commonly said to have lasted until the time of Childeric, who was deposed, shaved, and thrust into the cloister by command of the Roman Pontiff Stephen. But although, to all outward appearance, it ended with him, it had long since been devoid of vital strength, and conspicuous only from bearing the empty epithet Royal; the real power and authority in the kingdom lay in the hands of the chief officer of the court, the so-called Mayor of the Palace [*maior domo*], and he was at the head of affairs. There was nothing left [for] the King to do but to be content with his name of King, his flowing hair, and long beard, to sit on his throne and play the ruler, to give ear to the ambassadors that came from all quarters, and to dismiss them, as if on his own responsibility, in words that were, in fact, suggested to him, or even imposed upon him. He had nothing that he could call his own beyond this vain title of King and the precarious support allowed by the Mayor of the Palace in his discretion, except a single country seat, that brought him but a very small income.[3]

The political instability of the late Merovingian empire and the need for Charlemagne's father and former *maior domo* Pepin the Short (714–768 AD) to consolidate his papally-approved seizure of the throne in 751 AD from the Merovingians meant that the main reforms necessary to strengthen the Church and education fell to Charlemagne.

The first Carolingian king and son of Charles Martel, Pepin had nevertheless set a small foundation for the later Renaissance named after his son by supporting the missionary work of the

---

[3] Einhard, *The Life of Charlemagne*, trans. Samuel Epes Turner (The University of Michigan Press, 1966), 23–24.

Anglo-Saxon Winfrid, or St. Boniface (675–754 AD), the apostle to the Saxons. Pepin's aim to raise the intellectual and moral level of the clergy would be a central concern of Charlemagne. Such policies aligned with Christian tradition and educational practice. Centuries earlier, the Church Fathers had seen the spiritual and moral value of the liberal arts. In letter 53 to Paulinus, for example, St. Jerome (c. 347–420 AD) argued that the study of the Bible depends on mastery of the pre-Christian writers: "In the holy scriptures you can make no progress unless you have a guide to show you the way. I say nothing of the knowledge of grammarians, rhetoricians, philosophers, geometers, logicians, musicians, astronomers, astrologers, physicians, whose several kinds of skill are most useful to mankind, and may be ranged under the three heads of teaching, method, and proficiency."[4] These disciplines remained largely unchallenged during the medieval centuries.

The Carolingian Renaissance and its work of *renovatio* and *correctio* (as the Carolingian reformers called their work of renewal) emerged as a reaction against the terrible condition of the Church in the Frankish realms, particularly in its education for the clergy. The dire state of the largely unlettered rural priests impeded catechesis and preaching, parish administration, and the development of a uniform and correct liturgy, all of which required an educated priesthood. Some areas of the empire essentially needed to be re-Christianized, even as the still-pagan regions on the fringes of the empire, such as across the Rhine among the Saxon pagans or the Frisian areas in the north, required missionaries.

The fact that Gregory the Great's *Regula Pastoralis* featured in the writings of Rabanus Maurus, the major scholar of the second Carolingian generation, demonstrates the pastoral concern behind the educational renewal. The connection between educational and religious renewal emerged from the ultimate

---

[4] St. Jerome. *The Letters of St. Jerome*, trans. W. H. Fremantle (T&T Clark, 1892), Letter 53, Lightly edited.

purpose of *correctio,* which was to save souls for the next life.
Correctio sought "the ordering and improvement of the spiritual
life of Empire. Sometimes referred to as 'reform', this was a
political and chiefly spiritual mission, one intended to impose
'correct' but not necessarily uniform religious practice on the
Carolingian Emperor's subjects."[5] Charlemagne meddled in
the religious lives of the laity and clergy as much as Byzantine
emperors did, seeing himself, as his Byzantine counterparts did,
as the leader of the Church in the territories that he ruled. The
salvation of the souls of the realm was the duty of the king.[6]

The idea that the liturgy, and Church affairs in general, could
only be corrected with a simultaneous renewal of education
stems from the fact that Greek paideia had become fully Christian paideia based on the belief that knowledge and study served
the salvation of souls. The moral, pastoral, and eschatological
sense that this knowledge and study took reflected the holistic
appproach of the Carolingian intellectuals in their work of *correctio.*[7] In an episode from *The Deeds of Charles the Great* (also called
The Life of Charlemagne), Notker the Stammerer (c. 840–912
AD) reveals the connection between education (in this case, the
training of chanting) and liturgy in the mind of Charlemagne:

> Charles, that never-wearied lover of the service of God,
> when he could congratulate himself that all possible progress
> had been made in the knowledge of letters, was grieved to
> observe how widely the different provinces — nay, not the
> provinces only but districts and cities — differed in the
> praise of God, that is to say in their method of chanting. He
> therefore asked of Pope Stephen of blessed memory — the
> same who, after Hilderich King of the Franks had been
> deposed and tonsured, had anointed Charles to be ruler of

[5] Alexandra Elizabeth Jordan, *The influence of Carolingian political initiatives and correctio in ninth-century Brittany and the march: a study of the hagiographical dossiers of saints Machutus, Maglorius and Melanius and their political and eccle-siastical contexts* (University of Durham, Durham E-thesis, 2021).

[6] Rutger Kramer, "'Ecce fabula!' Problem-solving by numbers in the Carolingian world: The case of the *Propositiones ad Acuendos Iuvena,*" (Austrian Academy of Sciences, 2017), 17–18.

[7] Ibid., 20.

the kingdom after the ancestral custom of the people — he asked of Pope Stephen, I say, that he should provide him with twelve clerks deeply learned in divine song. The Pope yielded assent to his virtuous wish and his divinely inspired design and sent to him in Frankland from the apostolic see clerks skilled in divine song, and twelve in number, according to the number of the twelve apostles.[8]

The failure of the clerks to sing in a uniform way led to their abrupt dismissal and, according to Notker, their later imprisonment. Charlemagne continued to work at improving liturgical chant by trying to establish the practices of the famed monastery in St. Gall as the norm in his realms.

The Carolingian Renaissance can be divided into three eras or generations, roughly equaling the reigns of Charlemagne (748–814 AD), Louis the Pious (778–840 AD), the son of Charlemagne, and Charles the Bald (823–877 AD), one of the three sons of Louis who became rulers. The Renaissance was a pan-European project, with the leading scholars hailing from across Europe:

- The first generation included the Anglo-Saxon Alcuin of York (c. 735–804 AD), the Italians Peter of Pisa (aka Peter the Grammarian, 744–799 AD), Paulinus of Aquileia (726–802 AD), and the Lombard Paul the Deacon (c. 725–796/799 AD), the Austrian Arno of Salzburg (750–821 AD), the Frankish layman Einhard (775–840 AD), the Burgundian Remigius or Remi d'Auxerre (c. 841–908 AD), and the Spaniard Theodulf of Orleans (c. 750–821 AD).

- The Frankish Rabanus Maurus (780–856 AD) and Angilbert (c. 760–814 AD), the Irishman Dicuil (died after 825 AD), and the Swabian Walafrid Strabo (808–849 AD) counted among the leading second generation of scholars.

- The third generation included the most outstanding, yet perhaps most controversial of these men, the Irishman John Scotus Eriugena (800–877 AD), and the great humanist and Frankish-Bavarian Loup de Ferrières or Loup Servat (805–862 AD), the tutor of Charles the Bald.

---

[8] Notker the Stammerer, "Life of Charlemagne," in *Early Lives of Charlemagne*, ed. A. J. Grant (Alexander Moring, 1905), book I, §10, 53.

Charlemagne personifies the concept that Christianity simultaneously constructs and requires civilization. Baptizing and Christianizing the heathen amount to civilizing him and his society. Charlemagne was keenly concerned with the health, including the intellectual health, of the Church, as, according to Einhard, "he cherished with the greatest fervor and devotion the principles of the Christian religion, which had been instilled into him from infancy."[9] Paideia and pastoral care were one and the same. Put differently, paideia's main objective was pastoral. Incidentally, the Irish and Anglo-Saxons also believed this, as we have seen. Born in 748 AD, crowned king of the Franks in 768 AD, king of the Lombards in 774 AD, and Emperor in 800 AD, Charlemagne left a legacy that survived for centuries after his death in 814 AD, even if Europe went through another bleak period in the tenth century. In his *Life of Charlemagne*, Einhard idealizes and values the emperor's learning, noting that "Charles had the gift of ready and fluent speech, and could express whatever he had to say with the utmost clearness. He was not satisfied with command of his native language merely, but gave attention to the study of foreign ones, and in particular was such a master of Latin that he could speak it as well as his native tongue; but he could understand Greek better than he could speak it. He was so eloquent, indeed, that he might have passed for a teacher of eloquence." Even though Einhard is once again exaggerating the scholarly brilliance of Charlemagne, there is truth that the emperor (and his family members) took their own studies seriously, which raised the prestige of learning in the eyes of many. While much of the above words of Einhard are likely more fiction than reality concerning the emperor's command of Latin and Greek, the following observation comes clearer to the truth: "He most zealously cultivated the liberal arts, held those who taught them in great esteem, and conferred great honors upon them." Thus, Einhard leaves us with a mixture of the imagined and real learning environment of the court:

---

[9] Einhard, *The Life of Charlemagne*, xxvi, 54.

> He took lessons in grammar of the deacon Peter of Pisa, at
> that time an aged man. Another deacon, Albin of Britain,
> surnamed Alcuin, a man of Saxon extraction, who was the
> greatest scholar of the day, was his teacher in other branches
> of learning. The King spent much time and labor with
> him studying rhetoric, dialectics, and especially astronomy;
> he learned to reckon, and used to investigate the motions
> of the heavenly bodies most curiously, with an intelligent
> scrutiny. He also tried to write, and used to keep tablets
> and blanks in bed under his pillow, that at leisure hours he
> might accustom his hand to form the letters; however, as
> he did not begin his efforts in due season, but late in life,
> they met with ill success. [10]

The great Frankish warlord-emperor is depicted as a meticulous
schoolboy. Even though much of the above was an exaggeration,
the fact that a scholar king had once again become the ideal,
as in the days of Plato and the Greek *polis*, does tell us just
how seriously Charlemagne and his scholars at court took the
renovatio and *correctio*. The great Frankish warlord realized that
building an empire required more than arms.

The traditionalist Charlemagne wished to strengthen the
teachings of the past, not to produce anything new in terms
of content or culture. Nevertheless, what he and the scholars of his palatial school—whose first master was Alcuin of
York—accomplished was nothing short of revolutionary. The
Carolingian Renaissance cemented the value of the liberal arts of
the Greco-Roman canon, the pre-Christian poets, philosophers,
and grammarians. The idea of *Christian civilization* became the
reality in Christendom. The Carolingian Renaissance consolidated the Christian appropriation of Greco-Roman paideia,
particularly in the language arts.

As a pan-European project, the Carolingian Renaissance
was in many ways an outgrowth and continuation of the work
of the Irish and Anglo-Saxons. Indeed, men from the British
Isles remained central figures in European classrooms at this
time. Similar to education among the Irish and Anglo-Saxons,

---

[10] Einhard, *The Life of Charlemagne*, xxv, 54.

Carolingian education was largely monastic as well as court-centered. The Carolingians' long-lasting contribution to European and Catholic pedagogy stemmed largely from the development of the trivium, particularly grammar. They developed the foundations that Augustine, Boethius, Cassiodorus, Benedict, and Isidore had laid. The third generation of scholars even developed a renewed passion for Martianus Capella's poem on the liberal arts, *On the Marriage of Philology and Mercury*. Despite these accomplishments, the *renovatio* was only a beginning. Developments in logic or dialectic and the higher disciplines such as philosophy, law, and medicine, along with permanent schools and colleges, would mostly have to wait for the high Middle Ages and the advent of the universities.

Educational renewal not only concerned religion. Worldly forces were also at work. More than in previous medieval centuries, education played a role in statecraft and social policy. Charlemagne's support for the study of literature was based on the need to develop competent administrators who were knowledgeable about the law. The lack of such competence was a large obstacle to his empire building.[11] The Carolingians—most effectively Charlemagne—also imposed their wills throughout the empire via the Church, because this was the only institution capable of bringing unity to a scattered realm. Charlemagne's son and grandsons, upon falling into disunity and war, ultimately failed to maintain the *renovatio* beyond the third generation. The *renovatio* was always highly dependent on the active support of a strong Frankish leader.

10.2 FOUNDATIONAL DOCUMENTS

The Carolingian Renaissance was founded on the orders of Charlemagne, which were written on documents that were then sent out across the realm by the *missi*. These messengers communicated the emperor's will to local authorities. The most

---

[11] Georges Minois, *Charlemagne* (Perrin, 2010), 563.

important of these legal documents were the *Epistola de litteris colendis* (*Letter on the Cultivation of Letters*), written in 784/785 AD, the *Capitulary* of 787 AD, and the *Admonitio generalis*, particularly chapter 72, decreed in 789 AD. The *Letter on the Cultivation of Letters*, which concerned Church leaders in particular, echoed Gregory the Great in emphasizing the need for educated monks and clergy. Charlemagne endeavored to put his own stamp on the Frankish kingdom, which in living memory had been ruled by the centuries-long Merovingian dynasty. The *renovatio* aimed to give Charlemagne and the Carolingian dynasty a higher status than the Merovingians had ever had by acting as more than simple warlords. The Carolingians were the builders of civilization and culture, of *Christian* civilization and culture. This Christian component, anchored in shared knowledge and culture, established a very clear sense of this Christian civilization.[12] With one goal of the educational renewal being the salvation of souls, the *Epistola* took on an eschatological as well as political purpose.[13]

The *Capitulary* of 787 AD, which outlined the basic requirements of education, was a letter from the court addressed to abbots. It scolded these churchmen for illiteracy among monks and directed them to focus on priests' education, according to the ability of each.[14] An observation from Einhard supports this: Charlemagne "was at great pains to improve the church reading and psalmody, for he was well skilled in both, although he neither read in public nor sang, except in a low tone and with others."[15] The *Capitulary* justifies the trivium: "Those who seek to please God by living aright should also not neglect to please him by right speaking. It is written 'by thine own words shalt thou be justified or condemned'; and although right doing be preferable to right speaking, yet must the knowledge

---

[12] Kramer, "'Ecce fabula!' Problem-solving by numbers in the Carolingian world: The case of the *Propositiones ad Acuendos Iuvena*," 16–17.
[13] Ibid., 19.
[14] West, *Alcuin and the Rise of the Christian Schools*, 49–50. The words in quotation marks are from the capitulary, as cited by West.
[15] Einhard, *The Life of Charlemagne*, XXVI, 55.

of what is right precede right action."[16] The *Capitulary* clearly makes the traditional connection between education and proper behavior. The author, likely Alcuin on Charlemagne's behalf, places special importance on the virtue of priests: "And if false speaking is to be shunned by all men, especially should it be shunned by those who have elected to be the servants of the truth."[17] The author then offers a stinging rebuke for poor Latin: "During the past years we have often received letters from different monasteries informing us that at their sacred services the brethren offered up prayers on our behalf; and we have observed that the thoughts contained in these letters, though in themselves most just, were expressed in uncouth language, and while pious devotion dictated the sentiments, the unlettered tongue was unable to express them aright."[18] Poor Latin apparently impeded Christian piety. The author was not the first ancient or medieval Christian to think so.

The *Capitulary* then comes to the crux of the issue, a matter that greatly concerned the Church Fathers and that was at the heart of the Carolingian *correctio*. The author expresses the fear that the lack of writing skills would disrupt the proper understanding of Scripture and warns of the danger of verbal error and, even more so, of errors in understanding.[19] Incorrect language contains the specter of heresy. The *Capitulary* comes to the call to action: "We exhort you, therefore, not only not to neglect the study of letters, but to apply yourselves thereto with perseverance and with that humility which is well pleasing to God; so that you may be able to penetrate the mysteries of the Holy Scriptures. For as these contain images, tropes, and similar figures, it is impossible to doubt that the reader will arrive far more readily at the spiritual sense according as he is the better instructed in learning."[20] Here we have the heart

---

[16] West, *Alcuin and the Rise of the Christian Schools*, 50.
[17] Ibid., 50.
[18] Ibid.
[19] Ibid., 50–51.
[20] Ibid., 51.

of the eschatological mission of the Carolingian Renaissance. Renewed learning will prevent heresy and produce pious clergymen who will lead the faithful to their salvation. The author next asserts the Carolingians' holistic approach in declaring that "it is our wish that you may be what it behoves the soldiers of the Church to be, — religious in heart, learned in discourse, pure in act, eloquent in speech; so that all who approach your house in order to invoke the Divine Master or to behold the excellence of the religious life, may be edified in beholding you and instructed in hearing you discourse or chant, and may return home rendering thanks to God most High."[21] Education is virtue education because it develops not only capable readers and grammatically correct writers and preachers, but also the moral conduct that underpins the Christian life and that priests need to model to the laity.

The underlying principles of this *Capitulary* put education at the forefront of Western medieval society in a fresh way. One of these principles was the idea that the king could force individual subjects to study and the Church to establish schools.[22] Another principle was the belief, held by many Church Fathers and now made into official state policy, that the teaching of non-theological subjects such as grammar or philosophy were required to enable churchmen to carry out their functions and correctly understand the Bible.[23] Charlemagne undoubtedly knew that his orders were not instantly put into action, and that follow-up was needed. Capitularies in 789 and 802 AD further addressed the issue of the education of priests.

In the *Admonitio*, Charlemagne expresses his desire that children learn to chant and read music in order to follow the religious office.[24] The close connection of the educational aspect of the Carolingian *renovatio* to liturgy was natural in a monastic-centered society in which an oblate to a monastery underwent

---

[21] West, *Alcuin and the Rise of the Christian Schools*, 51.
[22] Ibid., 53–54.
[23] Ibid., 54.
[24] Riché and Verger, *Maîtres et élèves au Moyen Age*, 47.

an apprenticeship in the liturgy, a learning-by-doing process, alongside his classroom-based studies. The Carolingian era's ideal of a unified liturgy based on Rome's model led to the emergence of schools in Metz, Saint-Wandrille, Salzburg, Lyons, and St. Gall that were well-known for training cantors.[25] The intellectual renewal of the clergy through the palace school and its *docti viri* (scholars), along with cathedral schools, monasteries, and even parishes were at the heart of the renewal of the empire itself. This renewal would bear fruit long after the empire's breakup. The centers of higher education founded by Charlemagne throughout his lands were in some cases the seeds of future universities even if institutional continuity was lacking.[26] In addition to Charlemagne's palace school, important centers of learning were located in Germany (Corbie and Fulda) and France (St. Wandrille Fontenelle, St. Martin de Tours, Lyons, and Orléans).

10.3 EDUCATIONAL IDEAS AND PRACTICES

The palace school at Aachen was the "university" of the time, the Frankish equivalent of the *Pandidakterion*, the Imperial University of Constantinople, which had been established in 425 AD. Below the palace school were the monastic schools, alongside some cathedral schools offering a similar curriculum of the trivium and perhaps parts of the quadrivium. The head of a monastic school was the abbot, and that of a cathedral school the *scholasticus*. Some monasteries operated both external schools, for future secular priests and laymen, and internal schools, for the *oblati* (oblates), the boys who had been offered to the monastery to be monks in the future. Rabanus Maurus had been an oblate, and later, when this practice faced criticism, he wrote *De oblatione puerum* in support of it. These schools provided education without cost to free-born boys. Below the

---

[25] Riché and Verger, *Maîtres et élèves au Moyen Age*, 48.
[26] Newman, *The Benedictine Schools*, 80.

monastic and cathedral schools were the village parish schools run by the local priest, which provided the basics of reading (including Bible passages), writing, and *computus*.[27]

The Carolingian Renaissance designated grammar as key to its search for doctrinal and catechetical clarity because of the realization that the basics of the language and culture were in such poor shape. Dialectic and rhetoric took distant secondary places. A solid grammatical foundation was deemed essential for the improvement of the clergy. As such, grammar represented both an educational and spiritual undertaking, almost a worldview as it had been with Isidore of Seville. Charlemagne's preoccupation with doctrine, as exemplified in his robust reaction to the Second Ecumenical Council at Nicaea in 787 AD, required precise language. The ecumenical councils of the early Church had been dominated by Greek philosophical concerns and Greek speakers due in no small part to the sophisticated language capacities of the Greek Church leaders. A lack of advanced philosophical studies in the West, and even inferior dialectic and rhetoric, may have impeded greater input from the Latin West in these councils. Charlemagne wanted to be considered the equal to the Byzantine emperor, and was undoubtedly aware of the much more robust educational traditions and philosophical sophistication of the Christian east at the time.

10.4 CAROLINGIAN STUDENTS

Notker the Stammerer relates a very dramatic episode from the court of Charlemagne that, even if not completely true, colorfully portrays Charles the Great's passion for learning and some idea of his approach to it. First, we see that the more motivated students come from more economically restricted classes: "Then when Charles came back, after a long absence, crowned with victory, into Gaul, he ordered the boys whom he

---

[27] West, *Alcuin and the Rise of the Christian Schools*, 56–58.

had entrusted to Clement to come before him and present to him letters and verses of their own composition. Now the boys of middle or low birth presented him with writings garnished with the sweet savours of wisdom beyond all that he could have hoped, while those of the children of noble parents were silly and tasteless."[28] Notker then describes the holy and even practical use of education that the emperor identifies: "Then the most wise Charles, imitating the judgment of the eternal Judge, gathered together those who had done well upon his right hand and addressed them in these words: 'My children, you have found much favour with me because you have tried with all your strength to carry out my orders and win advantage for yourselves. Wherefore now study to attain to perfection; and I will give you bishoprics and splendid monasteries, and you shall be always honourable in my eyes.'"[29] Then as now, hard-working students were promised the future rewards of money and higher social status.

Charlemagne then chastises the poorly-performing students, who have neglected their studies for a life of ease and enjoyment:

> Then he turned severely to those who were gathered on his left, and, smiting their consciences with the fire of his eyes, he flung at them in scorn these terrible words, which seemed thunder rather than human speech: "You nobles, you sons of my chiefs, you superfine dandies, you have trusted to your birth and your possessions and have set at naught my orders to your own advancement: you have neglected the pursuit of learning and you have given yourselves over to luxury and sport, to idleness and profitless pastimes." Then solemnly he raised his august head and his unconquered right hand to the heavens and thus thundered against them, "By the King of Heaven, I take no account of your noble birth and your fine looks, though others may admire you for them. Know this for certain, that unless you make up for your former sloth by vigorous study, you will never get any favour from Charles."[30]

---

[28] Notker the Stammerer, "Life of Charlemagne," Book 1, §3, 48.
[29] Ibid., Book 1, §3, 48.
[30] Ibid., 48–49.

As Notker has it, Charlemagne cared more about education than about noble birth. There was likely some truth to that, given his empire's need for able bureaucrats and churchmen.

Carolingians wrote on traditional educational concerns, such as managing student behavior. Such writings, which are found throughout the Middle Ages, reflect a keen sense of developmental psychology, particularly the notion that children and adolescents differ psychologically from adults, and their resulting need to be treated with special care. Children and adolescents were not typically seen as simply smaller versions of adults. Children and adolescents were not held to the same standards as adults were. In his *Commentary on the Rule of St. Benedict*, Paul the Deacon counsels teachers to discipline moderately, not harshly, and to ensure plenty of exercise for boys: "In order to strengthen the children and satisfy the needs of human nature, they need to be taken weekly or monthly, according to the choice of the master, in a meadow or other place where the children can play for an hour under the supervision of their master."[31]

Paul's concern for student safety seems contemporary, although the second piece of advice is no longer accepted: "Three or four masters must supervise a group of boys, as the blessed Benedict said that they will be under the supervision of everyone and because they cannot go anywhere without their master [chapter XXXVIII]. The master must act with moderation towards the children, and not whip them too much, because after the whip and other punishment, they will quickly return to their naughty behavior [chapter XXXVII]."[32]

Perhaps Paul the Deacon had learned from experience that severe punishment has little long-term positive effect on behavior. In fact, he warns that harsh discipline will have the opposite effect as intended. The abbot has to prevent masters from punishing boys excessively, such as by whipping or

---

[31] Riché and Verger, *Maîtres et élèves au Moyen Age*, 45, Paul the Deacon, *Commentary on the Rule of St. Benedict*, Chapter XXXXVII.
[32] Ibid., 45.

excommunication.[33] Paul also warns that adolescents must also be dealt with carefully. This stage represents the most unstable years in life, which means that too much discipline could trigger teenage revolt.[34] Once again we see a surprisingly contemporary appreciation of developmental psychology. Was there something of a generation gap in Carolingian Europe?

10.5 ALCUIN OF YORK

On the way back from his third trip from York to Rome in 781 AD, when he was already in his mid-forties, Alcuin met Charlemagne, perhaps not for the first time, in Parma, Italy. The king (crowned emperor on Christmas Day, 800, in Rome) invited him to the court to help renew education. Notker the Stammer gives his own version of events and describes the close, collaborative relationship between the two that seemed to overturn the typical ruler-subject hierarchy:

> But when Albinus (Alcuin), an Englishman, heard that that most religious Emperor Charles gladly entertained wise men, he entered into a ship and came to him. Now Albinus was skilled in all learning beyond all others of our times, for he was the disciple of that most learned priest Bede, who next to Saint Gregory was the most skilful interpreter of the scriptures. And Charles received Albinus kindly and kept him at his side to the end of his life, except when he marched with his armies to his vast wars: nay, Charles would even call himself Albinus's disciple; and Albinus he would call his master. He appointed him to rule over the abbey of Saint Martin, near to the city of Tours: so that, when he himself was absent, Albinus might rest there and teach those who had recourse to him. And his teaching bore such fruit among his pupils that the modern Gauls or Franks came to equal the ancient Romans or Athenians.[35]

---

[33] Riché and Verger, *Maîtres et élèves au Moyen Age*, 45, Paul the Deacon, *Commentary on the Rule of St. Benedict*.

[34] Ibid., 45.

[35] Notker the Stammerer, "Life of Charlemagne," Book 1, § 2, 48. (Notker Balbulus)

The last sentence reveals the respect and love that the Carolingians had for the pagan writers and their attempts to raise their own society to the educational levels of these esteemed societies.

Another episode reported by Notker would, if true, reveal the close, even familiar, relationship between the Frankish ruler and the master from York:

> So the most glorious Charles saw the study of letters flourishing throughout his whole realm, but still he was grieved to find that it did not reach the ripeness of the earlier fathers; and so, after superhuman labours, he broke out one day with this expression of his sorrow: "Would that I had twelve clerks so learned in all wisdom and so perfectly trained as were Jerome and Augustine." Then the learned Alcuin, feeling himself ignorant indeed in comparison with these great names, rose to a height of daring, that no man else attained to in the presence of the terrible Charles, and said, with deep indignation in his mind but none in his countenance, "The Maker of heaven and earth has not many like to those men and do you expect to have twelve?"[36]

The Anglo-Saxon seemed to have a more realistic understanding of how difficult it was to produce a generation of scholars than Charlemagne had, the latter being not unlike the Roman centurion of Matthew 8:5–13 who is used to having his orders followed immediately and with near-instant outcomes.

Alcuin wrote poems and a number of education- and specifically language-related treatises that formed the backbone of the liberal arts-oriented Carolingian *correctio*. These include *On Grammar (De grammatica)*, *On Orthography*, *On Dialectic*, *The debate of the wisest king Charles and the teacher Alcuin, about rhetoric and the virtues (Disputatio de rhetorica et de virtutibus sapientissimi regis Carli et Albini magistri)*, *The dispute of the royal and most noble young man Pippin with the teacher Albinus (Disputatio regalis et nobilissimi juvenis Pippini cum Albino scholastico)*, *On Virtues and Vices (De virtutibus et vitiis)*, *De animae ratione*, and perhaps *Problems to Sharpen the Young*.[37]

---

[36] Notker the Stammerer, "Life of Charlemagne," Book I, §9, 52–53.

[37] *Propositiones ad acuendos iuvenes* has also been translated as *Propositions for Sharpening Youths*.

The content of the 53 problems of *Problems to Sharpen the Young* exemplifies how Christian belief was included in every possible aspect of education, as the logical and mathematical problems, which are of a practical nature, also contain references to moral issues such as sexual purity. The *Problems* emerged from the Anglo-Saxon and Irish love for riddles, which we saw in Chapter 9. Each scenario is normally given a title, followed by the problem and answer.[38] The *Problems* include the first examples of river-crossing riddles:

> 18. Proposition concerning the man, the she-goat, and the wolf. A certain man needed to take a wolf, a she-goat and a load of cabbage across a river. However, he could only find a boat which would carry two of these [at a time]. Thus, what rule did he employ so as to get all of them across unharmed?[39]

The following is a more explicit fusion of logic with morality:

> 17. Proposition concerning the men who had unmarried sisters.
>
> There were three men, each having an unmarried sister, who needed to cross a river. Each man was desirous of his friend's sister. Coming to the river, they found only a small boat in which only two persons could cross at a time. Let him say, he who is able, How did they cross the river, so that none of the sisters were defiled by the men?[40]

---

[38] Peter J. Burkholder, "Introduction," *Alcuin of York's 'Propositiones ad Acuendos Juvenes.'* Certain manuscripts have 56 problems.

[39] Peter J. Burkholder, "Introduction." The number indicates the problem number in the manuscript. "Solution. In a similar manner, I would first take the she-goat and leave behind the wolf and the cabbage. When I had returned, I would ferry over the wolf. With the wolf unloaded, I would retrieve the she-goat and take it back across. Then, I would unload the she-goat and take the cabbage to the other side. I would next row back, and take the she-goat across. The crossing should go well by doing thus, and absent from the threat of slaughter.

[40] Burkholder, "Introduction." Solution. First of all, my sister and I got into the boat and crossed. Having crossed the river, I let my sister out and recrossed the river. Then the sisters of the two men who remained on the bank got in. When these women had gotten out of the boat, my sister, who had already gone across, got in and brought the boat back to us. She then got out, and the two brothers crossed in the boat. Then, one of the brothers and his sister crossed over to us. However, I and the brother who piloted the boat went across while my sister remained behind. When we had been taken to the [other] side, one

There is a brief story or human interaction behind most of the problems:

> 36. A certain old man greeted a boy, saying to him: "May you live, boy, may you live for as long as you have [already] lived, and then another equal amount of time, and then three times as much. And may God grant you one of my years, and you shall live to be 100." Let him solve, he who can, How many years old was the boy at that time?[41]

The mixture of virtue education with training in numeracy or logic reflected the belief of school masters at the time that the pastoral element was at the core of teaching, and would ideally be included even in mathematics.[42]

The story-telling nature of the riddles offers a glimpse into certain characteristics of Carolingian society. The following problem reflects the hierarchical nature of medieval society, which determined relations among the clergy:

> 47. A certain bishop ordered 12 loaves of bread divided amongst the clergy. He stipulated that each priest should receive two loaves; a deacon, half a loaf; and a lector, a quarter part. Hence, it should turn out that the number of clerics and loaves is the same. Let him say, he who can, How many priests, deacons and lectors must there have been?[43]

The narrative structure of these mathematical puzzles reflects the concern to make the classroom enjoyable, personable, and relevant, whether this pragmatism concerned the real world

---

of the other women took the boat back across, and my sister came across to us with her at the same time. Then the man whose sister had remained on the other side got in the boat and brought it back with her. Thus the crossing was accomplished, with no one being defiled.

[41] Burkholder, "Introduction." Solution. When [the old man] said "may you live for as long as you have lived," [the boy] had [already] lived eight years, three months. Another equal number of years make 16 years, six months, while another equal span makes 33 years. Three times this makes 99 years, which with one more year added makes 100.

[42] Kramer, "'Ecce fabula!' Problem-solving by numbers in the Carolingian world: The case of the *Propositiones ad Acuendos Iuvena*," 25–26.

[43] Burkholder, "Introduction." Solution. Twice five is 10; that is, five priests received 10 loaves. The deacon got half a loaf, and there was a loaf and a half for the six lectors. Add five and one and six, making 12. Then add 10-and-a-half and one-and-a-half, making 12, this being the number of loaves. Hence, there are 12 men altogether and 12 loaves. Therefore, the number of clerics and loaves is the same.

of moral challenges (trying to protect a sister's purity) or the world of agriculture. Sheer repetition of mathematical problem-solving was avoided. Real-world analytical skills were honed with the *Problems to Sharpen the Young*.[44]

10.6 THE LIBERAL ARTS

Given the religious and philosophical concerns of Carolingian society, a treatise on grammar could include more than grammar basics. Alcuin wrote *On Grammar* as two dialogues, the first addressing the liberal arts and philosophy in general, and the second more specifically on grammar. The first dialogue addresses the cultivation of wisdom. True and eternal happiness contrasts with fleeting pleasure and is defined as the highest goal of the life of a rational creature such as a human being. Happiness is ordered to the nature of the soul, not to the things that are foreign to the soul.[45] Wisdom, as part of the eternal soul, is itself eternal, but, Alcuin warns, the attainment of wisdom is a difficult journey.

A letter Alcuin wrote on the occasion of his commentary on the Gospel of John reflects his "timorously conservative attitude"[46]:

> I have reverently traversed the storehouses of the early fathers, and whatever I have been able to find there, I have sent of it for you to taste. First of all, I have sought help from St. Augustine, who has devoted the greatest study to expounding the most holy words of this holy gospel. Next, I have drawn somewhat from the lesser works of St. Ambrose, that most holy doctor, and likewise from the Homilies of the distinguished father, Gregory the Great. I have also taken much from the Homilies of the blessed presbyter Bede, and from other holy fathers, whose interpretations I have here set forth. For I have preferred to employ their thoughts and words rather than to venture anything of my

---

[44] Kramer, "'Ecce fabula!' Problem-solving by numbers in the Carolingian world: The case of the *Propositiones ad Acuendos Iuvena*," 40.
[45] West, *Alcuin and the Rise of the Christian Schools*, 94.
[46] Ibid., 90.

> own audacity, even if the curiosity of my readers were to
> approve of it, and by a most cautious manner of writing
> I have made it my care, with the help of God, not to set
> down anything contrary to the thoughts of the fathers.[47]

Augustine, Isidore, Bede, and to a lesser degree Cassiodorus, influenced Alcuin, though Martianus Capella — celebrated by some Carolingians — seems to have had little impact on the first two Carolingian generations of reformers.

Theodulf of Orleans, whose family was originally from Zaragosa, Spain, arrived at Charlemagne's court in 780 AD, where he contributed to the establishment of the trivium. His poem *De septem artibus liberalibus in quadram picture depictis* employed allegorical symbols and imagery to convey his vision of the liberal arts and of knowledge in general. Along with many other theologians throughout the ancient and medieval centuries, such as Clement of Alexandria, Origen, and John of Salisbury, Theodulf saw the seven liberal arts as preparation for the interpretation of Scripture.[48] Secular education, these ancient and medieval theologians believed, could have a powerful impact on a person's salvation, even if not directly. This indirect contribution was vital, as the liberal arts trained the mind in reason and in the contemplation of God's created order even while it defended dogma against heresy. Theodulf envisioned knowledge as a tree whose branches included rhetoric, dialectic, the cardinal virtues, and the elements of the quadrivium, all of which led to wisdom. Grammar formed the roots of this tree, and wisdom crowned it. Centuries later, Ramon Llull[49] (c. 1232–1316 AD) would characterize grammar as the key that unlocks the doors to the other arts. He too used a tree in his *Arbre de ciencia* [*Tree of Knowledge*] in his description and classification of the mechanical and liberal arts.[50] As bishop

---

[47] West, *Alcuin and the Rise of the Christian Schools*, 90–91.

[48] Guadalupe Lopetegui Semperana, "Teodulfo de Orleans y las Artes Liberales," in *VELEIA* (2003), 459–476, 459–460.

[49] Variously written *Lull* and *Lully*.

[50] Ricardo da Costa, "Las definiciones de las siete artes liberales y mecánicos en la obra de Ramón Llull," in *Anales del Seminario de Historia de la Filosofía,*

of Orléans, Theodulf most faithfully applied the principles of the Carolingian *renovatio* and *correctio*, essentially through ensuring that a tuition-free school was attached to every parish in his diocese.[51]

The spiritual significance of the liberal arts in the eyes of the Church gave medieval clerics a generous, at times almost servile, view of ancient pagan writers. Even when beset by frequent theological errors or questionable ethics, these ancient writers carried out God's work according to the typical medieval view. The ancient association of gods, such as Mercury, with literature, or temples dedicated to justice and virtue, did not cause the Church to reject the study of literature or the valuing of justice and virtue.[52] Many medieval churchmen saw their vocations as rearranging these ancient concepts to accord with Scripture and the Christian life. Virgil was central to the medieval trivium, largely because Donatus and Priscian took most of their examples from the *Aeneid*. St. Gall had a particular esteem for Virgil, as exemplified with Ekkehard I's close imitation of him in the *Walthariuslied* or Notker the Stammerer's citation of him in the *Gesta Caroli Magni*. The Abbot Grimald gave his personal copy of a text of Virgil to the abbey's library. The numerous German glosses in the surviving manuscript testify to its heavy use.[53] Christian poets such as Sedulius, Juvencus, and Prudentius were also studied at St. Gall. Martianus Capella's *On the Marriage of Philology and Mercury* was extremely popular at St. Gall. The work's mythological content and references to classical literature meant that it was used only in rhetoric class, as it would have been too challenging for grammar students.[54] As for Horace at St. Gall, Notker writes in a letter to Salome that while the Latin poet expressed the truth, his poetry was immoral and therefore to be avoided.[55]

Volume 23 (2006), 154.

[51] West, *Alcuin and the Rise of the Christian Schools*, 55.

[52] De Bruyne, *Etudes d'esthétique médiévale*, 331.

[53] Clark, *The Abbey of St Gall as a Centre of Literature and Art*, 102.

[54] Ibid., 97.

[55] Ibid., 102.

10.7 ST. GALL

St. Gall was a center of the liberal arts, and played a key role in the Carolingian *renovatio*. Begun as an Irish monastery, as we have seen, it adopted the Rule of St. Benedict in 760 AD under Abbot Johannes. The abbey had already been thriving as a pilgrimage center because of the relics of its famous founder. It received another boost in 747 AD when Pepin, the father of Charlemagne and the first Carolingian king of the Franks, gave an endowment to the abbey, thus ensuring steady finances.[56] While Charlemagne had curbed the power of the monastery by placing it under the bishop of Constance, Louis the Pious and later Louis the German proclaimed it a royal monastery, which granted it the independence that it needed to turn into a center of culture and learning.

The abbey reached its greatest fame in the late ninth and early tenth centuries, beginning under Abbot Gozbert (in office 816–836 AD). Gozbert did for St. Gall what Benedict Biscop had done for Wearmouth and Jarrow by promoting scholarship and learning while also building up the library.[57] The following abbot, appointed by Louis the Pious in 841 AD, was the Frankish nobleman Grimald. A former student of Alcuin and a scholar in his own right, he built on St. Gall's reputation. It was under the Abbot Salomo (in office 890–920 AD) that St. Gall experienced its golden age.[58] The two most important masters were the famous musician Notker the Stammerer and the multi-talented Irishman Tuotilo, a poet, musician of string and wind instruments, artist, and architect.[59] Obviously, scholarly lineage was central to St. Gall's accomplishments and status in Europe. The second half of the tenth century saw numerous scholars who followed in the spiritual and scholarly lineage of

---

[56] Clark, *The Abbey of St Gall as a Centre of Literature and Art*, 4.
[57] Ibid., 6–7.
[58] Ibid., 9.
[59] Ibid., 10.

Notker the Stammerer.[60] These included Notker Labeo and Ekkehard I, Ekkehard II, and Ekkehard III. St. Gall continued to flourish in the following centuries, playing a central role in the renaissance under the Ottonian emperors.

---

[60] Clark, *The Abbey of St Gall as a Centre of Literature and Art*, 14.

CHAPTER II

Rabanus Maurus: On the Formation of Clergy

It is not ignoble, then, to know the metrical rules which are learned through the art of grammar, because among the Hebrews, as blessed Jerome testifies, the Psalter now gallops in iambic, now resounds in alcaics, now swells in sapphic, now is advanced by half-foot meter. Indeed, consider Deuteronomy and the canticle of Isaiah and also of Solomon and Job, all these works composed by them run in hexameters and pentameters, as Josephus and Origen write.
— Rabanus Maurus[1]

II.I THE HEART OF THE CAROLINGIAN *RENOVATIO*

THE SECOND GENERATION OF CAR-
olingian scholars reaped the benefits of the efforts of Charlemagne and the leaders of the palace school. One leading second generation figure, Rabanus Maurus, demonstrated the strong interpersonal links of the three generations of the Carolingian Renaissance. The name "Rabanus" came from the Old German word for raven, likely due to the schoolboy's striking black hair. Alcuin called him "Maurus" in honor of St. Benedict's favorite student of the same name. Rabanus was an oblate at Fulda monastery, one of Christendom's leading learning centers at that time, which was established, as we have seen, by St. Boniface. Various streams of the Carolingian Renaissance came together in Fulda.

Rabanus moved to France in 801 AD to continue his learning under Alcuin. The first *Praeceptor Germaniae*, Rabanus closely

---

[1] Rabanus Maurus, *On the Formation of Clergy*, trans. Owen M. Phelan (The catholic University of America Press), 3.17, 180. Variations on his name include *Hrabanus* or *Raban*, and *Maur*.

parallels many other early medieval writers on education, such as Cassiodorus or Isidore of Seville, in bringing together the achievements of the past for the edification of future clergymen and the health of the Church. Influenced by Isidore's encyclopedia, he wrote *De universo* or *De rerum naturis* around 830 AD. He was most noted, perhaps, for *De institutione clericorum* (*On the Training of the Clergy*) and also wrote a polemic against those who wanted to ban child oblates, *De oblatione puerorum* (*On Child Oblates*). His writings reflect the concern of Charlemagne's *Letter on the Cultivation of Letters* for an educated priesthood, which itself expressed the spirit of Pope Gregory the Great's *Regula pastoralis*.

Similar to Isidore's *Etymologies*, much of the three-book *On the Formation of Clergy* consists of citations from previous authorities such as Augustine and Gregory the Great. Written in 819 AD, the treatise reflects the aims set out by Alcuin on the three pillars of the *res ecclesiasticae*, the things that concern the Church. These are Revelation, the moral life, and the liberal arts.[2] The first two books discuss the first two pillars, often in quite practical terms. Some chapters of book one, for example, deal with the three orders that make up the Church: monks, clerics, and the laity. Other chapters discuss practical liturgical matters for the clergy and priestly vestments such as the amice, linen tunic, cincture, and maniple. Catechumens, baptism, and the office of the Mass are also treated. Turning to the Christian life, book two includes chapters on the daily office, types of prayers, fasting, penance, and religious festivals. In book three, which addresses the content of education, Rabanus justifies the need for training the clergy in virtuous living by citing Gregory the Great's *Regula pastoralis* (1.2): "And there are some who with expert care study spiritual precepts that they penetrate with understanding but violate in living. Unexpectedly, they teach what they have learned not by deed

---

[2] José Francisco García Juan, "La Biblia En '*De Institutione Clericorum*' De Rabano Mauro," in *Estudios Bíblicos* 75, no. 2 (2017), 285–286.

but by thought, and what they preach with words, they attack by their behavior."[3] These words remind us of the Church's continuation of the Greek paideutic tradition wherein education is essentially virtue education.

Book three reflects the entire project of the Carolingian Renaissance. The topic of the first chapter, "What is appropriate for those who wish to approach to holy orders to know and to have," describes the educational nature of the priestly vocation. Rabanus argues that an uneducated priest cannot fulfill his duties. Given the dire state of the Frankish Church before and likely during much of the Carolingian Renaissance, the following words would have rung painfully true for readers of the time concerning the low level of education among the lower clergy, who would have been the Church's main contact with the laity: "It is not permitted to them to be ignorant of any of those things with which they ought to instruct either themselves or those subject to them, that is: the knowledge of Holy Scripture, the pure truth of histories, the methods of figurative speech, the meaning of mystical things, the usefulness of all the disciplines, integrity of life in uprightness of behavior, elegance in advancing a speech, discernment in the presentation of doctrine, and differentiating among medicines for a variety of diseases."[4] This was an imposing to-do list for the *renovatio* to cover, yet included many of the traditional disciplines of Greek paideia.

The next part argues that it is vital for leaders to have these skills in order to lead the people. Rabanus envisions Church life in militaristic terms, which calls for the proper training of the priest for armed combat so that he may "powerfully overcome enemies and adequately defend the flock entrusted to him." Given the grave stakes involved, "it is dangerous to place the burden of instruction on him—even strongly supported by the help of learning—who is not able to bear it."[5] Rabanus

---

[3] Maurus, *On the Formation of Clergy*, 3.1, 154.

[4] Ibid., 152.

[5] Ibid.

cites Gregory the Great's *Regula pastoralis* (1.1) when he calls attention to the practical connection between education and the priestly vocation. As we have seen with countless other Church authorities, the ultimate objective is to foster the spiritual life, starting with the precept that "no one dares to teach any art unless he has first learned by deep contemplation. Therefore, because the direction of souls is the art of arts, with what rashness is the pastoral office taken up by the unskilled? Who, moreover, does not know that wounds of thoughts are more hidden than wounds of flesh? And, nevertheless, frequently those who know absolutely nothing of spiritual laws do not fear to profess themselves physicians of the heart."[6] These were biting words against the state of the ninth-century Church. The connection between contemplation and education is clear. This spiritual training in contemplation, which seems to have fallen short in Rabanus's era, is necessary to the priest's spiritual direction of the laity, so that the priest can impart something of this contemplation of the truth to the lay believer.

Rabanus continues his citation of Gregory's *Regula pastoralis* 1.1, which highlights the teaching duties of the priest:

> The ignorance of pastors is rebuked by the voice of Truth, when through the prophet it is said: "Those pastors themselves knew no understanding" (Is 56:11); "and they that held the Law knew me not" (Jer 2:8). Therefore, the Truth complains that He is not known by them and protests that He does not know the leadership of those who do not know Him, because these ones who do not know things that are of the Lord are not known by the Lord, as Paul witnesses, who says: "But if anyone does not know, he will not be known" (1 Cor 14:38). This ignorance of pastors without doubt often corresponds to the merits of their subjects, those who, although they may not have the light of knowledge (driven out by their own faults!), nevertheless, by severe judgment it happens that those who through their ignorance follow them [these pastors] also should stumble. Hence, for instance, the Truth says through His very Self

---

[6] Rabanus Maurus, *On the Formation of Clergy*, 3.1, 152–153.

in the Gospel: "If a blind man guide a blind man, both fall
into a pit" (cf. Mt 15:14).[7]

After this practical part, book three turns to more theoretical
concerns.

II.2 THE SPIRITUAL NATURE OF KNOWLEDGE

The fourth chapter, "Concerning the grades of wisdom and
charity," adheres to the Neoplatonist viewpoint that the Church
Fathers had generally adopted. Much of it consists of references to book one of Augustine's *De doctrina christiana* and
the stages or grades of the Christian ascent to God. After we
grow first in the fear of both God and death (stage one), and
then in piety (stage two), the Christian reaches the third grade,
which is knowledge. The study of Scripture is the surest way
to arrive at this knowledge. The next chapter points out the
close relationship between wisdom and the virtuous life as one
rises in the spiritual life. The pursuit of perfect wisdom is the
pursuit of perfect charity. The level of wisdom that is attained
is equal to the level of charity that is attained.[8] This outline of
the spiritual life was remarkably consistent throughout these
medieval Christian centuries. Its Neoplatonic spirit testifies to
the Church as the inheritor of the Greek tradition.

In the sixth chapter of book three, Rabanus then informs
the reader that he is returning to the third level on the Neoplatonic ladder, which is knowledge. He discusses the necessity
of studying Scripture. A pastor's knowledge of the Word of
God will help him counter his own potential misreadings and
resulting susceptibility to heretical thoughts. In 3.7 he classifies the Hebrew Scriptures into "the Law (*legis*), the Prophets
(*prophetarum*), and the Holy Writings (*hagiographorum*)" before
making important didactic points that once again justify the
study of the Bible. Like countless ancient and medieval writers,

---

[7] Rabanus Maurus, *On the Formation of Clergy*, 3.1, 153–154.
[8] Ibid., 3.5, 160.

he emphasizes the central role of memory, but only after noting the necessary spiritual disposition that the student or reader of Scripture needs to adopt. The various books of the Bible testify to the need for the fear of God and for docile piety when seeking to do God's will. The first step in this process is to study Scripture, even if the reader has difficulty in understanding its books. These sacred writings need to be committed to memory or, if that is not possible, at least be made familiar to the seeker of God's will. After this familiarity, the next step is to note the guiding principles by which to live one's life along with the guiding principles of dogma. Rabanus assures his reader that, in this process, the more intelligent one is, the more treasures one will find, and that "among the things that are placed openly in Scriptures is found everything that contains faith and habits of living, that is, hope and charity."[9]

Rabanus then borrows from book two of Augustine's *De doctrina christiana* in discussing why readers may not always correctly interpret everything in the Bible. Many truths are hidden by unknown or ambiguous signs, which may be literal or metaphorical, he notes. The literal sense is easy to spot, as it is the reference to everyday things such as "ox" denoting the common farm animal. The metaphorical sense occurs when the literal sign refers to something other than the direct real-world thing.[10] Rabanus's concern over the various levels of meaning in Scripture prompts him to directly address the difference between figurative and literal language. He refers to 2 Corinthians 3:6, "The letter kills, but the spirit gives life." Rabanus observes that if a passage "is already clear, it should not be thought of as a metaphorical saying. If an imperative sentence forbids either a shame or a crime or orders something useful or a kindness, it is not metaphorical. If, however, it seems to order a shame or a crime, or to forbid something useful or a kindness, it is metaphorical."[11] Rabanus seems to be telling

---

[9] Rabanus Maurus, *On the Formation of Clergy*, 3.7, 162–163.
[10] Ibid., 3.8, 163.
[11] Ibid., 3.13, 171.

his readers to use their common sense. He is also following the more ancient Greek tradition of practicing allegorical interpretation to smooth out the unethical or otherwise difficult passage so that it can fit into the desired religious, moral, or philosophical perspectives. Pagan Greeks and Christians desired the fullness of their literary or religious canons, which required the adoption of this more flexible way of interpretation.

Proper Biblical interpretation requires more than the skill of choosing the literal and figurative meaning. In Chapter 10, Rabanus justifies the encyclopedic knowledge that he desired for students by arguing that without this all-encompassing type of knowledge, readers of Scripture will misinterpret the text. He again borrows from the second book of *De doctrina christiana* when he warns that the ignorance of numbers and of music prevents a clear mystical or figurative understanding of certain passages.[12] He then returns to demonstrating the dangers of ambiguous readings of Scripture, and why they so easily lead to heresy. Even poor pronunciation endangers the truth because it is also a source of ambiguity.

II.3 DIFFERENT TYPES OF KNOWLEDGE

While Rabanus offers little new information here, his arrangement of this information is interesting. Like Isidore, this structure often leads to fresh ways of perceiving or using things known to the ancients. Chapter 16 examines different kinds of knowledge. This includes the two kinds that pagans establish, one based on their own thoughts and the other based on their observations of God's creation. The first type is a mixture of superstition and legitimate thinking. Superstition refers to anything that humans make that is related to the worship of idols or of anything that is not God, or anything that is related to demons. These all encompass the magical arts, which, Rabanus notes, some poets do mention.[13] Superstition,

---

[12] Rabanus Maurus, *On the Formation of Clergy*, 3.10, 167.
[13] Ibid., 3.16, 175.

in other words, is forbidden because it is the worship of false gods. Anything related to this area is not to be pursued. But other types of known things, "convenient and necessary signs" mostly related to culture (such as appropriate attire for the two sexes) and commercial procedures and standards (such as weights and measures), ought to be accepted and studied. This human-established knowledge from culture or business is derived from custom, not from the worship of false gods.

The next chapter addresses two types of knowledge of "divinely instituted things" that have been discovered by humans: that which can be perceived by the senses and that which is attainable through "the soul's reason."[14] The first type includes history because it is based on experience. We readily believe and understand the knowledge that is derived from sensory experience. We often use this as parts of an argument. This experience-based knowledge makes the study of history valuable, as it aids in understanding Scripture, even if it is not learned from a Church source.[15] The author of *On the Formation of Clergy* warns that a lack of this type of knowledge can cause errors in the most basic Christian facts. This raises the specter of heresy, a constant worry of so many Christian writers on education. Rabanus gives an example: "Ignorance of the consulate in which the Lord was born and in which He suffered has driven some to err so that they think the Lord suffered when he was forty-six years old because the Jews say such was the number of years to build the Temple (cf. Jn 2.20), which is the image of the Lord's body."[16]

Rabanus then turns to knowledge pertaining to the reason that is found in the soul, which is central to dialectic and the quadrivial disciplines.[17] He singles out one trivial discipline, connecting dialectic to proper exegesis of the Bible. He warns against the misuse of dialectic. While the skill of disputation

---

[14] Rabanus Maurus, *On the Formation of Clergy*, 3.17, 176.
[15] Ibid., 3.17, 176.
[16] Ibid.
[17] Ibid., 178.

provides valuable insight into the meaning of Biblical passages
which are otherwise confusing, scholars need to be wary of
an inordinate desire for disputation and the immature exhi-
bitionism of defeating opponents.[18] In all of this discussion,
Rabanus expresses his enthusiastic support for grammar, dialectic, and rhetoric, and points out their central roles in the
life of the Church.

II.4 THE LIBERAL ARTS

Rabanus adopted the traditional Pythagorean orientation of the
quadrivium, which likely comes from his reading of Boethius.
He asserts that humans have not created numbers and their
properties, but only discovered these.[19] The eternal validity of
numbers gives them an almost divine-like quality for thinkers
like Boethius and certain Carolingians. This quality can be seen
when comparing their truths to those of grammar. Unlike the
pronunciation of *Italia*, Rabanus notes, the nature of numbers
is unchanging. This unchanging nature holds regardless of
whether numbers are studied in themselves or are applied to
more practical things, such as "the laws of shapes, of sounds,
or of other motions."[20] Rabanus then connects numbers to
the Neoplatonic elevation of the soul towards the unchanging
truth, which involves the attainment of wisdom. He adds a
warning for those who learn for their pride, not in the service
of truth and wisdom. Instead of being boastful and proud of
their superior stations, they need to continue down the path of
learning, knowledge, and wisdom by further seeking to know
why it is that the immutable truths that they have already
studied are indeed true and immutable, and therefore higher
than the things of the perceptible world that are only present
in the human mind. Rabanus warns that whoever has learned
about the lower mutable things and the higher immutable

---

[18] Rabanus Maurus, *On the Formation of Clergy*, 3.17, 178.
[19] Ibid.
[20] Ibid.

truths, but does not investigate further into the truths of these, is merely learned, not wise, especially if he has not pursued such knowledge as a way to praise and love God.[21] Pride is dangerous because it impedes progress towards the higher things, and can even lead to heretical thoughts. A proud mind cannot be purified through the study of mathematics for the contemplation of God.

On the Foundation of Clergy includes a chapter on each liberal arts discipline before turning to philosophy. For Rabanus, grammar encompasses the wide range of learning that most ancient and medieval authorities accepted. While the discipline starts with letters and shows their connection to sounds, it then moves on to correct speaking and writing, and the interpretation of the poets and historians.[22] This makes grammar "both the origin and the foundation of the liberal arts."[23] Ultimately, as with all else in education in this period, there is a religious reason to grammar. Grammar enables not only proper understanding of the Bible and the prevention of false interpretations, but also correct copying and interpretation of Scripture. Rabanus borrows from the third book of *De doctrina christiana* when he notes grammar's role in orthodox Biblical exegesis. Tropes are found in abundance throughout the Scriptures, and add greatly to proper interpretation. The inspired authors cannot be understood, particularly in ambiguous passages, without familiarity with tropes because "when the literal sense of the words — if it is accepted — is absurd, it should by all means be sought whether what we do not understand was said with this or that trope, and in this way a great part of what was hidden is found."[24]

Rabanus explains that pastoral concern is the standard for sifting through the non-Christian canon. The most basic requirements are truthfulness to Christian belief, support for

---

[21] Rabanus Maurus, *On the Formation of Clergy*, 3.17, 178.
[22] Ibid., 3.18, 179.
[23] Ibid.
[24] Ibid., 179–180.

other Christians, and the avoidance of scandal. Useful passages and books are to be retained, but those with excessive attention to false gods or to the cares of the world are to be eliminated or trimmed just as we trim our fingernails. Christian teachers need to beware that even if they are left unaffected by troubling passages, their Christian brothers might not be. Less well-read brothers might turn to idolatry.[25] Yet pastoral concerns also support instruction in the pagan disciplines. Regarding rhetoric, Rabanus adopts Augustine's attitude from *De doctrina christiana* that because skills in the art of rhetoric are commonly available to everyone, and can therefore be exploited by unscrupulous or treacherous individuals to hurt Christians and the Church, leaders of the faithful must be educated to defend the truth with rhetoric and thereby nullify the trickery employed on behalf of "iniquity and error."[26] In other words, liars and opponents of Christianity should not be the only ones armed with the trivium and philosophy.

Rabanus cites Isidore at the beginning of his chapter on dialectic to provide a definition that was familiar to generations of students and masters: "Dialectic is the discipline of rationally questioning, defining, and discussing, and also is the power of distinguishing truth from falsehood. It therefore is the discipline of disciplines. It teaches to teach. It teaches to learn. In it, reason shows itself and reveals what it is, what it wants, and what it can accomplish. It alone knows how to know, and so, knowing, it not only wishes to do so, but is also able so to do."[27] Dialectic establishes the methods for learning, teaching, investigating, and analyzing knowledge. It helps those who reason to know what they are and where they came from because dialectic separates truth from falsehood, and God from creation. In addition to this differentiation, dialectic provides the skills to make conclusions, identify consequences, and separate the truth from what only appears as truth but is inwardly false.

---

[25] Rabanus Maurus, *On the Formation of Clergy*, 3.18, 180.

[26] Ibid., 3.19, 181.

[27] Ibid., 3.20, 182.

Unsurprisingly, dialectic is crucial in the fight against heresy: "It is fitting that clerics know this most respected art and have its laws for their constant contemplation so that they are able to discern the subtle craft of the heretics and refute their poisonous words with the truthful reasoned conclusions of syllogisms."[28] The study of dialectic sharpens the faculty of judgment.

The author of *On the Formation of Clergy* turns to Augustine, Cassiodorus, and Isidore for the quadrivium. The study of num-bers improves understanding of the Bible and its use of numbers, such as the meaning of forty. It is only natural that readers will wonder about the meaning of the forty day fasts of Moses, Elijah, and Jesus. It takes an appropriate understanding of the Biblical meaning of this number to know whether forty should be applied figuratively or literally.[29] Rabanus notes a similar connection between geometry and the Bible. The author then turns to music, which is so noble and useful that Church office must be reserved only for those who have acquired a suitable level of understanding of the discipline because "whatever is gracefully announced in readings, and whatever is sung sweetly from the Psalms in the Church, is governed by the knowledge of this discipline. And not only do we read and chant Psalms in the Church through it, but we also duly fulfill every service of God."[30] He then presents the thoughts of Augustine and Cassiodorus on the discipline before differentiating astronomy from astrology as Isidore does. He ends by justifying the study of astronomy for calculating the date for Easter.

Overall, Rabanus combined the concerns of Pope Gregory the Great and Augustine on education, which needs to be pursued for its spiritual and pastoral rewards.

---

[28] Rabanus Maurus, *On the Formation of Clergy*, 3.20, 183.
[29] Ibid., 3.22, 186.
[30] Ibid., 3.24, 188.

CHAPTER 12

John Scotus Eriugena

*Where there are reason and intellect I should not believe
that the Image of God is absent.*[1]

—John Scotus Eriugena

12.1 THE THIRD GENERATION
OF CAROLINGIAN SCHOLARS

THE THIRD GENERATION OF THE
Carolingian Renaissance begins with Charlemagne's
grandson, Charles the Bald (King of West Francia,
843–877 AD), who led the Second Carolingian Renaissance.
The most important educational and cultural centers of the
Frankish realms were under his authority. These included
Saint-Vaast, Saint-Riquier, Saint-Amand, Corbie, Saint-Denis,
Saint-Germain-des-Pres, and Saint-Germain-d'Auxerre. Charles
himself had received a decent education, certainly more than
Charlemagne had, and was interested in the monastic life. He
was a book collector and was not only personally interested in
philosophy, but promoted its teaching, particularly as a support for theology. As well, he had a love for Hellenism, Greek
Orthodox liturgical splendor, and the use of Greek forms of
address for him as king, including *"anax, archos, autokrator,
kurios, monarchos, agathos, orthodoxos."*[2]

The most famous scholar at the palace school of the third
generation was John Scotus Eriugena,[3] perhaps the most richly-
educated and insightful western philosopher of the period from
500 to 1050 AD. He shared the king's love for the liberal arts,

---

[1] Eriugena, *Periphyseon*, Book 2, 732D, 368.
[2] John O'Meara, "Introduction," in *Periphyseon*, trans. by John O'Meara (Bel-larmin, 1987), 12. The information from this paragraph is from O'Meara.
[3] Eriugena is often confused with the great Franciscan scholastic, John Duns Scotus (c. 1265–1308), who hailed from Scotland.

and believed that they were found within each human and offered a path to salvation. He declared that "no one enters into heaven except through philosophy" and echoed Augustine's temporary thinking at the time of his conversion in 386 AD that authority did not need religion, but that "authority aided by reason was more desirable than authority alone; reason depended on some authority so that it might begin to operate; and reason could arrive at an understanding of what was taught by authority."[4]

Eriugena continued and renewed earlier currents of philosophical thought and practice that were highly relevant to the Christian life. In fact, he represents the best of several strands in early medieval Christian education: the Irish, the Carolingian, and the Christian philosopher. He brings together, perhaps more fully than any other thinker since Origen, the notion of the philosophical and the Christian life. To pursue philosophy means to pursue the wisdom that Christ personifies, that Christ *is*. He was the most important thinker on Christian education since Augustine in his revelation of the spiritual aspects of the liberal arts and philosophy, and how the study of these disciplines fit into the Christian life.

12.2 THE LIBERAL ARTS

The third generation of Carolingian scholars passionately took to Martianus Capella's allegorical work *On the Marriage of Philology and Mercury*. This enthusiasm contributed to the central place of allegory in later medieval centuries. Some earlier Carolingian scholars had also been influenced by Capella's work. Remi d'Auxerre, one of the earlier Carolingian scholars to analyze *On the Marriage of Philology and Mercury*, authored a commentary on Capella's text.[5] The later Carolingians, who were keen admirers of Capella's synthesis of Greco-Roman culture,

---

[4] O'Meara, "Introduction," 13.
[5] Guillaumin, "Introduction," in Martianus Capella, *Les Noces de Philologie et de Mercure. Livre VII. L'Arithmetique*, xxxii.

based their own educational program on his work.[6] Eriugena
produced a commentary on Capella's poem. *On the Marriage
of Philology and Mercury* strongly influenced his thinking on
the liberal arts. Central to this influence was the Neoplatonic
ordering of reality as progressing out from the One, the monad,
and then returning to the One. In his *Periphyseon* (*On the
Division of Nature*), Eriugena adopts this scheme.[7] He followed
both Augustine and the Greek Fathers in regarding created
things as proceeding from God, who alone is permanent, in
two stages. The intelligible world, which is created and creates,
emerged first. The intelligible world then created the world of
things that can be perceived by our sensory organs and that is
created and does not create.[8] This follows Capella's main idea.

For Eriugena, such matters were not merely abstractions,
but had practical relevance. In the same vein as some Church
Fathers who blamed heretical thoughts on deficient reason,
Eriugena believed that heretical thoughts arose from a lack of
knowledge of the liberal arts.[9] In the *Periphyseon*, he closely
links reason, which is developed through the study of these
disciplines, with contemplation. The mind that contemplates
and discourses on the divine and primordial causes and its
order is granted knowledge of these causes. The pious philosopher—by which Eriugena undoubtedly means the Christian
philosopher—can start this contemplation from any one of the
primordial causes and let his reason arrive at the other causes
in any order. He can contemplate any number of these causes
and cease his contemplation at any one of them.[10] Reason
constitutes the core of this activity. As we saw in chapter three,
reason runs through all the liberal arts and brings unity and

---

[6] Guillaumin, "Introduction," in Martianus Capella, *Les Noces de Philologie et
de Mercure. Livre VII. L'Arithmetique*, xxxiii.

[7] O'Meara, "Introduction," 13.

[8] Marenbon, *Early Medieval Philosophy (480–1150)*, 61. The most important
Greek influences on the *Periphyseon* were the Platonist Church Fathers Gregory
of Nyssa, Dionysius the Areopagite, and Maximus the Confessor.

[9] O'Meara, "Introduction," 14.

[10] Eriugena, *Periphyseon*, Book 3, 624C, 239–240.

sense to them. From the ancient Greeks onward, it was believed that wisdom developed not only through spiritual practice and maturity, but also through learning about the physical world, in large part guided and processed by reason.

As we have seen with other Christian authorities, there is a contemplative aspect at the heart of this learning. A reasonable God created a reasonable world that can be investigated by human reason, a process that leads to contemplation of God's creation. This alignment of human reason with the reason behind the universe and its creation reflects man's position as a microcosm of the macrocosm. This view or practice remained remarkably consistent for centuries and was a central pillar of the Christian appropriation of Greco-Roman paideia. Contemplation is not anti-intellectual. It does not turn away from reason or sensory perception, but fulfills it.

12.3 REASON AND INTELLECT

Like many early medieval thinkers, then, Eriugena saw an under-lying *ratio* to everything and found inspiration in this idea to guide his own thinking. In the *Periphyseon*, he equates *ratio* with *rationabilis investigatio*, rational or reasoned investigation. A reasoned investigation of something must follow from *vera ratio*, true reasoning. With this scheme, Eriugena proved to be the sharpest dialectical thinker in the West since Boethius. He was certainly the most innovative western thinker in the Early Middle Ages. He informs us that division is the starting point of his investigation. The first and most basic division that the mind can grasp is into things that are and that are not.[11] Thus the Irishman begins his dialectic work with ontology.

This use of dialectic is ambitious, though it is based on the teachings of previous authorities. Eriugena adopts Boethius's notion of "beginning with the simplest and most directly obvi-ous concepts." Boethius argues that every inquiry needs to begin

---

[11] Eriugena, *Periphyseon*, Book I, 441A, 25.

with *conceptiones communes*, commonly understood ideas.[12] The second element is the *iter rationis*, the rational path or method that guides an investigation from the lower questions to those that only the educated can grasp.[13] This is followed by justification, or demonstration, based on assertions that remove doubt. The fourth, and most controversial, is the requirement that reason (*recta ratio*) and authority (*vera auctoritas*) agree (*vera ratio*). The author of the *Periphyseon* foreshadows another famous dialectician, Abelard, in asserting that reason can sort out contradictions among Church authorities. As we have seen, he notes that authoritative assertions are weak if not confirmed by reason, but that true reason does not need confirmation from authority.[14] The next stage is the meeting of rational discourse with the intellectual vision, which is the experience of a kind of intuition. This is a necessary step because not all contradictions can be resolved at the level of rational discourse.[15] The person at this stage is passing to the illuminative stage. This scheme combines dialectic, ontology, psychology, and contemplation.

The last step involves a transformation in cognition, as the "movement of reason" passes to "the movement of the intellect, which is the simple understanding of things and their multiple causes in a unique cause." This correspondence between the activity of the intellect and "the mode of existence of things" is the macro-micro correspondence. This relationship reveals the alignment of the cosmos and man, as they are both made by the same Logos Creator, and based on identical principles.[16] The spiritual reality of this creative principle calls forth contemplation as the only appropriate response. Contemplation, man's humble gaze upon the created order and his place in it, is the attitude of receptivity and passive, yet total attention.

---

[12] Agnieszka Kijewska, "La Conception de la *Vera/Recta Ratio* dans le *Periphyseon de Jean Scot Erigene*," 25–38, 27.

[13] Eriugena, *Periphyseon*, Book 1, 503D–504A, 98–99.

[14] Thomas Cahill, *How the Irish Saved Civilization*, (Sceptre, 2018), 209.

[15] Kijewska, "La Conception de la *Vera/Recta Ratio* dans le *Periphyseon de Jean Scot Erigene*," 32.

[16] Ibid., 33.

Eriugena reminds us that beauty is the attractive force for contemplation. This last level is the ultimate goal of cognition. The external natures of things, which are known to humans in their physical forms, and are perceived by the senses, vary greatly in time, location, and the other accidents. Their beauty, which is displayed through these accidents, attracts the carnal mind. This mind becomes more distant from truth and unity, and wastes its energy in its dissipation in this multiplicity of the physical and temporal world, when it excessively loves these physical things. In contrast, the wise mind is attracted to the interior natures of things, that is, to the intelligible essences. The wise mind can perceive "their simple and indivisible unity within themselves and among themselves," and find delight in these ontological realities, particularly in the contemplation of "the beauty of their harmony and fellowship."[17] Eriugena provides perhaps the best explanation of the purpose of the trivium and quadrivium of nearly any early medieval writer. The study of these disciplines leads to the contemplative mind beholding the universe. This is enabled by the parallelism between the orders of being and of knowledge.

Learning about the world develops reason through the ascent and descent between *intellectus* (gk. *noesis*) and *ratio* (gk. *logos*).[18] Eriugena takes the reader through the trajectory of this unity of knowledge, from wisdom to science to virtue. He starts by identifying the relationship between wisdom and contemplation. Wisdom "is that power by which the contemplative mind, whether human or angelic, contemplates the eternal and immutable things of God, whether it concerns itself about the First Cause of all things or about the primordial causes of nature which the Father created at once and all together in His Word; and this species of reason is called by the wise theology."[19]

---

[17] Eriugena, *Periphyseon*, Book 3, 544B–C, 144–145.
[18] Kijewska, "La Conception de la *Vera/Recta Ratio* dans le *Periphyseon de Jean Scot Erigene*," 34.
[19] Eriugena, *Periphyseon*, Book 3, 629A, 245.

The author of the *Periphyseon* next points out the nature
and task of science, which is quite different from the place
and nature of wisdom. Science's nature and task include the
division of things into genera and species. Interestingly, Eriugena does not associate any decline in contemplation with
science. He defines science as "the power by which the contemplative mind, whether human or angelic," enquires into and
"discourses on the nature of the things which proceed from the
primordial causes through generation and which are divided
into genera and species by means of differences and properties,
whether it is susceptible to accidents or free from them, whether
joined to bodies or altogether free from them, whether it is
distributed over places and times or, outside place and time, is
unified and indivisible by reason of [its] simplicity; and this
species of reason is called physics."[20] He finishes this section
by observing that the teaching of virtues properly comes after
physics, because this latter deals with the natures of things as
apprehended by the senses.[21]

Eriugena achieved the fusion of scholastic Neoplatonism
(in the sense that the liberal arts and philosophy elevate the
soul to the One, God), Biblical exegesis, and the Christian
ascetic life of contemplation. His writings, more than almost
any other authority since Origen, show how Greek paideia
complements the Christian life. Ultimately, Eriugena follows
Plato and Augustine in assigning the highest knowledge to the
intellect, although the Irishman's scheme requires grace because
while the human must seek, "to find is His alone Who illumines
the hidden places of darkness. His also is the demonstration
because He [alone] can open the sense of those who seek and
the intellect. For of what use is a demonstration from without
if there is not illumination within?"[22] This is the receptivity
that enables the contemplation of the universe. One scholar
reminds us of how tremendous Eriugena's achievement here

---

[20] Eriugena, *Periphyseon*, Book 3, 629A–B, 245.
[21] Ibid., 629B, 245.
[22] Ibid., 656D–657A, 278.

is in applying dialectic in a way that no one else in the early medieval Latin West could, in a world that was producing much less advanced philosophy. Reading his *Periphyseon* is therefore striking because it returns us to "the world of Plato. Here is a mind that could grasp the most rarefied distinctions of the Greek philosophical tradition and, far more important, could elaborate a new system of thought, one that is balanced and internally consistent."[23]

12.4 PSYCHOLOGY AND NUMBERS

Eriugena's psychology is unparalleled in the early western Middle Ages in its elegant fusion of Greek paideia and Neoplatonic philosophy with Christian spirituality. He begins by outlining the unity and multiplicity found in numbers. He defines force as "the substantial virtue by which they ['numbers in the Monad'] subsist eternally and immutably in the Monad" and power as "the possibility, innate in them, by which they are able to be multiplied and *become* manifest to intellects by certain terminological distinctions, quantitative diversities, differential intervals, (and) the wonderful equality and indissoluble harmony of proportion and proportionalities."[24] At the heart of this is not the language of the trivium, but the number logic or numerology of the quadrivium.

The following is likely the clearest description of the contemplative nature of the quadrivial disciplines that exists. It also indicates that the concept of the monad is more than simply an eccentric, long-forgotten concept, but that it is at the heart of the quadrivium. The mind contemplates numbers by moving from the monad into the diversity of genus and species, and from there, with "the eye of the intellect," beyond quantity, quality, time, and place, beholding their simple, purest nature, devoid of body or imagery.[25] There is a sense of movement in

---

[23] Cahill, *How the Irish Saved Civilization*, 209.
[24] Eriugena, *Periphyseon*, Book 3, 657D, 279.
[25] Ibid., 657D, 279–280.

this, which ultimately refers to the mind's upward movement in its contemplation of numbers.

Erigiuna then refers to the metaphysical properties of the content of the quadrivium and their apprehension by the contemplative mind. He describes the operation of the mind as it consigns to memory the pure numbers that it considers in themselves and that come to be embodied by physical images. This operation works to put these numbers into order so that the mind can more easily deal with them. It is at this point, after having connected the pure number to the physical world, that the contemplator or scholar can convey the truths of these numbers to others. This master must not forget, however, that these numbers were not established by the human intellect (which his pride might trick him into believing), but by "the Creator and Multiplicator and Ordainer of all things Himself." Eriugena claims that the immutability and harmony that is found within them is proof enough to believe this.[26]

In the next section, Eriugena describes the ascent and descent of the student- or scholar-ascetic based on the operations of the *intellectus* and *ratio*. He first establishes a Neoplatonic approach to the connection between the Creator and the monad. He reminds his reader that it is erroneous to think that simply because the intellect contemplates the intellectual numbers, it creates them. Instead, it is God who created these numbers in the human and angelic intellects, just as He established them for all eternity in the monad even though from there they descend to human knowledge via the intellect.[27]

Given the intellect's central role in all of this, unsurprisingly, the author of the *Periphyseon* then provides insight into the nature of the intellect. This includes the connection between the intellect and the liberal arts, and how the intellect discovers the individual arts. The liberal art in question is initially "contained within the most hidden recesses of the intellectual

---

[26] Eriugena, *Periphyseon*, Book 3, 657D–658A, 280.
[27] Ibid., 658A–658B, 280

nature, is all together and a simple unity without parts or divisions, without quantity or quality, without place or time, and altogether free from all accidents and barely known to the intellect alone." Through the intellect's contemplation, this art "begins to descend by an intelligible progress into the reason from its secret places in which it is all one in the mind in which it is, soon it gradually begins to reveal by evident divisions and differences its hidden structure, though as yet in a most pure form free from all imagery—and this initial process of the art out of that science in which it originally subsists is directed by the act of the intellect itself through the intellect to the reason."[28] Here we have a clear understanding of an academic discipline or liberal art that is based on uncreated truths.

Eriugena described the connection between reason and the intellect in the understanding of an individual liberal art. It is the operation of the intellect that is responsible for everything that is hidden in nature to come into the purview of reason. This is the first descent of this truth. A second descent of this truth occurs when this moves from reason to memory. The art in question then becomes associated with images, which enables its clearer distinction from the other arts. The third descent is its apprehension by the physical senses, "where by sensible signs it exhibits its powers by means of genera and species and all its divisions and subdivisions and particulars."[29] Eriugena then gives an overview of this process. He highlights that the descent of the intellectual numbers, which starts with the monad, enables their lights to be present in the mind, and from there to reason, by which "they reveal themselves more openly; next, descending from the reason into the memory they receive from the nature of the memory itself phantasmal appearances in which they clearly reveal the powers of their multiple forms to those that inquire into them, [then into the senses, lastly into figures]."[30]

---

[28] Eriugena, *Periphyseon*, Book 3, 658B–658C, 280.
[29] Ibid., 658A–658D, 280–281.
[30] Ibid., 658C–658D, 281.

The conclusion of this brings together the highest aspect of human psychology and the eternal, unchanging, and objective metaphysical reality of numbers that underpins the cosmos: "Do you then see the three things which you had searched for, the How, and the Where, and the Whence? From the Monad. Where? In the intellect. How? By different stages: first they descend from themselves into the intellect; from the intellect into the reason; from the reason into the memory; from the memory into the corporeal senses; and, if it is required for the benefit of students, by a final stage from the senses into visible figures."[31] In addition to the quadrivium, the sole trivial discipline that plays a significant role in this process is dialectic through its direction of reason. This is the dialectic that Plato imagines to be capable of acting as a guide to the truth. Eriugena is therefore faithful to Platonism with this schema.

The author of the *Periphyseon* provided a powerful philosophical foundation to the quadrivium. This foundation starts from his description of numbers in terms that closely parallel Plato's eternal Ideas. The intellectual numbers that are found in each science exist eternally in the monad from the moment of creation, and are made manifest through their expression as numbers from two onward (assuming that the monad, One, is not counted as a number).[32] Eriugena adheres to the thinking of Boethius and Capella on the quadrivium. He describes the philosophical aspect of the first quadrivial discipline, which does not consider the counting function of numbers, noting that "the wise say that it is *not* the numbers of animals, fruits, crops, and other bodies or things that belong to the science of arithmetic, but they assign to arithmetic only the intellectual, invisible, incorporeal (numbers) which are constituted in the science alone but reside in no subject" other than themselves.[33] Eriugena outlines the psychological process to this. Humans cannot discern them as they truly are in any physical or imagined

---

[31] Eriugena, *Periphyseon*, Book 3, 658D–659A, 281.

[32] Ibid., 656C, 278.

[33] Ibid., 651B, 272.

object, which is one reason why they are not connected to the countable things of this world. Because incorporeal numbers are beyond any academic discipline, only the intellect, through wisdom and science, can discern them. "The excellence of their divine nature" is another reason why these pure numbers do not have any relationship with the countable things of this world.[34] Following the practice of the Church Fathers, the Irishman brings Greek philosophy together with Scripture: "The infinite multitude of all things visible and invisible assumes its substance according to the rules of numbers which arithmetic contemplates, as the supreme philosopher Pythagoras, the first inventor of this art, testifies when he gives good reason for asserting that the intellectual numbers are the substances of all things visible and invisible. Nor does Holy Scripture deny this, for it says that all things have been made in measure and number and weight."[35]

The philosophical foundation to arithmetic begins with the monad, as we saw in chapter four. The monad was not considered to be a number by many ancient and medieval authorities, including Eriugena:

> The first progression of the numbers is from the Monad; and the first multiplication is Δυάς, that is, the number two, the second Τριάς, the number three, the third thereafter the number four, then all the terms, each established in its own place. And the number two is the source of all parity which falls within (the view of) the intellect, but the number three is the source of all disparity. And from these, I mean from parity and disparity, all kinds of numbers are generated whether simple or composite. [The simple are the even and the odd, the composite those that are made up of both these, the evenly even, the evenly odd, the oddly even.][36]

Much of this discussion of the metaphysical reality of numbers could have been developed independently of Revelation, yet Eriugena endeavored to give this number philosophy a Christian sense.

---

[34] Eriugena, *Periphyseon*, Book 3, 651C–651D, 272.
[35] Ibid., 652A, 273.
[36] Ibid., 654A–654B, 275.

12.5 ERIUGENA'S NEOPLATONISM

When discussing the creation of the world, Eriugena brings up the fourfold division of wisdom in the second book of the *Periphyseon*. This division reflects the ascendent trajectory of Neoplatonism and demonstrates its connection to the Christian life. It begins with virtue, also called the practical (πρακτική or *pratiké*), which is followed by the natural (φυσική or *phusiké*), the theological (θεολογία or *theologia*), and the rational or logical (λογική or *logiké*). The rational reveals the means by which the first three are to be discussed. The virtues are examined by replacing and eradicating the vices. Nature is investigated through causes and effects. Theological reason is concerned with the pious thinking regarding God, the ultimate cause of all.[37]

In a later part of the *Periphyseon*, Eriugena notes that both man and the angels have rational and intellectual powers. The primary division in the life of the universe in between rational and irrational life. Rational life can be separated into humans and angels. The rational life in humans is called rational, but intellectual in angels, although both angels and men have both the rational and the intellectual faculties, "and therefore intellectual and rational life is predicated of both as a common form . . . and where there are reason and intellect I should not believe that the Image of God is absent."[38] The last sentence provides a key insight that supports the Christian development of Greek paideia. It is the connection of "rational life" with God.

Yet, this rationality cannot by itself bring us into the metaphysical realm. It cannot provide us with the pure knowledge of the metaphysical properties of numbers or of anything else. As we have seen, for this we need another psycho-spiritual organ, the intellect. Contemplation enables man to pass from the lower, rational understanding to higher intellect-based understanding. Eriugena's anthropology expresses the tremendous esteem that

---

[37] Eriugena, *Periphyseon*, Book 3, 705B, 336.
[38] Ibid., 732C–732D, 368.

the Church has always had for humans, and why the Church prioritized education, at least for the elite and the leaders of the Church, in the medieval period. Man has great potential, and this explain, Eriugena poetically acknowledges, "why man is not inappropriately called the workshop of all creatures since in him the universal creature is contained. [For] he has intellect like an angel, reason like a man, sense like an [irrational] animal, life like a plant, and subsists in body and soul: [there is no creature that he is without]. [For] outside these you (will) find no creature."[39] This is a clear definition and image of man as the microcosmos.

Eriugena's impact on the Church did not match his brilliant insights into all these truths. William Turner in his entry on him at *The Catholic Encyclopedia of 1913* sums up the thinker's influence on the Church as marked by controversy:

> Eriugena's influence on the theological thought of his own and immediately subsequent generations was doubtless checked by the condemnations to which his doctrines of predestination and of the Eucharist were subjected in the Councils of Valencia (855), Langres (859), and Vercelli (1050). The general trend of his thought, so far as it was discernible at the time of his translations of Pseudo-Dionysius, was referred to with suspicion in a letter addressed by Pope Nicholas I to Charles the Bald in 859. It was not, however, until the beginning of the thirteenth century that the pantheism of the "De Divisione Naturae" was formally condemned. The Council of Paris (1225) coupled the condemnation of Eriugena's work with the previous condemnations (1210) of the doctrines of Amalric of Chartres and David of Dinant, and there can be no doubt that the pantheists of that time were using Eriugena's treatise. While the great Scholastic teachers, Abelard, Alexander of Hales, St. Bonaventure, St. Thomas, and Albert the Great knew nothing, apparently, of Eriugena and his pantheism, certain groups of mystical theologians, even as early as the thirteenth century, were interested in his work and drew their doctrines from it. The Albigenses, too, sought inspiration from him. Later, the Mystics, especially Meister Eckhart, were influenced by

---

[39] Eriugena, *Periphyseon*, Book 3, 733B, 369.

him. And in recent times the great transcendental idealists, especially the Germans, recognize in him a kindred spirit and speak of him in the highest terms.[40]

Given the subtleties of Eriugena's thought in an age of grammar, in other words, in an age that was simply trying to get the basics correct, it is unsurprising that he would run into trouble, including long after his death. There is a basis for asserting that his thought is indeed pantheistic, though Thomas Cahill points out that for Eriugena *nature* denotes *reality*, "all of reality, our natural world as well as the reality of God. In Scotus there is no useful distinction between natural and supernatural. Though the system is both subtle and elaborate, one sees immediately his debt to Patrick's simple worldview. Reality is a continuum, and all God's creatures are theophanies of God himself, for God speaks in them and through them."[41] Cahill seems to be suggesting that Eriugena was misinterpreted because this element of the Irish sense of nature was not appreciated by minds on the Continent.

The controversies that surrounded the Irish scholar made him into a theological underground figure, similar to Meister Eckhart and Jakob Boehme, whose thought systems were never fully integrated into mainstream theology. Perhaps Eriugena's attempts to Christianize his Neoplatonic perspective were too metaphysical or mystical for the age of grammar. The influence of Dionysius the Areopagite created a gulf between Eriugena and most of the Middle Ages, as the Areopagite's theology had also not been assimilated into the Latin Church at that time, if it ever has been. Yet in one notable area of Christian education, Eriugena retains a theologically-orthodox anthropology. This is in his sense of the power of original sin to distort the intellect (*nous*), which he places above the human reasoning faculty (*logos*). His sense of original sin prompts him to place important limits on human knowledge even as he adopts the

---

[40] William Turner, "Eriugena, John Scotus," in The Catholic Encyclopedia, Knight of Columbus Special Edition 1913, Volume 05, Charles G. Herbermann, et. al, eds. (New York: The Encyclopedia Press, 1913), 519–522, 521.
[41] Cahill, *How the Irish Saved Civilization*, 209.

ascendant and ambitious Neoplatonic understanding of the liberal arts and philosophy.

12.6 THE TENTH AND EARLY ELEVENTH CENTURIES

Eriugena represents the highest philosophical achievement of the Early Middle Ages in the Latin West, a bright spot in an intellectual landscape that would not truly awaken for more than two centuries after him. The growing social and political instability of the tenth century compared to the three great generations of the Carolingian Renaissance led to a sharp decline in education. The monasteries once again played their role as reservoir of knowledge and learning until the renowned cathedral schools of northern France in the twelfth century. The monastery at St. Gall, for example, was a bright spot of learning in the tenth century, with Notker the Stammerer (died in 912 AD),[42] Tuotilo (died in 915 AD), Ekkehard I (died in 973 AD), and Moengal among others. Many of these scholars, such as Notker, built their reputations on their music theories.

The love for science, technology, and learning of Gerbert of Aurillac (946–1003 AD, Pope Sylvester II, 999–1003 AD) included "Arabic" numerals, mathematics, astronomy, the abacus (from the Spanish Arabs), and the armillary sphere. He taught at France's leading cathedral school in Reims from 972 to 996 AD, eventually becoming headmaster, though he left in disgrace. In addition to geometry and arithmetic, he taught a pre-rhetoric course that included the poetry of Virgil, Statius, and Terence, the satirical writings of Juvenal, Persius, and Horace, and the histories of Lucian.[43] "Gerbert's letters hint at his teaching philosophy. He speaks of the importance of 'a mind conscious of itself,' of studying mathematics 'for the utmost exercise of the mind' and astronomy 'in order not to grow inwardly lazy.'"[44]

---

[42] Also known as Notker of St. Gall.
[43] Richer of Reims, *Histoire de Richer*, tome deuxième, trans. J. Gaudet (Jules Renouard, 1845), p. 59.
[44] Nancy Marie Brown, *The Abacus and the Cross* (Basic Books, 2010), p. 69.

There were oft-repeated reasons for studying the liberal arts. Yet there is little of Eriugena's metaphysical ambitions here. One continuation from the Irish, Anglo-Saxons, and Carolingians is the fondness and expressions of love that Gerbert expresses in letters to his former students, which reflect the close tutor-student relationship, a relationship that recognized virtue in the other: "Gerbert's school at Reims was founded on this Ciceronian code of friendship, on the mutual desire of friends to better each other."[45] Etienne Gilson describes Gerbert as the very embodiment of the seven disciplines of the liberal arts. That this could be said of a figure in this era of decline reveals the staying power of the liberal arts through the medieval era's ups and downs.

Gerbert's experimental, empirical approach to the quadrivium foreshadowed that of Robert Grosseteste (1161–1253 AD), as exemplified in Gerbert's search for "a law for computing the dimensions of an organ pipe that would sound the same note as the string of a certain length on the monochord."[46] This reflects the Christian spirit of the medieval quadrivium. Gerbert's surprisingly modern approach to science was prompted by his typically medieval search for the unity of God's creation. The mathematical order that Gerbert sought was the one that God had established and about which Augustine had already written.[47] Therefore, even though Gerbert adopted certain empirical methods, his quadrivial science differed notably from modern science and retained a core metaphysical and contemplative dimension.

---

[45] Brown, *The Abacus and the Cross*, 72.
[46] Ibid., 106.
[47] Ibid.

CHAPTER 13

Education in the Byzantine Empire up to the Macedonian Renaissance

Every soul that delights in instruction will revel and find joy..., and in its love for God it will be aroused by a sacred passion to pious imitation.
— The Life of St. John the Almsgiver[1]

13.1 CONTINUITY WITH ANCIENT ROOTS

WHILE EDUCATION IN THE BYZAN-tine Empire shared many commonalities with western education, it also diverged in significant ways. Most notably, the Church did not directly dominate education as thoroughly as it did in the Latin world, even though many priests taught at all levels, from grammar to rhetoric. Second, education thrived when supported by a single, dominant ruler, the emperor, even if most first- and second-level schools were private, whereas western education in Spain or Ireland had done without the same level of political support. Third, Greek, not Latin, was the classroom language. Byzantine students knew little-to-nothing of Donatus, Priscian, Cicero, or Virgil. Lastly, education remained an urban phenomenon, while in the West education was largely centered on the mostly-rural monasteries. However, a significant parallel with the West was the centrality of the trivium and quadrivium, though even here, there was a distinction. While grammar was of the greatest concern in

---

[1] *The Life of St. John the Almsgiver* in *Three Byzantine Saints: Contemporary Biographies of St. Daniel the Stylite, St. Theodore of Sykeon and St. John the Almsgiver,* trans. Elizabeth Dawes, and introductions and notes by Norman H. Baynes, (London, 1948).

the early medieval West, rhetoric was the most highly-regarded trivial discipline among the Byzantines. There was nevertheless a common spirit here too, as the concern in the Byzantine Empire for proper language usage mirrored that of the West.

There was not as much of a Christian ascetic sense in certain aspects of Byzantine liberal arts education as there was in the West in the same period, as both laymen and priests taught the foundational liberal arts in cities. Educators in the empire still maintained the original meaning of *paideia*, that is, education and culture. Similar to Ireland's dual cultural-educational model which continued the pre-Christian culture and teaching, support in the Byzantine Empire for Greek-based education reflected enthusiasm for secular Greek culture alongside the dominant Christian culture. Rejected by the majority for much of the Byzantine period was the notion that this secular culture and education were somehow in competition with Christianity. Education in the liberal arts and philosophy therefore retained a stronger secular quality and greater independence than in the Latin West.

As in the West, the foundational discipline of grammar was the most common course. Most students did not go beyond this instruction. Education began with the *propaideia* (προπαιδεία), from whence comes the word *propaedeutic*, denoting *prerequisite*. This foundational content, *grammata* (γράμματα), was taught by the *grammatistes* or, less commonly, the *paidodidaskalos*, *paidotribes*, or *paidagogos*. George Choiroboskos's textbooks on grammar and philology, mirroring those of Donatus for Latin students in the West, contained the expected commentaries on orthography, Greek verb declensions, and prosody. It kept to the older grammar of Denys of Thrace (170–90 BC). The propaideia cycle was succeeded by the paideia (παιδεία) cycle, which was offered in privately-run schools in cities and taught by the *grammatikos* or *maistor*.[2] This teaching, rooted in the pre-Christian world and its numerous pagan texts, was called

---

[2] Markopoulos, "Education," 788.

Hellenike sophia (ἑλληνικὴ σοφία) or *enkyklios paideia* (ἐγκύκλιος παιδεία). Throughout the Byzantine era, the Church was intimately involved in this supposedly secular tradition of education, with lessons even being held in churches or monasteries because of the large numbers of clergy serving as *grammatistai*.

Instead of being set once and for all, the curriculum depended on the school. The typical school had one master with several assistants, who were normally upper year students helping to instruct the lower levels. Even monastic novices received a basic secular education in writing, reading, grammar, and calligraphy for future service in the monastery, often as a secretary or copyist.[3] The grammar-rhetoric boundary was, as always, unclear, even though one tool, the progymnasmata, was in constant and consistent use. The progymnasmata referred to the series of exercises that developed oratorical skills based on the texts of the second century Hermogenus of Tarsus and the fourth century Aphthonios of Antioch. These exercises provided a bridge from grammar to rhetoric class. Over the centuries, school masters updated these manuals. The mid-twelfth century professor of exegesis, Nicephorus Basilakes, for example, wrote a textbook on the progymnasmata. Just like in the Latin West, there was little attempt or reward for innovation. The ultimate objective of Byzantine rhetoric was the faithful reproduction of the prescribed, age-old models.[4]

Philosophy was the most highly-esteemed discipline after rhetoric. Byzantine philosophy closely continued the pagan foundations, particularly Neoplatonism, even while, over the centuries, philosophy took on a wider range of meanings in the empire. The considerable overlapping of rhetoric and philosophy meant that philosophy could refer to eloquence, but also to education in general, which idealized encyclopedic knowledge. It could even signify Christian spirituality, including monasticism and martyrdom.[5] The following standard six items in fifth

---

[3] Lemerle, *Le premier humanisme byzantine*, 102.
[4] Ibid., 255.
[5] Katerina Ierodiakonou and Dominic O'Meara, "Philosophies," in *The Oxford*

and sixth-century schools in Athens and Alexandria took into account the etymology of *philo-sophia* while also expanding the sense: (1) the knowledge of beings (ontology); (2) the knowledge of God and man and what concerns them (anthropology and theology); (3) the preparation for death; (4) man's fullest possible assimilation to God; (5) "the art of arts and the science of sciences"; and (6) the most literal meaning of all, the love of wisdom.[6] At the same time, out of the Byzantine Church, as out of its Latin counterpart in the West, came a lively and expressive stream of Church leaders opposed to Greek paideia. For example, Theodore of Cyrus (393–458 AD) set himself against Hellenism in general in the *Cure of the Greek Maladies: The Truth of the Gospel proved from Greek Philosophy*. But such public opinions remained in the minority.

13.2 HELLENISM AND CHRISTIANITY

The relative independence of education in the empire raised the never ending issue of Hellenism and its place among a mostly faithful Christian population, even if Alexandria's Catechetical School under Clement and Origen had supposedly worked out the relationship of ancient Greek pagan culture and education with Christianity. The Catechetical School accomplished this by adapting the most favorable elements of the ancient pagan canon to Christianity as tools for developing the necessary skills in Biblical exegesis and theology.[7] The relative independence of Hellenism was not the result of indifference or hostility on the part of the Church, and a resulting attempt to wall off pagan culture and education from the faith. In fact, the foundations of Byzantine education came from the support for classical learning by the ancient Greek Church Fathers themselves. In his

---

Handbook of Byzantine Studies, ed. Elizabeth Jeffreys (Oxford University Press, 2008), 712.

[6] The authors further note that these definitions were Aristotelian (1,5), Stoic (2), and Platonic (3,4). Ierodiakonou, "Philosophies," 712.

[7] Tatakis, *Byzantine Philosophy*, 5.

oft-cited eulogy for St. Basil in 379 AD, Gregory of Nazianzus describes how his friendship with Basil developed from their shared passion for learning:

> Athens, which has been to me, if to any one, a city truly of gold, and the patroness of all that is good. For it brought me to know Basil more perfectly, though he had not been unknown to me before; and in my pursuit of letters, I attained to happiness; and in another fashion had the same experience as Saul, 1 Samuel 9:3, who, seeking his father's asses, found a kingdom, and gained incidentally what was of more importance than the object which he had in view.... We were contained by Athens, like two branches of some river-stream, for after leaving the common fountain of our fatherland, we had been separated in our varying pursuit of culture, and were now again united by the impulsion of God no less than by our own agreement. I preceded him by a little, but he soon followed me, to be welcomed with great and brilliant hope. For he was versed in many languages, before his arrival, and it was a great thing for either of us to outstrip the other in the attainment of some object of our study. And I may well add, as a seasoning to any speech, a short narrative, which will be a reminder to those who know it, a source of information to those who do not.[8]

Gregory's characterization of his shared love of learning with Basil idealizes Athens and its secular learning.

Gregory does concede, however, the secular motivations for the pursuit of Greek paideia for most students in his description of the decidedly non-Christian behavior of his peers. Countless students sought glory, not the Lord. There was always much truth to the oft-made connection of Greek education with materialism and a worldly mindset. The following from Gregory supports this connection:

> Most of the young men at Athens in their folly are mad after rhetorical skill — not only those who are ignobly born and unknown, but even the noble and illustrious, in the general mass of young men difficult to keep under control. They

---

[8] Gregory of Nazianzen, *Oration 43. Funeral Oration on the Great S. Basil, Bishop of Cæsarea in Cappadocia*, §14, in *New Advent*, https://www.newadvent.org/fathers/310243.htm.

are just like men devoted to horses and exhibitions, as we
see, at the horse-races; they leap, they shout, raise clouds
of dust, they drive in their seats, they beat the air, (instead
of the horses) with their fingers as whips, they yoke and
unyoke the horses, though they are none of theirs: they
readily exchange with one another drivers, horses, positions,
leaders: and who are they who do this? Often poor and
needy fellows, without the means of support for a single
day. This is just how the students feel in regard to their
own tutors, and their rivals, in their eagerness to increase
their own numbers and thereby enrich them. The matter is
absolutely absurd and silly. Cities, roads, harbours, mountain
tops, coastlines, are seized upon — in short, every part of
Attica, or of the rest of Greece, with most of the inhabitants;
for even these they have divided between the rival parties.[9]

The thirst for such glory was likely encouraged by the fact
that this education was primarily for the training of future
bureaucrats, not monks. At least as Gregory describes it, there
did not seem to be any accent on the training of holiness. This
sharply contrasts with the educational ideals of the West, in
this same period, as seen so powerfully with the role of the
nutritor as spiritual father in Anglo-Saxon and Irish education.
Nevertheless, Gregory of Nazianzus's argument that pagan
works benefited Christians would remain the enduring and
dominant view for centuries. It led Christian churchmen and
Hellenists to work out a *modus vivendi* between the Christian
life on the one hand and Greek literature and philosophy on
the other, that would impact each side for centuries, despite
the frequent inclination towards the ascetic and mystical life
in the Byzantine Empire.[10]

The wide acceptance of Greek paideia did not avert the
need for continuous negotiation over the precise relationship
between Hellenism and Christianity. Iconoclasm complicated
this relationship.[11] With the end of Iconoclasm in 843 AD,

---

[9] Nazianzen, *Oration 43. Funeral Oration on the Great S. Basil, Bishop of Cæsarea in Cappadocia*, §15.

[10] Markopoulos, "Education," 786.

[11] The strife between iconoclasts and iconophiles occurred from the early eighth to the mid-ninth centuries. The veneration of icons was prohibited in 730. After

Hellenism took on a higher, more venerable status, and the *intelligentsia*, if not the Eastern Church itself, became comfortable with a mostly-harmonious relationship between Eastern Christians on the one hand and the heirs of Socrates and the Sophists on the other hand. The resolution of this problem put another issue into the spotlight, which concerned the importance of Atticism for Hellenism. Would the written Greek of the Byzantine Empire follow in the spirit of the *koine* Greek of the New Testament, the common language of the first century Hellenic world, or emulate the high literary language of Attic Greek? The Byzantines followed the Church Fathers in favoring the latter. The ability to write in this high literary language became a point of pride for many Byzantine authors. Atticism encouraged a traditionalist spirit to Byzantine thought that may at times have discouraged innovation and change.[12] Though the *Septuagint* and the New Testament were studied, the preference for Atticism encouraged the continuous study of the classical authors Homer, Plato, Isocrates, Aristophanes, Euripides, and Thucydides and the development of lexica of Attic Greek vocabulary.[13] One reason Hellenism did not pose a threat to most Byzantines was the feeling that the empire was the continuation of the Roman Empire and that the Christian nature of society meant that the people were the heirs of the ancient Israelites as people of the new covenant.[14] Despite Atticism's triumph, the main figures of the Second Sophistic, from the first through sixth centuries AD, were also very influential, such as with Photios.

---

decades of iconoclast emperors, iconophiles held power from the 780s to 814, starting with the ascendency of Empress Irene in 780. In 788, the icons were restored. Icons were again prohibited in 815 after the iconoclasts took the throne back. The veneration of icons was restored definitively in 843 after the death of the last iconoclast emperor in the previous year.

[12] Tatakis, *Byzantine Philosophy*, 9.
[13] Herbert Hunger, "The Classical Tradition in Byzantine Literature: The Importance of Rhetoric," pp. 35–47 in *Byzantium and the Classical Tradition*, eds. Margaret Mullett and Roger Scott (Birmingham: Centre for Byzantine Studies, 1981), 43.
[14] Ibid., 54.

One reason for the difference between education in the East and West was that the Byzantine Empire did not face the same historical and cultural disunity that the West did. There was no break in schooling or institutions. Even in the so-called Dark Ages of the sixth-to-eighth centuries, this cultural and perhaps even institutional continuity meant that the Greek-speaking Church did not come to dominate education in the way that the western Church did through the cathedral schools and monasteries, which emerged in the educational and cultural vacuum of the West, when the bishops were forced by dire circumstances to take over public duties that had traditionally been ensured by government or local traditions. Byzantine monasteries did not become famous centers of learning as their western counterparts did.[15] There were no Fuldas or St. Galls.

13.3 A NEW CENTER OF LEARNING

The fourth and fifth centuries saw great intellectual activity, particularly in rhetoric and philosophy, with masters and students moving from one city to the next. Famous centers of learning operated over the length and breadth of the empire, including at Antioch, Alexandria, Nicomedia (until devastated by an earthquake in 357 AD), Caesarea of Palestine, Athens, Berytos, Gaza, Edessa, and Nisibus. Most of these schools were either fully Christian or combined traditional learning with catechism.[16] For example, Aeneas of Gaza (c. 450–534 AD), the author of the philosophical dialogue *Theophrastus*, developed a model of thinking that reflected the tendencies of other ancient Christian intellectuals. This model is "Greek philosophy in form and method, and an heir to Greek thought, but above all it is Christian in its aspirations and principles."[17] The ancient pedigrees of these schools could not prevent the emergence of Constantinople as the empire's seat of learning.

---

[15] Lemerle, *Le premier humanisme byzantine*, 47.
[16] Ibid., 51.
[17] Tatakis, *Byzantine Philosophy*, 23.

In the fourth century, the city became not only the educational capital of the empire, but also of text production with the establishment of the imperial scriptorium, which produced codices of parchment. This material lasted much longer than papyrus.[18] The operation of a large scriptorium indicates the presence of one or more sizable libraries.

The Christian spirit of learning in the capital (even with the continued reverence for pagan writers and the liberal arts) meant that the city's development into an educational center contributed to the decline of paganism and the pagan schools of Athens. Constantinople represented the future of education in the Byzantine Empire, Athens the past. Ironically, it was the pagan Themistios the Eloquent (317–c. 388 AD) who played a major role in Constantinople's emergence as the heart of Byzantine education after the mid-fourth century. He arrived in the city on the invitation of Emperor Constantius II (317–361 AD) to teach. He rose to the rank of senator. Themistios's contribution to education set the foundation for Emperor Theodosius II (408–450 AD) to establish the Pandidakterion, the Imperial University of Constantinople, in 425 AD. This was the first official foray of the Byzantine state into intellectual affairs, with the objective of establishing an educational system in parallel to the centuries-long and still-vibrant secular system.[19] As its professors were forbidden from teaching elsewhere, it would become the only non-ecclesiastical center of higher education in the empire.[20] Teachers and students from all over the empire and abroad were attracted to the city.[21]

The Pandidakterion reflects the enduring secular nature of state education in this most Christian city in the empire, as

---

[18] Lemerle, *Le premier humanisme byzantine*, 59.
[19] Markopoulos. "In Search For 'Higher Education' In Byzantium." 29–44, 34. The new institution was also called the School of Advanced Christian Studies.
[20] Lemerle, *Le premier humanisme byzantine*, 63. Lemerle agrees with the historian Émile Bréhier that "from the foundation of Constantinople to its end, an imperial university did not cease to exist." Lemerle, *Le premier humanisme byzantine*, 84. Others, such as Warren Treadgold, disagree.
[21] Tatakis, *Byzantine Philosophy*, 11.

the university specialized in educating state bureaucrats. In the rivalry between philosophy and rhetoric that took place in the institution, the latter won out, with Sophists and grammarians outnumbering philosophy professors. This was similar to the situation in Athens' pagan schools.[22] The Pandidakterion also reflects the rivalry between Latin and Greek in the fourth century, when students ambitious for government positions would have opted for Latin rhetoric over Greek. The school originally struck a rough balance between Greek and Latin teachers.[23] The number of masters was set at three *oratores* and ten *grammatici* for Latin, five *sofistae* and ten *grammatici* for Greek. One master in philosophy and two in law rounded out the teaching personnel.[24] The Byzantine tendency to develop polymaths instead of more specialized scholars is exemplified by the student of John Philoponos, Stephen of Alexandria, a professor at the Pandidakterion. Stephen gave instruction in Plato, Aristotle, and the quadrivial sciences.

The fifth century saw a sharp decline in educational or cultural unity between East and West. The linguistic rivalry between Latin and Greek lasted until 395 AD, when the empire was split into Latin- and Greek-speaking halves, after which it was only natural for the Byzantines to fully embrace their Hellenic roots. With the Latin West characterized and delimited by Latin, linguistic and cultural alienation rapidly grew between East and West. From the fifth century onward, except for a few cases, Greek was no longer known in Spain or the British Isles, nor in Gaul by the early sixth century. In many parts of Italy, by the year 600 AD the Greek Fathers were no longer read in the original.[25] Gregory the Great, papal legate to Constantinople and then pope from 590 to 604 AD, did not know Greek. John Scotus Eriugena was the only notable Hellenist in the West in the Early Middle Ages, which reflects some level of

---

[22] Tatakis, *Byzantine Philosophy*, 11.
[23] Markopoulos, "In Search For 'Higher Education' In Byzantium," 34.
[24] Tatakis, *Byzantine Philosophy*, 11.
[25] Lemerle, *Le premier humanisme byzantine*, 9–10.

Greek instruction in Ireland. The medieval Byzantine Empire was as alienated from the West as the West was from it. Thus, while from the western perspective, the most groundbreaking translations were from Greek or Arabic into Latin, rarely did translations go in the other direction. The monk Maximus Planudes (1260–1305 AD), famous for *The Greek Anthology*, translated from Latin (a mostly unknown language among Byzantine scholars of the time) Cicero, Ovid, Boethius, and Augustine. He was a rarity. On the whole, Latin authors were not well known in the empire. The empire's relatively secular Hellenism, whose impact on culture and education waxed and waned throughout the centuries, fostered a cultural identity primarily through Constantinople's classrooms that was separate from the identity fostered by the Church in its catechesis and training of monks and priests. No separate cultural entity would exist in the West for centuries.

Emperor Justinian (482–565 AD) played a pivotal role in bringing Greek paideia under the auspices of Christianity while giving it the freedom to flourish and maintain a relatively separate identity. He tried to increase the Christian influence over education with his edict in 529 that banned heretics, Jews, and pagans from teaching. For the same reason, he ordered the school of Athens closed in the same year. Its master, Damascius, was the last of "the 'golden chain' of the Platonic succession."[26] With this decision, Justinian destroyed the final rival to Christianity's cultural, social, and political domination of the empire and, as a sign of the success of this policy, Constantinople thrived as never before in its role as the center of Christianity. Athens' schools had been the last surviving outposts of paganism, and their closures were an attack on paganism. The crucial point is that the closures were not an attack on Hellenism in general or philosophy in particular. Classical literature not only flourished in Justin's era, but exerted a strong influence on

---

[26] John Edwin Sandys, *A History of Classical Scholarship* (Cambridge: Cambridge University Press, 1903), 368. Incidentally, 529 is traditionally taken as the year that St. Benedict of Nursia founded Monte Cassino.

Christian writers. There was no interruption in the study of the classical literary texts, which would remain popular throughout the history of the Byzantine Empire.[27] The argument that the closure of Athens was an attack on classical Greek paideia falls flat when we see that Byzantine writers continued the practice of many Church Fathers of developing their theology from the tools of pagan Greek philosophy, logic, and rhetoric. For example, Leontios of Byzantium (c. 475–543 AD), a well-known scholastic philosopher of the sixth century, systematically applied dialectic and Greek philosophy to theology.[28]

The succession of theological controversies in the sixth century, followed by Iconoclasm and the related polemics, required a sophisticated thought process to develop and present orthodox theology.[29] Christian leaders needed the intellectual riches of the pagan Greek past. Philosophy became a support for theology because the philosophical and theological issues surrounding the debate over the nature of Christ, for example, involved not only substance and hypostasis, but also the relationship between substance and qualities.[30] The fact that such sophisticated discussions went on for so many centuries, including the centuries of supposed educational and cultural decline, demonstrates a very robust and successful school system that imparted the best of ancient Greek philosophy, logic, and rhetoric.

Most Christian thinkers took a conciliatory approach by attempting to bring harmony to Christian and Greek thought. The convert to Christianity, John Philoponos (c. 490–c. 570 AD), also known as John the Grammarian, adopted an approach that was more scientific than philosophical.[31] In his attempt to reconcile philosophy and Christian thought, he directly continued the approach of the Church Fathers before him in

---

[27] Tatakis, *Byzantine Philosophy*, 12.
[28] Ibid., 14.
[29] Ibid.
[30] Ibid., 14–15.
[31] Another John the Grammarian headed the iconoclast research commission into the Church Fathers in the early ninth century.

not uncritically accepting Greek thought, but in adopting only the ideas that he deemed to be correct. He turned to Aristotle for this-world applications such as logic, physics, and problem-based modes of investigation, but relied on Plato for the higher things of metaphysics to investigate the teachings of Revelation on God, the human soul, and the created order.[32] He did not rely solely on Scripture and Church authorities for dealing with the ultimate questions.

This attempt to reconcile two traditions did not prevent Philoponos from falling afoul of ecclesiastical authorities, as he allowed his Aristotelian methods to lead him into heresy over the natures of the Trinity and Christ. Leontios of Byzantium responded to Philoponos' heresy by pointing out that the truths of revelation necessitate a different kind of dialectic than the one wielded for worldly concerns.[33] The Aristotelian Leontios succeeded in increasing the influence of the Stagirite in the empire, at a cost to Plato's standing. Leontios's application of Aristotle's categories and logic in his own teaching and writing established what can be called "Byzantine Scholasticism."[34] This was a particularly significant achievement because instruction in philosophy in the empire, mirroring that of the early medieval Latin West, normally ended with logic, with occasional forays into ethics, physics, and mathematics.[35]

13.4 DECLINE IN THE SEVENTH AND EIGHTH CENTURIES

The early sixth century saw the end of the previous strong cultural and educational development and the beginning of a period of relative inactivity that, however, retained enough of the essentials to allow for something new to eventually emerge — a gestation period of sorts according to historian

---

[32] Tatakis, *Byzantine Philosophy*, 28.
[33] Ibid., 34.
[34] Ibid., 53.
[35] Ierodiakonou and O'Meara, "Philosophies," 713.

Paul Lemerle.[36] A succession of setbacks for the empire led to overall decline in a host of fields, including education and culture. The earthquake of 551 AD destroyed the law school at Berytus. Territorial losses to Islam brought definitive educational losses, as with the centuries-old Christian educational traditions of Antioch and Alexandria. The consolidation of education at Constantinople encouraged the itinerancy of scholars that marked the Latin and Greek early medieval worlds. An extreme case concerned the Armenian Anania of Shirak (Anania Shirakatsi, died after 667 AD). The father of Armenian science, Anania traveled to Trebizond in search of a master after having found few teachers in his own country. His educational aspirations did not seem to have been particularly religious. He was in search of science. After a disappointing six months in Trebizond, he moved to Constantinople, and studied under the Armenian-speaking Tychikos. Anania's history demonstrates the rarity of professors in his day outside of Constantinople.

The capital's status as the imperial center of education did not shield it from the cultural and educational decline. In the early seventh century, the Emperor Phocas (reigned 602–610 AD) suspended the operations of the University of Constantinople. A new Church-controlled school, the Ecumenical College, opened in the next reign. The Church, it seems, remained as the last institution that still worked to disseminate and control ideas.[37] The Ecumenical College initially employed twelve professors responsible for theology and other disciplines, including those of Greek paideia. Despite this promising development, the battle over icons in the eighth century was a disaster for Hellenism, as some iconoclasts apparently wished to purify Christianity of pagan Greek ideas.[38] Iconoclasm's attacks on the Hellenic elements that remained at work in the Church

---

[36] Lemerle, Le premier humanisme byzantine, 73.
[37] R. R. Bolgar. The Classical Heritage and its Beneficiaries (Cambridge: Cambridge University Press, 1973), 62.
[38] Ibid. As mentioned, the iconoclast era lasted from 726 to 843.

seemed to have brought about the lean centuries of Byzantine education and culture, though it remains unclear how responsible iconoclasm was for this low point.[39] The ensuing polemics from both iconophiles and iconoclasts—based as they were on grammar, logic, and rhetoric—ironically helped to keep these skills sharp.[40] Education still suffered. The iconoclast Emperor Leo the Isaurian (685–741 AD) issued an edict in 726 AD that forbade all religious statues and pictures. He closed down the Ecumenical College after the institution refused his request to support his iconoclastic beliefs. The Pandidakterion also faded into obscurity in the seventh century. Perhaps the most important reason for the educational and cultural decline of the empire was the decline in the fortunes of Constantinople's educated class, which was mostly comprised of civil servants. They felt the decline of the state's fortunes more keenly than almost anyone else in the capital, as the fortunes of the military leaders rose due to the campaigns against the empire's enemies.[41]

Education undoubtedly continued in the empire in these more obscure times from the sixth through eighth centuries, as testified by hagiographies.[42] However, aside from the lives of the saints, there is scant evidence of the nature of the Church's activity in education or connections to Byzantine educational institutions from the sixth to the ninth centuries. Presumably, much Church-related education took place in monasteries and under the leadership of bishops, and would have concerned training in the liturgy, including chanting and Scripture reading. The lack of state-sponsored higher educational institutions after the sixth or seventh centuries left the schools run by the *grammatikoi* as the sole non-ecclesiastical educational institutions for many decades.

---

[39] Bolgar. *The Classical Heritage and its Beneficiaries*, 64, 65.
[40] Lemerle, *Le premier humanisme byzantine*, 75.
[41] Warren Treadgold. "The Macedonian Renaissance," in *Renaissances Before the Renaissance: Cultural Revivals of Late Antiquity and the Middle Ages*, ed. by Warren Treadgold (Stanford University Press, 1984), 78.
[42] Markopoulos, "In Search For 'Higher Education' In Byzantium," 35, 36.

13.5 JOHN OF DAMASCUS

There was a bright spot in this intellectual decline. In *The Fount of Knowledge*, the monk and priest John of Damascus (675–749 AD)[43] included chapters on philosophy and elevated Aristotelianism to a dominant position, the first time Platonism had been eclipsed in Byzantine history.[44] He added to the Byzantine scholastic tradition that Leon the Byzantium had earlier established. John's interest in philosophy was entirely Christian. He wanted philosophy to serve as the tool of the explanation of dogma. Philosophy and the other secular disciplines, the handmaidens of theology, were to explain Revelation to the world. John offers a metaphysical explanation for the relationship between man and the cosmos through reason, according to which man is the microcosm of the universe, the meeting point of mind and matter that connects the visible and invisible worlds. Man's spirit, "the purest part of the soul but not distinct from it, connects man with both the incorporeal and the intelligible and with the rational appetite of the spirit, the will, the prime mover of the spirit."[45] In other words, John of Damascus put forth a Christian perspective from the metaphysical insights of philosophy. This was not a fusion of philosophy and Christian theology, as each discipline kept its separate identity. The two disciplines were complementary to each other, as testified by the fact that philosophy's deepest questions could be answered by Christianity.

The four books of *The Fount of Knowledge*, which is regarded by some as the first *Summa Theologica*,[46] represent an innovative synthesis of the dogma that was established by the Greek Church Fathers. As such a synthesis, it is the first theological work with an introduction consisting of philosophy. This

---

[43] Also known as John Mansur or Yanah ibn Mansur ibn Sargun. The work is also known as *The Fountain of Knowledge*.
[44] Tatakis, *Byzantine Philosophy*, 15.
[45] Ibid., 93.
[46] Frederic H. Chase, "Introduction," pp. v–xxxviii, in *Saint John of Damascus: Writings*, v, xxvi.

organization arose from the author's belief in the vital role of this discipline in the explication of dogma. The philosophical chapters of book one are known as the *Dialectica*. The Aristotelian parts of the *Dialectica* are mostly based on the *Introduction to the Categories of Aristotle* (Porphyry) and the *Commentary on the Isagoge of Porphyry* (Ammonius Hermeae). The *Dialectica* discusses "the Five Universals and the dialectic method."[47] The philosophical chapters, oriented towards the later theological section (which itself comes after chapters on heresies and the history-focused second book), contain terms from philosophy which had acquired new theological meanings and had been important to the development of Christian doctrine.[48] In short, the *Dialectica* is the first Christian philosophy text specifically devoted to aiding in the comprehension of theology. While Leontios of Byzantium, as we have seen, had used Aristotelian dialectic in his theological writings, unlike John of Damascus, he did not write any text specifically focused only on dialectic and philosophy.[49]

In the Preface to *The Fount of Knowledge* that precedes the *Dialectica*, John follows the general spirit of the Church Fathers in identifying Greek pagan philosophy as an effective tool for the investigation of the truth. He refers to James 1:17: "I shall set forth the best contributions of the philosophers of the Greeks, because whatever there is of good has been given to men from above by God, since 'every best gift and every perfect gift is from above, coming down from the Father of lights.'"[50] Continuing to echo the Fathers, John next acknowledges the imperfect nature of the pagan Greek sources and the necessity to separate the good from the harmful and bad. Anything contrary to the truth of Christian dogma comes from Satan or another evil spirit. Only that which conforms to the truth

---

[47] Chase, "Introduction," xxvii.
[48] Ibid., xxvii–xxviii. Such terms included *hypostasis, person, union, nature.*
[49] Ibid., xxviii.
[50] John of Damascus, *The Fount of Knowledge* in *Saint John of Damascus: Writings,* 5.

can contribute to theology, whereas "all that is worthless and falsely labeled as knowledge I shall reject."[51] Philosophy is once again read through the lens of Revelation.

The first chapter of Book 1, "On Knowledge," highlights the need for reason and wisdom for the spiritual life. In the tradition of the Fathers, John associates heresy with deceit and the proper contribution of reason to the spiritual life, particularly in the understanding of Scripture: "Let us learn the true knowledge of all things that are. Let us approach with attention and in all sincerity and proceed without letting the spiritual eye of our soul be dulled by passions."[52] It is through the repeated study of Scripture that knowledge and understanding are acquired. Interestingly, in a brief reference to the third trivial discipline, which was held in the highest esteem throughout Byzantine history, he associates it with deceit: "Let us not belittle that which is good. Nor let us use the art of rhetoric for the deception of simpler folk. On the other hand, although the truth stands in no need of the service of subtle reasonings, let us definitely use them to overthrow both those who fight dishonestly and that which is falsely called knowledge."[53]

At the end of this opening chapter, John acknowledges both reason's vital role, in ascending to the heights of the spiritual life, and reason's limits. Once again we see nothing original in the following, but the assertion of a central part of the Christian appropriation of Greek *paidea*: "May those who happen upon this work have it as their purpose to bring their mind safely through to the final blessed end which means to be guided by their sense perceptions up to that which is beyond all sense perception and comprehension, which is He who is the Author and Maker and Creator of all."[54] This is the Neoplatonic-Christian spirituality that was normative to the liberal arts in the Middle Ages. Unsurprisingly, in the same

---

[51] John of Damascus, *The Fount of Knowledge*, 5.
[52] Ibid., Chapter 1, 8.
[53] Ibid., Chapter 1, 9.
[54] Ibid., Chapter 1, 9–10.

paragraph, he calls on his readers to apply themselves meekly and humbly to acquire knowledge, as this attitude will enable them to achieve their objective. Ultimately, education and the pursuit of knowledge are spiritual endeavors, and must be undertaken with the appropriate Christian disposition, however Neoplatonic they also happen to be.

John's discussion of philosophy maintains this focus on the truth and on the spiritual nature of knowledge. This focus gives an ontological orientation to the following definition: "Philosophy is knowledge of things which are in so far as they are, that is, a knowledge of the nature of things which have being. And again, philosophy is knowledge of both divine and human things, that is to say, of things both visible and invisible."[55] He notes in the same section the ascendant aspect of philosophy: "Philosophy is the making of one's self like God. Now, we become like God in wisdom, which is to say, in the true knowledge of good; and in justice . . . and in holiness." He then comes very close to Isidore of Seville's definition in the *Etymologies* (2.24.9) when he notes that "philosophy is the art of arts and the science of sciences" because philosophy is the origin and heart of every art and science.[56] This role, as we saw in earlier chapters, is ascribed by many (such as, centuries later, by Petrus Ramus) to dialectic. Ultimately, for John, because philosophy is the love of wisdom, and God is wisdom, the love of God is true philosophy. There is no division between philosophy and the Christian life because the Christian life is philosophy. This reflects the six-part definition of philosophy that we saw at the beginning of this chapter and continues the attitude that Clement of Alexandria had established centuries earlier.

John followed pagan Greek and the subsequent Christian tradition in breaking philosophy into speculative and practical parts. Speculative philosophy consists of theology, physiology, and mathematics, and practical philosophy can be divided

---

[55] John of Damascus, *The Fount of Knowledge*, Chapter 3, II.
[56] Ibid.

into ethics, domestic economy, and politics. After noting that "the speculative is the orderly disposition of knowledge," he describes the numerical basis of the quadrivium.[57] John notes that practical philosophy deals with the virtues. John must have encountered opposition to philosophy from some churchmen, as he ends the section with a clever note on the illogical reasoning of those who want to eliminate philosophy:

> There are, however, some people who have endeavored to do away entirely with philosophy by asserting that it does not exist and that neither does any knowledge or perception exist. We shall answer them by asking: How is it that you say that there is neither philosophy, nor knowledge, nor perception? Is it by your knowing and perceiving it, or is it by your not knowing and perceiving it? If you have perceived it, well, that is knowledge and perception. But if it is by your not knowing it, then no one will believe you, as long as you are discussing something of which you have no knowledge.[58]

In other words, no one can escape philosophy. After this foundational definition and justification for philosophy, John turns to the nature of being. He makes a distinction between substance and accident. Later chapters discuss definition, difference, genus and species, predicates (including univocal and equivocal predication), genera, and form. Chapter 67, "Six Definitions of Philosophy," echoes the standard list that we saw earlier.[59]

---

[57] John of Damascus, *The Fount of Knowledge*, Chapter 3, 12.

[58] Ibid., Chapter 3, 12–13.

[59] "Philosophy is knowledge of things which are in so far as they are; that is to say, a knowledge of their nature. Philosophy is a knowledge of divine and human things. Philosophy is a study of death, both that which is deliberate and that which is natural. Philosophy is a becoming like God, in so far as this is possible for man. Now, it is in justice, sanctity, and goodness that we become like God. And justice is that which is distributive of equity; it is not wronging and not being wronged, not prejudicing a person, but rendering to each his due in accordance with his works. Sanctity, on the other hand, is that which is over and above justice; that is to say, it is the good, the patience of the one wronged, the forgiving of them that do wrong, and, more than that, the doing of good to them. Philosophy is the art of arts and the science of sciences, for, since through philosophy every art is discovered, it is the principle underlying every art. Philosophy is love of wisdom. But, the true wisdom is God. Therefore, the love of God this is the true philosophy." John of Damascus, *The Fount of Knowledge*, chapter 67, 105–106.

CHAPTER 14

Rebirth of Learning in the Byzantine Empire

The labors of Plato and Aristotle resulted in my own intellectual birth. They brought me into the world and educated me.

— Michael Psellos[1]

I owe my mother a double debt since she both gave me my physical existence and dazzled me with the beauty of words.

— Michael Psellos[2]

14.1 THE MACEDONIAN RENAISSANCE

T HE MACEDONIAN RENAISSANCE, from the ninth through eleventh centuries, takes its name from the Macedonian Dynasty (867–1056 AD), whose emperors played leading roles in educational and cultural renewal. A reconstructed understanding of the Byzantine Empire and culture contributed to the advances and even innovation. Just like in the Latin West, the era of greatest cultural and educational decline in the empire had managed to maintain a certain level of paideia, even if much of that teaching and learning was limited to one or a few cities. The achievements of the ninth century were the outcome of a slow developmental process that had been triggered by the loss of lands to the Muslim Arabs and the ensuing transformation of the empire to deal with this challenging situation.[3] Territorial loss led to political and cultural consolidation of the remaining lands before some of these territories were reconquered. The

---

[1] Tatakis, *Byzantine Philosophy*, 149.
[2] Michael Psellos, "The Encomium of His Mother," trans. Jeffrey Walker, in *History of Rhetoric*, Volume 8 (2005), §10.
[3] Lemerle, *Le premier humanisme byzantine*, 120.

greater unity and cohesion impacted education. The empire
became less multicultural and more Greek. This encouraged a
nationalism that identified with both Hellenism and orthodox
Christianity.

This new era in Byzantine history began with the death
of the last iconoclast ruler, Theophilos (reigned 829–842 AD),
though the strong impetus for learning had been building since
the 780s AD with the Empress Irene's sponsorship of research
into the Church Fathers to buttress iconophile arguments and
work towards an ecumenical council that would end Iconoclasm
once and for all. A notable increase in the copying of manuscripts also began in the late eighth century, which reflected
a larger reading public eager for more texts.[4] A synod in 843
AD officially ended Iconoclasm and permitted the veneration of
images. This encouraged a revival of Hellenism, as Iconoclasm,
it seems, had at times experienced a tense relationship with
pagan Greek culture.[5] While the iconoclasts may not have been
responsible for the decline in education and culture as this had
set in before the strife over icons had begun, the iconophiles
had convinced themselves of the link between this era of intellectual decline and Iconoclasm, and this made them all the
more fervent about learning.[6] The reintroduction of Iconoclasm
in 815 AD by Emperor Leo V did not lead to another decline
in learning, but to even more intellectual activity because the
iconoclasts had come to realize, since 780 AD, that research into
supporting arguments for their side from the Church Fathers
was vital. The emperor therefore set up his own commission,
just as Irene had previously done, headed by the iconoclasts'

[4] Treadgold. "The Macedonian Renaissance," 75–98 in *Renaissances Before the Renaissance: Cultural Revivals of Late Antiquity and the Middle Ages*, ed. Warren Treadgold (Stanford University Press, Stanford, 1984), 78.
[5] The triumphant iconophile party destroyed countless iconoclast documents, such as decrees by iconoclast emperors. This destruction makes it impossible to know precisely the iconoclasts' stance (or stances) on Hellenism. "We know the basic principles of Iconoclasm, but what has been totally lost are the nuances, the development and variation, and the richness of the argumentation." Tatakis, *Byzantine Philosophy*, 79.
[6] Treadgold. "The Macedonian Renaissance," 84.

intellectual leader, John the Grammarian.[7] His cousin Leo the Philosopher was another iconoclast.

Even before the end of Iconoclasm, the state's view of education had already shifted radically from Themistios's perspective of Hellenism and Christianity as two opposite yet coexisting worldviews to Justinian's vision of a united empire under one language and one faith.[8] Education was seen as serving that unity. Maximus the Confessor (580–662 AD), for instance, integrated the liberal arts with his theology and introduced Dionysius's Neoplatonic thought into Christian theology.[9] Ironically, while there was little conflict between paganism and Christianity in these early medieval centuries, pagan opposed pagan and Christian opposed Christian over what constituted orthodox belief or practice within their respective traditions.[10] The birth of a new, unitary culture would come about as each stream, the Christian and the Hellenic, worked out its respective inner problems. The newfound unity did not lead to the submersion of Hellenism in the dominant Christian culture. Instead, Hellenism's relative independence from the Church (even with the participation of churchmen in teaching), would emerge once again. Naturally, this would have enormous implications for education in the empire even if it did not put an end to all conflicts between the Church and those espousing ancient Greek culture and education.

During the iconoclast struggle, iconophiles and hellenophiles found themselves in common cause, which led to a fruitful interaction between the two. Christianity came to be seen as a strong supporter of Hellenism. The Church saw Hellenistic education as a propaedeutic for Christianity. After 843 AD, the newly-confident Church took the lead in rebuilding tradition and educational institutions, and had little to fear from Hellenistic thought challenging its supremacy.[11] This created

---

[7] Treadgold. "The Macedonian Renaissance," 84.

[8] Markopoulos, "In Search For 'Higher Education' In Byzantium," 35.

[9] Tatakis, *Byzantine Philosophy*, 54, 65.

[10] Lemerle, *Le premier humanisme byzantine*, 54.

[11] Bolgar. *The Classical Heritage and its Beneficiaries*, 67.

an interesting paradox whereby orthodox doctrine and the Church's role in society became increasingly inflexible just as an 'orthodox' view and practice of Attic pagan culture, which provided the intellectual backbone to the empire, increasingly embraced more flexible and varied ways of thinking. Leaders of this more intellectually adventurous secular culture could always seek the Church's protection when they came under attack by claiming to be faithful sons of the orthodox Church.[12] Michael Psellos, as we will see, was particularly adept at this balancing act. Overall, the end of Iconoclasm freed Byzantine minds, previously held captive to theological conflict, to focus on philosophy, rhetoric, and the sciences due to this feeling of certainty regarding theological orthodoxy. It also freed the members of the civil service, who tended to be iconophiles, to return to their traditional role as the empire's main source of Attic culture.

14.2 PHOTIOS

The polymath Photios (820–891/893 AD) was at the heart of the ninth century renaissance, and grammar was at the heart of his work. With his brother Tarasius, he had grown up at the end of Iconoclasm, and personified this newly-energized education with his own somewhat eccentric writings. A bureaucrat and the ecumenical patriarch of Constantinople (858–867; 877–886 AD), Photios focused on language in his *Lexicon*, which contains more than seven thousand entries, the shortest of which are two-word synonyms. Not meant for the public, the text lacks order and unity.[13] As for his *Bibliotheca*, it summarizes writings that were typically unknown even to the educated, while the entries of his *Amphilochia* are responses to queries from his friend Amphilochius. The three multivolume texts provide "excerpts, summaries, interpretations, and criticisms of

---

[12] Magdalino, "From 'encyclopedism' to 'humanism': the turning point of Basil II and the millennium," 4.

[13] Lemerle, *Le premier humanisme byzantine*, 192.

earlier Greek literature."[14] Photios' criticism of authors seems to favor the writers of the Second Sophistic, from the first to sixth centuries AD, over representatives of Atticism. He praised Pseudo-Phalaris, Pseudo Brutus, and Isidore of Pelusium, and criticized Isocrates, Aristotle, Plato, and Demosthenes. Other writers of the Macedonian Renaissance such as Leo the Mathematician had similar preferences.[15] One scholar notes that "it was perfectly natural that the Byzantines of the Macedonian renaissance took up Greek learning and literature from where these had left off before the Dark Ages, and not from the Golden Age of Athens. The Byzantine identified himself as a Christian and a Roman, not as a Greek or 'Hellene,' a name that meant 'pagan.'"[16] The spirit behind the writers of the Second Sophistic was also closer to the spirit of the Byzantines, particularly with the heavy influence of Neoplatonism.

As a defender of orthodox theology, Photios paralleled western educational leaders such as Charlemagne and the Latin and Greek Church Fathers with his concern for clarity. Logic needs grammar. Unambiguous language and clear thinking went hand-in-hand. The proper functioning of reason relied on this clarity. Reason guaranteed theological orthodoxy while irrationality and ambiguous language caused heresy. Photios, like Isidore of Seville, turned to etymology to find the eternal, precise, and genuine meaning of a given word. This certain meaning acted as a guarantee against the errors that could lead to misinterpretation and ensuing accusations of heresy. Such accusations could lead to grave consequences, such as the loss of Church office. Photios accordingly put considerable effort into getting to the core or basic meaning of words. His focus on the original meaning of this lexis, which he discovered in ancient dictionaries and grammars, continued the preference among the Byzantines for the Attic style over the New Testament *koine* Greek or their own early

---

[14] Treadgold. "The Macedonian Renaissance," 89.
[15] Ibid., 90.
[16] Ibid., 91. Treadgold reminds his reader that "Byzantine" is a modern term.

medieval colloquial Greek. Byzantine high culture, including the Greek that was taught in the classroom through the progymnasmata, was Atticist.[17] This paralleled the centuries-long love in the West for Virgil, Ovid, Horace and other exemplars of classical Latin.

An Aristotelian and Hellenist, Photios as patriarch opened his home and its famous library to students. His love for the Greek pagan classics raised the status of the ancient canon in the empire, and the Hellenic past became a more conscious part of the Byzantine present.[18] This intellectual climate proved fertile ground for later scholars such as Michael Psellos, because Photios's interest in, for instance, philosophy, was not limited to philosophy as a tool of Christianity, that is, to its being the handmaiden of theology, but in philosophy as a discipline in its own right. This love for many aspects of Hellenism itself and not for what it could do for the Church, was a ninth century shift in Byzantium that had profound long-term consequences for education.[19] This shift would not have been possible during the iconoclastic period. It required a more confident Church that was not riven by internal theological conflict. With Photios we see some innovation and independent thinking that was based on the ancients. His Aristotelianism, in an era that favored Plato, exemplifies this independence, though he failed to create a lineage of Aristotelian scholars, as the intellectual circle around his former student Arethas, Bishop of Caesaria (c. 850–944 AD), was Platonist. The ninth century did not resolve the question of which philosopher would take primacy, even with Photios's Aristotelianism.[20]

Humanism in the empire took a major step forward in 855/856 AD with the creation of a state college for higher education by the controversial brother of Empress Theodora and a powerful bureaucrat in his own right, Bardas (assassinated in

---

[17] Bolgar. *The Classical Heritage and its Beneficiaries*, 70.
[18] Tatakis, *Byzantine Philosophy*, 103.
[19] Ibid.
[20] Ibid., 105.

866 AD).[21] This foundation reflected greater official interest in the classical authors. Leo the Philosopher was named rector and philosophy master. Byzantine chroniclers dated the beginning of the ninth century intellectual renaissance from the foundation of the school.[22] The polymath Leo (c. 790–after 869 AD)[23] had received his elementary education in Constantinople in grammar and poetics. Given the absence of higher education in the capital at this time, he was forced to travel to the island of Andros to find a suitable tutor for more advanced studies. As even that was not sufficient, Leo was largely self-taught. He became a famous teacher in Constantinople before his appointment as Metropolitan of Thessaloniki in 840 AD (until deposed in 843 AD due to his iconoclastic beliefs). He headed the school in Magnaura. Emperor Theophilus was moved to financially support Leo's teaching after the caliph al-Mamun had invited the renowned mathematician to his palace in Baghdad. His renown had spread there after one of his students had been captured and dazzled the court with his Euclidean geometry, which surpassed any of al-Mamun's leading intellectual lights. Theophilus's financial support of John the Grammarian and Leo set a precedent of the emperors' financial support of intellectual work in secular disciplines.[24] Incidentally, the fact that Leo was both an iconoclast and the era's leading scholar indicates that we cannot jump to any conclusions in the association between Iconoclasm and anti-Hellenism.

14.3 WRITTEN MATERIALS

As we have seen in previous chapters, paideia was heavily impacted by the centuries-long notion of encyclopedism.[25]

---

[21] Lemerle, *Le premier humanisme byzantine*, 167. Lemerle gives 855 as an approximation.
[22] Ibid., 167.
[23] Also known as Leo the Grammarian or Leo the Mathematician, reflecting his polymathic education.
[24] Treadgold. "The Macedonian Renaissance," 85–86.
[25] Lemerle, *Le premier humanisme byzantine*, 267.

Paideia and encyclopedism were mutually reinforcing, as
encyclopedias were tools of learning. This was true in the
Byzantine Empire, and no more so than in the tenth century. Many encyclopedias were specialized. Simeon the Meta-
phraste (died c. 1000 AD) authored an encyclopedia on the
lives of the saints, the *Menologue*, while Nikephoros Ouranos
(died c. 1010 AD) wrote a military encyclopedia, *Taktika*. Some
scholars intentionally connected encylopedism to educational
goals. Photios had prioritized encyclopedism in an attempt
to strengthen orthodoxy by constructing a unified orthodox
culture based on the classical paideutic program of the first
through fifth centuries AD.[26] Ninth century encyclopedism
also benefited from the intellectual stimulation brought about
by the emperors. Near the end of the century, the bookish
Emperor Leo VI the Wise (866–912 AD), a former student
of Photios, opened the palace to scholars in order to promote
the intellectual achievements of his former master.[27] But it
was Constantine VII Porphyrogenitus (913–959 AD) who
personified encyclopedism. Reading literature, not governing,
dominated his time and passions. He financially supported
the intellectuals who flocked to him.[28] He pursued both
rhetoric and philosophy, and believed that the *praxis* of the
former and the *theoria* of the latter brought humans closer
to God.[29] There was a mixture of *praxis* and *theoria* in the
overall educational program of the Macedonian Renaissance.
Constantine VII ensured that students found appropriate positions in government and Church to spread *sophia*
throughout the state.[30] He also commissioned encyclopedia

---

[26] Magdalino, "From 'encyclopedism' to 'humanism': the turning point of Basil
II and the millennium," 7.

[27] Tatakis, *Byzantine Philosophy*, 101.

[28] Ibid., 105. Constantine VII's bookishness can also be attributed to the fact
that he was prevented from governing until almost 40 years of age by his regents.
In his boredom, he spent much time in the imperial library. Treadgold. "The
Macedonian Renaissance," 92.

[29] Magdalino, "From 'encyclopedism' to 'humanism': the turning point of Basil
II and the millennium," 7.

[30] Ibid., 7–8.

on history and political philosophy, and in practical subjects such as agriculture, medicine, and animal care, as a way to catalog existing knowledge.[31] His century became known as the age of the encyclopedia because many volumes of the genre were produced, largely because it represented the ideals of Byzantine education.

A technical development helped spur on the ninth-century renaissance, with obvious parallels to the Carolingian renaissance in the West. After the imperial scriptorium of the fourth century had saved ancient texts from oblivion through the copying of papyrus documents onto longer-lasting parchment, the ninth-century copying of uncial documents into minuscule script saved these texts a second time.[32] Minuscule allowed for the economizing of space in a manuscript, as the letters were smaller than uncial script and were joined together. Cursive's connected letters made writing faster, which naturally sped up the production of manuscripts. Minuscule's two other innovations, the separation of words and the introduction of signs for punctuation and accentuation, made reading easier and faster.[33] This new writing also contributed to the sense of *renovatio* in the Carolingian Renaissance. Historian Paul Lemerle even sees a parallel in the invention of minuscule and the printing press centuries later for the impact on reading and text production.[34] As an aside, despite the secondary role of monasteries in Byzantine education, the empire's monks also played an important role in copying manuscripts, so much so that Theodore of Stoudios' rules for this activity meted out harsh penalties for errors. The library at that monastery, which included both religious and pagan works, became a well-regarded center of manuscript production.[35]

---

[31] Bolgar. *The Classical Heritage and its Beneficiaries*, 71.
[32] Lemerle, *Le premier humanisme byzantine*, 59–60.
[33] Ibid., 119.
[34] Ibid., 121.
[35] Tatakis, *Byzantine Philosophy*, 76.

14.4 THE ELEVENTH CENTURY RENAISSANCE

At the beginning of the *Alexiad*, Anna Comnena (1083–1153 AD) describes her education: "I was not ignorant of letters, for I carried my study of Greek to the highest pitch, and was also not unpractised in rhetoric; I perused the works of Aristotle and the dialogues of Plato carefully, and enriched my mind by the 'quaternion' of learning. (I must let this out and it is not bragging to state what nature and my zeal for learning have given me, and the gifts which God apportioned to me at birth and time has contributed)."[36] Given that she was "born in the purple," as the daughter of the Emperor Alexios I Komnenos, this bookish upbringing was in no way typical, especially for girls, in the Byzantine Empire.

In the eleventh century, the Byzantine concern for rhetoric, far greater than that found in the West at the time, spurred on the development of one notable innovation to the teaching of the progymnasmata. The progrymnasmata, as we have seen, were the exercises that raised the grammar student to the capacity to give an oral and public declamation in rhetoric class. The new development concerned *schedography*, a novel form of classroom exercise. The verbal puzzles of the schede (σχέδη) aimed at improving orthography and grammar, while simultaneously familiarizing students with the various genres that they would see in the more challenging parts of the progymnasmata.[37] The puzzles of between twenty and twenty-five lines were written, usually by the masters, into the various prose exercises of the progymnasmata. The grammar or lexical faults that the students were to work out likely came from everyday

---

[36] Anna Comnena (Komnene), *The Alexiad*, ed. and trans. Elizabeth A. Dawes (Routledge, Kegan, Paul, 1928).
[37] Alexander Riehle, "Rhetorical Practice," in *The Oxford Handbook of Byzantine Literature*, ed. Stratis Papaioannou (Oxford University Press, 2023), 300. *Schedos* can mean "sketch" or "improvisation." Panagiotis A. Agapitos, "Grammar, genre and patronage in the twelfth century: A scientific paradigm and its implications," in *Jahrbücher des Österreichischen Byzantinistik* 64, (Österreichische Akademie der Wissenschaften, 2014), 4.

language. One scholar describes a typical schede: "The text was filled with strange sounds and phrases giving no meaning, and punctuated in an erratic manner. The pupils had to decode such a puzzle and to rewrite it correctly. The puzzles were based on ἀντίστοιχα ('sound correspondences'); these could be similarly sounding verbal or nominal forms, or they could be wrongly written words or phrases."[38] This sounds like the same concern for correct usage that western thinkers such as Isidore of Seville also had.

The academic culture surrounding schedography centered on the high place of rhetoric. Schedography contests were held in Constantinople, with students solving and even composing schede. This public performance aspect was central to schedography-based training, and helped to raise the profiles of teachers and schools for future patrons.[39] But not everyone was convinced that schedography boosted language development. John Tzetzes complained that the practice took classroom focus away from the classic texts, where it belonged, and thereby turned budding scholars into barbarians. He saw the exercises as reflecting the concerns of rhetoric teachers about form, not content.[40]

Anna Comnena also criticized certain aspects of schedography in the *Alexiad* (15.7), which she adds to a wider discussion of a few observations she makes on education in her day. She is describing the building that housed orphans and retired soldiers in Constantinople, the *orphanotropheion*: "On entering you would find the sanctuaries and monasteries to your left; and on the right of the large sanctuary stood the grammar-school for orphans collected from every race, in which a master presided and the boys stood round him, some puzzled over grammatical questions, and others writing what are called grammatical analyses." She laments the decline in

---

[38] Agapitos, "Grammar, genre and patronage in the twelfth century: A scientific paradigm and its implications," 5. Antistoika = ἀντίστοιχα .

[39] Ibid., 8.

[40] Ibid., 12.

education, as the cast-aside source texts were replaced by the above-mentioned grammatical analysis. She also laments more trifling things that occur: "But now the study of these lofty matters and of the poets and historians and the wisdom to be gained from them do not receive even secondary attention; but the absorbing occupation is the game of draughts and other unlawful things."[41] She uses this observation to turn to a larger concern about the state of learning: "I say this because I am grieved at the absolute neglect of general education and it makes me glow with anger because I myself spent so much time over the same things. And when I was released from that childish teaching and betook myself to the study of rhetoric and touched on philosophy and in between these sciences turned to the poets and historians, by means of these I polished the roughness of my speech, then with the aid of rhetoric I felt that the highly complex complications of grammatical parsing were to be condemned."[42] The daughter of the emperor expresses here the type of love that westerners had for their favorite academic discipline, though what she calls rhetoric, they would likely call grammar. In both cases, it was the ancient canon of poets, philosophers, and Sophists that had so enamored them.

As with the Carolingian Renaissance, political support for this education had practical purposes. The eleventh century Byzantine renaissance, the age of Hellenic revival, was encouraged by political forces. The cult of antiquity, which had always been present in Byzantine history, received a strong boost with the educational and cultural revolution and became a predominant part of Byzantine life. This cult of antiquity required not only the study of ancient texts, but the embrace of traditional methods and ideals from ancient Greece and Rome.[43] The cult of antiquity, the basis of the Greek nationalism of the empire, enabled the powerful landowning families to command greater

---

[41] Comnena (Komnene), *The Alexiad*, Book 5, vii.
[42] Ibid.
[43] Bolgar. *The Classical Heritage and its Beneficiaries*, 72.

loyalty from their subjects. Michael Psellos (1018–1078 AD) was the most renowned exemplar of a scholar who came from the Hellenizing political class.

14.5 MICHAEL PSELLOS'S EDUCATION

The eleventh century was the age of Psellos in the Byzantine Empire. Anna Comnena notes of him: "This man had not studied very much under learned professors, but through his natural cleverness and quick intelligence and further by the help of God (which he had obtained by his mother's ardent supplications, for she often spent whole nights in the church of God weeping and making invocations to the holy picture of the Virgin on her son's behalf) he had reached the summit of all knowledge, was thoroughly acquainted with Greek and Chaldæan literature and grew famous in those days for his wisdom."[44] Comnena's depiction does not reveal a vibrant educational scene. It seems that his achievements as an aspiring scholar were supernatural, or, like those of Leo the Grammarian, mostly based on independent self-study.

In his funeral oration for his mother, Psellos refers to his own education in less mystical terms than Comnena does:

> My mother was led to an embrace of education by the very loveliness of learned discourse and a desire for practical activity. Moreover, my own nature also encouraged her to this, as she was astonished at the quickness of my understanding, and convinced of my ability to learn. Most people related to the family say that when I was a child, nothing that was said passed through my ears in vain, and that every word was copied in my soul; and because of that my mother was guided to the better things, and at the end of my fifth year she fixed upon a teacher. My lessons were not only easy for me, but also more enjoyable than any other childish pastime. I would be vexed if given no lessons for an entire day. Study was play to me, and play was study — not because some things were play and others were study, but

---

[44] Comnena (Komnene), *The Alexiad*, Book 5, viii.

because I embraced some things because of their sweetness, and avoided others because of their harshness. I say these things not from a wish to praise myself, but to indicate the origins of my love of learning.[45]

When the young Michael wanted to pursue higher education at the age of eight, his mother supported this over the objections of other family members, he reports in the *Encomium*.

Here we have the first indication in the *Encomium* of the supernatural aspect of his education, as he mentions the divine mission that Psellos's mother saw in this education for her son:

> My mother told me that, once when she was dissolved in sleep, she seemed again to be disputing what my lot should be. Since she often was feeling overwhelmed by the arguments the family made against her, a certain man from among the servants of God, someone familiar to her and resembling the golden-tongued John (and I mean our Antiochene), I said to her, "Do not be distressed, O woman, by these considerations, but with a conquering resolve instruct your son in learned matters. I will accompany him as his guide and teacher, and I will fill him with learning."[46]

He recalls learning quickly and easily, and benefiting from a keen memory and good expression for the recitation of his lessons. He claims to have learned to correctly write and recite the whole of the *Iliad* in one year. Boastful as he was, he emphasizes that this learning was not merely memorization, but also based on the use of rhetorical tools such as figure, trope, diction, and metaphor in these texts.[47]

Psellos then relates a dream that, he believed, foretold in some way his future path as a rhetorician and philosopher:

> I was not yet ten years old (or perhaps I had just reached that age), and one night a dream lifted me up, and transported me into the open sky. I do not know whether or not I was hunting, but it seemed to me that I was pursuing two musical birds, one of which resembled a little parrot, and the other a magpie, and they both went in beneath the fold

---

[45] Michael Psellos, *Encomium of his Mother*, §5.
[46] Ibid.
[47] Ibid., §6.

of my robe! At this my spirit was lightened and gladdened, and by frequently using my hands I kept up with them and grasped their wings. But the birds said, "Neither rule tyrannically, in the way of men, nor seize power by force: rule, master, according to law! Rather, accomplish this by reason, and stay and converse with us. And should you persuade, then rule over us; but if not, give us back the freedom of our wings." It seemed to me that what they said was wise, and as I grasped each one firmly by the wings on either side, I imagined some philosophers exchanging arguments with them, and then and there the veil that birth casts over the soul was lifted from me. At the outset, then, equipoised arguments on both sides were established, and they opposed enthymemes and syllogisms to my antitheses; and when the conversation had played out the argument as far as possible and I was chattering on at length about one of their points, they said, "Stop, since even we have awarded you the victory!" At that time I did not fully understand my dream; rather, I supposed that what I had seen was a representation of the more irrational part of the soul. But later, once I had attained a grasp of music and the more exacting studies, I connected those apparitions to the verbal arts, since those twittering birds emitted a voice both musical and human.[48]

A Platonist and rhetorician, Psellos personifies the long-running duels in Byzantine intellectual history between philosophy and rhetoric, and between Platonism and Aristotle. Although the Byzantines inherited Neoplatonism from late Antiquity, principally through Pseudo-Dionysius, and therefore favored a synthesis of the major schools of philosophy, many thinkers favored one of the two foundational philosophers over the other. As for the other competition, the debate between philosophy and rhetoric, it could be seen as a rivalry between content and sequencing or style.[49] The Neoplatonist Psellos was most famous for his rhetoric.

---

[48] Michael Psellos, *Encomium of his Mother*, § 6.
[49] Tatakis, *Byzantine Philosophy*, 9. Tatakis notes: "Byzantine thought, interpretative par excellence, is concerned more with logical form [than content], and it is inclined towards the formalization of thought, seeing within form the substance of thought." (9–10) He also notes that Maximus the Confessor brought the writings of Pseudo Dionysius into the Church. (16)

CHAPTER 15

Michael Psellos

You must place your son between these two sources, philosophy and rhetoric, allowing him to drink from both, each in its turn. Otherwise you will turn your child into a mind without a voice, if he only studies philosophy, or a voice without a mind, in the opposite case.

—Michael Psellos[1]

15.1 A POLEMIC

AFTER BECOMING A RENOWNED LAW-yer, Psellos set out to improve the teaching of law, which he believed had greatly declined, by pairing its instruction with that of rhetoric. This desire led to a confrontation with John Xiphilinos (c. 1010–1075 AD), his former law teacher. The Emperor Constantine Monomachus (ruled 1042–54 AD) tried to settle the dispute over the new program by establishing faculties of law and philosophy under Xiphilinos and Psellos respectively. The latter was given the title *Consul of the Philosophers*.[2] This position as the leading philosopher of the empire did not prevent Psellos from furthering the cause of rhetoric. He wrote didactic poems on grammar and rhetoric, including his *Synopsis of Rhetoric*, in which he refers to the dispute between content (or philosophy), and style (or rhetoric), and highlights the need for both:

> A speech composed with art, master,
> has both body and soul, both head and feet:
> the thought [*dianoia*] is its soul, the style [*lexis*] is its body,
> the introductory matter [*ta prooimia*] is its head, and the
> epilogue is its feet.[3]

---

[1] Tatakis, *Byzantine Philosophy*, 130.
[2] Bolgar. *The Classical Heritage and its Beneficiaries*, 75.
[3] Psellos, *Synopsis of Rhetoric*.

It is as a philosopher, and not a rhetorician, that Psellos seems to have had a disagreement with Xiphilinos. Psellos claims in a letter to his former teacher that, contrary to Xiphilinos's accusation, his own interpretation and presentation of Plato's teaching adhered to the Church Fathers' formula: "'*My* Plato'? O most saintly and wise man! '*Mine*'? O by the earth and sun! — there, so I too may use words from tragedy upon this debate-stage! For if it is your reproach that I often conversed with that man [Plato] in his dialogues and that I admired the style of his expression and worshipped the power that lies in his proofs, why then did you not also hurl this charge against the Great Fathers, who overturned the heresies of Eunomios and Apollinarios by employing precisely those kinds of exact proofs."[4]

He carefully defends his judicious reading of Plato that weeds out the bad elements: Plato's "accounts of justice and of the immortality of the soul became the foundations for our own similar dogmas. It is not as though I contracted some disease of the eyes from those studies, but rather, in a fair way, I loved what was clear in those waters and washed off what was salty."[5] Psellos then describes what he sees as Plato's greatest act before laying an accusation against Xiphilinos: "But Plato discovered this thing, having raised himself up to Mind, and saw also that which is above Mind, finally stopping at the One. But you accuse him of everything, you *Plato-hater*."[6] Psellos expresses outrage at Xiphilinos's apparent accusation that he had turned his back on God and unduly loved the founder of the Academy. He adds to this his own sense of frustration, claiming that he cannot endure Xiphilinos' attacks much longer.[7] It is interesting to note that so many centuries after the Church Fathers had supposedly settled the place of Hellenism in Christian education and culture, Hellenism in this personal

---

[4] "Letter to Ioannes Xiphilinos," in *Psellos and the Patriarchs*, 168.
[5] Ibid., 169.
[6] Ibid.
[7] Ibid., 170.

conflict is wielded as a tool to attack an individual's position in society and adherence to Christianity.

The accused defends his Christian integrity with the two-pronged approach of Hellenism, represented here by reason, and theology. First, Psellos calls Xiphilinos a "misologist," a "hater of reason," before evoking the accomplished and highly-esteemed theologian for his cause, Maximus the Confessor, whom, he says, belongs to all Byzantines, but to himself in particular because Maximus was a philosopher who made natural science into a virtue.[8] Psellos then takes the opportunity to give his rival some advice on how to acquire basic reasoning: "But if there is a plain anywhere, or a deep valley, or a sundered gorge, or a hidden corner of the earth, secret and mysterious, go and hide yourself down there, and take a close look into all books, both our own and the profane ones. And, by first training your-self in reasoning, you can then ascend to the knowledge that makes no use of logic. For every virtue, when it is accompanied by arrogance and false notions, my dear brother, becomes an extreme evil and is the offspring of a state of wilful ignorance, which *my* philosopher [Plato], as you think, doubly condemns."[9] The personal and emotional defense then turns back to Psellos's own Christian beliefs and his appropriation, as a Christian, of the pagan past, which he claims to have accomplished in a judicious way, in the spirit of so many Church Fathers:

> But since that word [that you used] stings me again, lend me your ear for a moment and listen to what a Platonic philosopher is telling you. My dear brother, I have been made worthy of the divine name of Christ by the previous generations of Fathers and was the student of the crucified one (assuming no one reproaches me if that the word is too daring); I was instructed by the holy Apostles and fashioned into a most suitable vessel, I dare say, of the great and mysterious doctrine concerning the divine. As for the Platos and Chrysipposes whom you mention, I have loved them — how could I not? — but only for their beauty and

---

[8] "Letter to Ioannes Xiphilinos," 170.
[9] Ibid., 171.

surface smoothness. Of their doctrines, some I immediately
passed over, while those others that complement our suppo-
sitions I readily took on and mixed with our holy doctrines,
just as once Gregorios [of Nazianzos] and Basileios [of
Kaisareia], the great luminaries of the Church, did. As for
syllogisms, I have never despised their form.[10]

The general aim of this letter is to dispel the false opposition or
division between philosophy, personified by Plato, and Christ.
Following Christ does not require giving up the philosopher, a
theme that the Church Fathers had already repeatedly addressed.

Psellos breaks no new ground here, even with a rather bold
claim: "Plato *is* mine, brother, and so is Chrysippos! But Christ,
with whom I have been crucified, whose is he? On his account
did I not symbolically cut off the superfluity of my hair? On
his account did I not exchange one way of life for another?"[11]
Belonging to Christ prompts him to seek the truth, which
he implies is found in the achievement of the pre-Christians.
His faith in Christ drives him to embrace literature and "the
knowledge of beings, both those that are intelligible and those
that are sensible," while he also prays to be able to do this to
the utmost of his abilities. But he says that although this will
take him to tremendous heights, nature will bring him down,
and he will "walk through the meadows of rational discourse,
now plucking the saying of an elder father as though it were a
beautiful flower, and now gathering some other teaching of ours,
thereby culling the best for my soul."[12] Psellos links rational
discourse, or reason, to this world. He describes what the use
of this rational discourse looks like, including syllogistic and
natural reasoning, examining the causes of events, and inquiring "into Mind and that which lies beyond it," such as form.[13]

All of Psellos's writings were affected by his Platonism. His
lectures increased the status and knowledge of this thought
among Byzantine intellectuals. Philosophy's dominant place

---

[10] "Letter to Ioannes Xiphilinos," 171.
[11] Ibid., 174.
[12] Ibid., 174–175.
[13] Ibid., 175.

in the new school of law and philosophy was solidified when John Italos succeeded Psellos. Italos was not the polymath that Psellos had been, but focused entirely on philosophy, particularly Neoplatonism. As we will see, Italos's narrow focus on philosophy did not keep him out of trouble with the Church.[14]

Though Psellos endeavored to strike a balance between rhetoric and philosophy, and between Hellenism and Christianity, there was still one notable imbalance. The new university headed by Psellos and Xiphilinos was far more focused on literature and rhetoric than its ninth-century predecessor had been, but the sciences were all but ignored. Perhaps rhetoric had grown too powerful and dominant, like dialectic would at the University of Paris two centuries later. Under the leadership of Psellos, science was subordinated to rhetoric. Psellos himself exemplified this overuse of rhetoric. Apparently, he approached each discipline, such as mathematics or astronomy, as a rhetorician. He was uninterested in delving into the details and deeper meanings of concepts related to these subjects, in other words, the truths espoused by these subjects, but merely came up with the appropriate words to appear as a polymath. His real aim was to make memorable speeches, based on beautiful expressions, and thereby build his reputation as a skilled orator.[15] Psellos the Sophist apparently subordinated everything to rhetoric. Yet this was not all bad. His university faculty of philosophy emphasized the imitation of classical Greek models, which made antiquity a more living reality than it had been for centuries.[16] Psellos brought to the highest point Photios's attempt to bring back to life the paideia of late antiquity in the service of orthodoxy. He strove to establish the empire as a second Athens.[17]

---

[14] Bolgar. *The Classical Heritage and its Beneficiaries*, 75. "Psellus" is an alternative spelling.
[15] Ibid., 75–77.
[16] Ibid., 77.
[17] Ibid.

15.2 HELLENISM OR CHRISTIANITY

Psellos's views diverged not only from those of Xiphilinos. One episode in his life seems to reveal that he was not always able to unify Hellenism with Christianity in his own writing and teaching. It also demonstrates that Greek paideia, in this case represented by rhetoric, could clash with Christian practice. The problem seems in part to have stemmed from Psellos's overvaluation of rhetoric and alienation from the monastic life. He had been asked to write a *Vita* of Patriarch Kyr Michael Keroullarios. After describing his own wide-ranging academic achievements in a letter to the Patriarch, he describes how he regards the Patriarch, and how the two men differ so sharply in their intellectual outlooks. He claims he is unable to identify the "first principles" of the bishop's wisdom and theology, and notes that his reader, the bishop, lacked a formal education in philosophy and had not studied the necessary texts that made someone learned. There is a contradiction that the bishop did not ever learn from the wise (Greek or barbarian) or from any others, but "to us you have plainly appeared to be, as you would say, absolute science-in-itself and wisdom-in-itself."[18]

Psellos is not boasting in vain of his tremendous progress in Hellenism, as he came to personify the eleventh century Renaissance as the founder of a new era.[19] Perhaps the inner Christian-Hellenic split within himself emerged from his energetic promotion of the eleventh century renaissance, a re-creation of Byzantine culture and education. In the same letter, then, Psellos boldly describes his apparently unparalleled and world-renowned skills and powers as a rhetorician while noting the indifference of Keroullarios, the reader, to this speaking prowess. The writer seems to take personally that Keroullarios avoids the famous rhetor's friendship and company, and criticizes eloquence, reason, and Hellenic culture. He accuses Keroullarios of failing

---

[18] "Letter to the Patriarch Kyr Michael Keroullarios," 40.
[19] Tatakis, *Byzantine Philosophy*, 169.

to be charmed by anything he did, including the words of his improvised speeches, beautifully-rhymed language, apparently mild personality, "philosophical ethos," and "prosaic and supine character."[20] It seems, in other words, that the bishop failed to flatter Psellos' needy ego. The polymath puts the blame for this on the supposedly anti-Hellenic Patriarch, and not on his own inadequacies among which were clearly intellectual pride.

Psellos reminds his reader of his own renown in more than one empire, which he takes as proof of the validity of his position. He attracts admirers from far and wide:

> But I have made Celts and Arabs yield to me, and on account of my fame they regularly come down here to study even from the other continent; and while the Nile irrigates the land of the Egyptians, my speech irrigates their souls. And if you ask a Persian or an Ethiopian, they will say that they have known me and admired me and sought me out. And now someone from across the boundary of Babylon has come to drink from my springs through an insatiable desire of his. One of the nations calls me "a lamp of wisdom," another gives me the name "luminary," while others distinguish me in other ways, with the most beautiful names.[21]

Psellos then turns on the patriarch for the latter's supposedly incomplete education. It is this deficiency that, in Psellos's perspective, has caused their disagreement. The patriarch is simply not at his own intellectual level. Psellos attacks him by claiming that the bishop's educational deficiencies make him deaf to this brilliance: "You alone have not listened to my lyre, or rather you have heard it, but an oak tree is not fit to hear the Orphic harmony."[22] Then Psellos states that he has nothing more to say about this because of Keroullarios' inflexibility, which he once again imputes to the churchman's apparent lack of education. He is not shy to point out his worldly and worldwide fame, and is mystified why the bishop does not jump on the

---

[20] "Letter to the Patriarch Kyr Michael Keroullarios," 41.
[21] Ibid., 41–42.
[22] Ibid., 42.

bandwagon. Psellos ascribes this indifference to this greatness to the bishop's rigidity.

Psellos, an exponent of the liberal arts, highlights the work of these disciplines in elevating the soul. He seems to equate reason with Christian mysticism, claiming that he has reached the same heights as the bishop, though with a different path. He identifies the cause of the estrangement with the bishop by contrasting a certain type of wisdom with reason, the bishop's "ineffable and mystical wisdom" with his own knowledge "of that which proceeds from reason and the appropriate theory." Psellos claims equality with the bishop, as he also occupies a throne "in no way inferior to yours, lest I say far more self-sufficient, and you will neither theologize, nor expound the canons, nor perform any other divine service, without employing my eloquence. For I am the yardstick and ruler by which these things are measured."[23] The throne to which he refers is his chair in philosophy, in comparison with the episcopal seat. The equality of their respective seats arises from rhetoric's inescapable importance to the Church, which means that the bishop must adopt its methods. Psellos also notes that he surpasses the bishop in this skill. The use of rhetoric is inescapable for the Christian Patriarch, so he may as well embrace Psellos's position.

Psellos then expresses frustration at their inability to communicate, which is ironic given that he was the era's most renowned communicator. Are they living in two worlds? Is there a split between Christianity and Hellenism here? What is certain is that they followed two distinct spiritual paths, one based on mystical wisdom, the other on reason. Despite his high self-esteem, he does seem to admit that the bishop has reached a higher religious state than he has. He asks, "but from where do my words flow? It concerns the incongruence and incommunicability that exist between us. I was a lover of philosophy right from the start, while you were mystically involved with those lofty matters that are above us, through which, as

---

[23] "Letter to the Patriarch Kyr Michael Keroullarios," 43.

you yourself would say, you made your way upon the path of martyrdom, were proclaimed as the winner of the crown, and were judged the chief of the good and sacred company."[24] It seems that Psellos is practicing some of his sweet rhetoric on the bishop with these words.

Next, Psellos seems to distinguish between the patriarch's passive mysticism from his own active, independent actions that have brought him to his own heights. The bishop had achieved a higher "divine state" through his acceptance of "the better arguments of Scripture." Meanwhile, Psellos had focused on the grammarian's task of the research of "homonyms and synonyms, distinguishing individually between them and establishing their nature," and the philosopher's task of inquiring into nature, the Platonic Ideas, and "the causes of nature." He investigated philosophical terminology and logical discourse, and "how the two are in accordance and also divided from one another." He spots a gap between himself and the bishop, declaring that "*you would call these pursuits nonsensical and vain, but to me they are quite attainable.*"[25] Implied in this gap is Psellos's confession that he cannot bridge this alienation, that he cannot or does not want to pursue the path of mystical wisdom that the bishop took. He describes how he attained spiritual heights from the study of the trivium and, ultimately, philosophy. Is Psellos declaring Hellenism's independence from the Church? Does he not need Christ's grace that the Church provides?

Apparently not, because, despite all this boasting, Psellos tries to humble himself by depicting himself as a nobody, declaring "let him wear the golden sandal to whom it is destined. But I am so old-fashioned and ignorant that I have not risen above my lot, but rather I must deal with slaves as though they have political rights equal to my own. So then, if I am not invited as a guest to someone's house and share his hearth, I sit at the common table and drink from that same cup. And should

---

[24] "Letter to the Patriarch Kyr Michael Keroullarios," 44.
[25] Ibid., 43–44.

someone think less of me, I do not get very angry; should he laugh at me when I slip and fall, I do not cause trouble."[26] He contrasts his own humble position with the high social status of the patriarch, whom everyone feared and dared not oppose. Hellenism was inferior to Christianity in Byzantine society, it seems. Perhaps he was appealing to the bishop's sense of guilt at being so successful in the worldly sense despite the churchman's supposed mystical orientation. Psellos next compares his own struggles to those of Sts. Peter and Paul. After all the critical words about the patriarch, he ends the letter by promising to write a flattering biography that will bring fame, far and wide, to the patriarch. He will apply his rhetoric to the accomplishments of the man who followed the path of mystical wisdom, and thereby prove its utility.

Is this rhetorical interpretation of the Christian deeds of a churchman not the ultimate triumph of Hellenism (at least in Psellos's own mind)? He promises, "I will flowerily adorn the composition with rhythmical and supremely beautiful words, sowing my language with flatteries and graces and all the elements of euphony, so that when someone holds my book in hand he must simultaneously both admire the deed and applaud the word. And the man who was previously hidden even from us, well, Egypt too will know him in the future, as will the spice-bearing land [Arabia Felix] and the Ocean that lies to the west, to which places my text will travel."[27] Here we have a sense of why some accused Psellos of being short on content and philosophy and heavy on rhetoric, of having more style than substance.

Apparently, Patriarch Kerouollarios was not the only Byzantine intellectual to embrace mystical wisdom over the trivium. Many monks, such as Xiphilinos and Symeon the New Theologian, followed the mystical path of internal illumination. They undermined or opposed the rational foundations of knowledge,

---

[26] "Letter to the Patriarch Kyr Michael Keroullarios," 44.
[27] Ibid., 48.

though not always intentionally. They opposed dialectic. This is one reason why Psellos's voice was so precious and why he stood out so strongly.[28] Perhaps this implies that the split between Christianity and Hellenism had not been smoothed over during all of these centuries, but instead that a *detente* of sorts was attempted, with each side taking what it needed from the other, but otherwise keeping to its own field. No fusion of the two pillars of Byzantine culture took place. Yet such a conclusion is not entirely true, as Eustathios of Thessaloniki (1115–1195 AD), a famous commentator on Homer, was brought up in a monastery and taught rhetoric at the Patriarchal School. He acquired a significant level of humanist knowledge in the monastery. So certain individuals did indeed personify a fusion, as we saw in volume one with Clement of Alexandria, Origen, Augustine, and Boethius.

15.3. PSELLOS'S LINEAGE

Psellos's spirit lived on in the scholarly lineage that had begun with Photios all the way back in the ninth century. This lineage included Psellos's own students, Michael of Ephesus and "the Italian" John Italos (died 1112 AD), and in Italos's student Eustratios of Nicaea. From Calabria, Italos had come to the empire after political strife in his homeland. Anna Comnena notes his beginning in Constantinople while also giving her opinion of other scholars. Italos himself arrived at a Constantinople that was already teeming "with teachers of every subject and of the art of language. For from the time of Basil Porphyrogenitus down to the Emperor Monomachus, the study of letters, although neglected by the many, had nevertheless not entirely died out; it blazed up again and revived and was seriously pursued by the lovers of letters in the reign of the Emperor Alexius."[29] Anna criticizes the neglect of scholarly pursuits in

---

[28] Tatakis, *Byzantine Philosophy*, 159.
[29] Comnena (Komnene), *The Alexiad*, Book 5, viii.

the preceding era by associating this deficiency with a corresponding lack of manliness and a life of easy living: "Before that time men for the most part lived luxuriously and amused themselves, and due to their effeminacy they busied themselves with quail-hunting and other more disgraceful pastimes, and treated letters, and in fact any training in arts, as a secondary consideration."[30] According to the *Alexios*, Italos did not find such men attractive, and instead "consorted with the scholars, gloomy men of uncouth habits (for such were to be found in the capital even then)" until he finished his education and became close to Michael Psellos.[31]

After furthering his knowledge of science, Italos stayed on as professor of philosophy as Psellos's successor. He followed the perspective of his predecessor in his instruction in dialectic and history of philosophy, specializing in the Neoplatonists Porphyry, Iamblichos, and Proclus, the latter of whom deeply impacted Byzantine philosophy.[32] This philosophical teaching consisted of commentaries on these thinkers, a tradition that persisted throughout Byzantine history. Generally, throughout Byzantine history, notable shifts in philosophy, and therefore in the teaching of philosophy, resulted from the to-and-fro of scholars preferring either Plato or Aristotle. But this teaching itself did not always bring change. For example, unlike his master, Italos favored the Stagirite, though in fact the Aristotelianism of Italos and Psellos had much in common, and Italos's writings also reveal a strong Neoplatonist streak.[33] In other words, as with the majority of Byzantine thinkers, Platonic philosophy was applied to some issues and Aristotelianism to others. Rare was the attitude of Theodore Prodromos, a Platonist and rhetorician who strongly opposed Aristotle. In his treatise *Concerning the Great and the Small*, Prodromos attacked the sixth book of Aristotle's *Categories*. In general, Byzantine

---

[30] Comnena (Komnene), *The Alexiad*, Book 5, viii.
[31] Ibid.
[32] Tatakis, *Byzantine Philosophy*, 169.
[33] Ibid., 171.

philosophy was Neoplatonic in spirit, as it was in the Latin West until the age of the Parisian scholastics.

We read of the events surrounding Italos in the *Alexiad*, and how after Psellos had left public life for the tonsure, Italos became the most renowned philosopher in the empire and lectured on Plato and Aristotle.[34] The biased *Alexiad* then turns into riveting reading. The princess acknowledges Italos's high reputation, but expresses her disappointment of his level of Greek: "He was generally supposed to be very learned and he undoubtedly was far cleverer than all others in expounding that most wonderful philosophic system, the Peripatetic [Aristotelian], and especially the dialectics of it. But for other branches of literature he had not a very good head, for he stumbled over grammar and had never tasted the nectar of rhetoric."[35] Italos's deficiency in rhetoric would have been disappointing after the high standard set by Psellos.

Spiteful and petty, the princess depicts the Calabrian as lowbrow and finds fault with his demeanor: "Consequently his language was not adaptable nor at all polished. For the same reason, too, his character was austere and entirely unadorned with grace. His studies too had contracted his brows and he literally exhaled harshness."[36] She then criticizes his dialectic method, which she does not see as revealing the truth, but as causing confusion: "His writings were crammed full of dialectic exordiums and his language in disputations redounded with 'attempted proofs,' more so in his discourses than in his written works."[37] His dialectic was apparently counterproductive: "He was so strong in his arguments and so difficult to beat that his opponent would automatically be reduced to silence and to despair. For he would dig a pit either side of his question and hurl his interlocutor into a well of difficulties. Such skill the man had in dialectics, and by a rapid succession of questions

---

[34] Comnena (Komnene), *The Alexiad*, Book 5, viii.
[35] Ibid.
[36] Ibid.
[37] Ibid.

he would overwhelm his opponents by confusing and daunt-
ing their minds. And it was impossible for anyone, who had
once argued with him, to free himself from these labyrinths."[38]
She blames some of his pedagogical failures on his supposedly
uncultured and difficult personality: "In other ways he was
most unrefined, and subject to violent temper; and this fierce
temper annulled and obliterated the credit he gained from his
learning. For in arguments this man used fists as well as words
and he did not allow his interlocutor simply to lose himself in
embarrassment nor was he satisfied with sewing up his opponent's mouth and condemning him to silence, but forthwith
his hand flew out to tear his beard and hair, and insult quickly
followed insult, in fact the man could not be restrained in the
use of his hands and tongue."[39]

She returns to her criticism of his language, which is perhaps
unjust given that he was not a native Greek speaker, noting
that "his pronunciation was such as you would expect of a
Latin who had come to our country as a young man and learnt
Greek thoroughly but was not quite clear in his articulation,
for he mutilated his syllables here and there. This want of
clearness in his utterance and his dropping the last letters did
not escape even ordinary people and made rhetoricians call
him 'rustic' in his speech. As a result, although his writings
were crammed with dialectical commonplaces, drawn from all
sources, they were decidedly not free from faults of composition
and solecisms."[40]

Despite Italos's apparent shortcomings, the students flocked
to hear "the acknowledged master of all philosophy" in his
expounding of "the doctrines of Plato and Proclus and of the
two philosophers, Porphyry and Iamblichus, but especially the
rules of Aristotle; and he gave instruction in the system to
those who wished, as affording a serviceable tool and it was
on this that he rather prided himself and to this he devoted

---

[38] Comnena (Komnene), *The Alexiad*, Book 5, viii.
[39] Ibid.
[40] Ibid.

his attention."[41] But Anna can spot no greatness, as "he was unequal to exerting a very good influence on his pupils as his violent temper and his general instability of character stood in the way."[42] According to her, he failed to have any positive influence on his learners. After his instruction, they "knew no literary subject accurately, but would pose as dialecticians, making ungainly movements and mad contortions of their limbs, they understood nothing sound but put forth ideas, even those about metempsychosis, in a shadowy way and other similar equally monstrous notions."[43] Comnena is as petty and spiteful towards Italos's students as she is towards him.

The princess argues that Italos's personality negatively affected his teaching. She gives some of the background that may have led up to confrontation with the authorities. Italos "was never able to plumb the depths of philosophy for he was of such a boorish and barbarous disposition that he could not endure teachers even when learning from them. He was full of daring and barbarous rebelliousness and even before learning a thing, imagined he surpassed everybody else and from the very start he entered the lists against Psellus himself."[44] His dialectical approach seemed to lack the scholar's detachment, as he seems to have "caused daily commotions in public meeting places by stringing together sophistical quibbles, putting forward something of the kind and then maintaining an argument to match it."[45] Disappointingly for her, he had friends in high places, including Emperor Michael Ducas and his brothers. They esteemed Italos, though naturally less than they did the great Psellos, towards whom the Calabrian "would always cast heated, furious glances . . . when the latter, like an eagle, soared above his quibbles." Perhaps jealous of the attention Italos received, she notes that "yet they were fond of him, and used him in

---

[41] Comnena (Komnene), *The Alexiad*, Book 5, ix.
[42] Ibid.
[43] Ibid.
[44] Ibid., Book 5, viii.
[45] Ibid.

literary contests; for the Ducases, the Emperor's brothers, and even the Emperor Michael himself, were very literary."[46]

Italos ran into serious conflict when problems with his teaching flared up into open confrontation. He was forced to stand before the Holy Synod. The Church body condemned his Neoplatonist-inspired ideas and forbade him from teaching in any capacity, publicly or privately. Anna Comnena continues with her biased report, portraying Italos as very different from the spiritual fathers of the ideal Irish or Anglo-Saxon educational tradition: "When he was at the height of his popularity with the students, some of whom I have named, he treated them all with contempt and turned many of the feebler-minded to rebellion and made not a few of his own pupils tyrants. And I could mention several of them, had not time obliterated their names from my memory."[47]

The *Alexiad* notes the role of the emperor in education, including his management of the Italos affair: "All this took place before my father was elevated to the throne. On his accession he found all education here in a very poor way and the regular study of letters apparently banished afar, he lost no time in raking the ashes together to see whether some live sparks might perchance be hidden under them. Those who were inclined to learning (and they were but few and had not passed beyond the vestibule of Aristotelian philosophy) he did not cease from encouraging but bade them prefer the study of the sacred writings to Greek literature."[48] The level of philosophy was apparently not up to a high standard. Interestingly, the emperor put Hellenism in a secondary place in the curriculum.

Italos's disrespect of everyone and his poor dialectical skills finally caught up with him, according to the princess. Coming to see that Italos caused confusion and led many astray, the emperor had the Sebastokrator Isaac lead an investigation. Isaac was a *literati* and an experienced and reliable public servant.

---

[46] Comnena (Komnene), *The Alexiad*, Book 5, viii.
[47] Ibid., Book 5, ix.
[48] Ibid.

After agreeing with the report that had been written on Italos, Isaac "openly censured him in a public meeting and then passed him on to the ecclesiastical tribunal by order of the Emperor."

Italos's issues moved from the philosophical to the theological, as he was not merely a poor dialectician, but apparently also a heretic (perhaps proving that unsound reasoning leads to heretical dogma). The princess was harshly critical. She calls him a heretic, as he "was unable to hide his own ignorance, and there he vomited forth doctrines quite foreign to the church's, and in the midst of the ecclesiastical dignitaries he did not cease from acting like a buffoon, and doing other things of a boorish and uncultured nature; the president of the church then was Eustratius Garidas who condemned him to detention within the precincts of the great church in the hopes of bringing him to a better state of mind."[49] Italos apparently outwitted his opponent, with dramatic results: "But, [the] report says that Garidas would more quickly have shared the other's evil doctrines than brought him back to the right path, and Italus won him over entirely to his side. What was the consequence? The whole population of Constantinople surged into the church, shouting for Italus."[50] The *Alexiad* reports that Italos escaped and hid in the church roof.

But people at the court, eventually including the emperor, were troubled by his supposedly heretical doctrines. The report on Italos was given to the emperor, who made the philosopher "recite these chapters from the pulpit in the great church with his head uncovered, and pronounce a curse upon them, while all the congregation listened and repeated the curse."[51] By now, the reader of the *Alexiad* is unsurprised to learn that this did not have the expected effects on the seemingly incorrigible Italos, who went back to teaching heterodox doctrines. This finally led to his excommunication. Some time after that, Italos was brought under control, as reported by Comnena:

---

[49] Comnena (Komnene), *The Alexiad*, Book 5, ix.
[50] Ibid.
[51] Ibid.

Later on, when he professed penitence, his sentence of excommunication was lightened somewhat. And although his doctrines are still recited and cursed, his name is only mentioned indirectly, as it were, and secretly, and the anathema pronounced on him by the church is not pronounced in a voice audible to the congregation. For in his later years he changed his opinions and repented of the error into which he had been led. Furthermore, he denied a belief in metempsychosis and retracted his insulting words about the holy icons of the saints; he also remodelled his teaching about "ideas" so as to make it conform to orthodoxy, and it was quite evident that he condemned himself for having formerly strayed from the straight path.[52]

The defeated Italos was left with no choice but to withdraw to a monastery. His students Leo of Chalcedon, Neibos, and Eustratios of Nicaea went through a similar process, though they were all eventually acquitted.[53] The result of this entire episode was the attempt, however brief, to cordon off theology from philosophy, as the Church banned the application of rational thought and a Hellenistic spirit to theology. In support of the Church, Euthymios Zigabenos wrote *The Dogmatic Panoply* and Niketas Akominatos penned *The Treasure of Orthodoxy*.

Rhetoric seemed to have created far fewer problems in the empire than philosophy or dialectic did. The rhetorician Michael Italikos, the *oikoumenikos didaskalos* at the Patriarchal School in Constantinople, closely followed the teaching of Psellos in literature and philosophy. He likened philosophy to a hermit, and declared rhetoric to be superior because it brings beauty and civility to society. He echoed Psellos in noting the ultimate superiority of theology, as the unique source of understanding the truths that are beyond human expression. As one comes closer to the ineffable, the soul naturally cleanses itself of the ideas from philosophy, rhetoric, and other worldly disciplines.[54] This reveals how the strong eastern Christian preference for

---

[52] Comnena (Komnene), *The Alexiad*, Book 5, ix.
[53] Tatakis, *Byzantine Philosophy*, 171–172.
[54] Ibid., 177.

mysticism, arrived at through ascetic practice, impacted attitudes towards philosophy.

The scholarly achievements of the ninth through twelfth centuries set the stage for later intellectual advancements in the Byzantine Empire and beyond, particularly in fifteenth century Italy. Psellos's writings were at the heart of this for the rest of the empire's history. Gemisthos Plethos used them in his own teachings. The independence of philosophy from Church oversight only grew, as Neoplatonism, inspired by Proclus, increasingly turned against the eastern Church.[55]

---

[55] Tatakis, *Byzantine Philosophy*, 171.

CONCLUSION

THE YEARS 500 TO 1050 AD SAW NO DECI-
sive break with the previous era. Church leaders molded
Greco-Roman paideia to suit their needs. Since it had been
decided that Homer and Virgil were needed to understand the
Bible correctly, these and other Greek and Latin authors were
embraced. Philosophy and dialectic were equally required for
logical expression and the understanding of complex theological
ideas. The Queen of the Sciences, theology, along with its close
partner, Biblical exegesis, could not be undertaken without the
Greek intellectual tools. The Greek New Testament itself was
in fact a product of that Greek intellectual world, as evidenced
by the referral to the *Logos* at the beginning of the Gospel of
John. Clement of Alexandria and Origen had been quite daring
in seeing Christianity as the last and greatest philosophy, in fact
as *the* philosophy, as the true philosophy at which the others
had only been hinting. Nevertheless, Greek paideia remained
at the heart of the Christian classroom.

The forming of this paideia in the half millennium that
we have just seen gave to education and culture a decidedly
Christian orientation. Dialectic, for instance, was clearly in
the service of theology. Christians, however, did not feel the
sort of debt to the Greeks that would oblige them to retain
unnecessary elements. Thus, while the discipline of music grew
by leaps and bounds in some ways, in other ways, it developed
into a more practical and less philosophical discipline, as the
vast majority of teaching and learning related to music was
liturgy-related. Some Greek musical theorists would likely
have dismissed the practical developments as meaningless. As
noted throughout this volume, the most notable advances in
the West involved language, particularly grammar. This set a
very strong foundation for the next period, with the rise of the
scholastics and dialectic as the newly dominant discipline of
the trivium. And natural philosophy would reach new heights

with optics and illumination theory, as represented by Robert Grosseteste. Sciences at the University of Oxford would far outpace early medieval science. Perhaps this was due to the stability brought about by the end of the Viking invasions and the unique institutional stability of the university.

The pedagogical accomplishments of the early medieval western Church are remarkable considering the almost constant political instability, the lack of institutional continuity, and the small libraries. The personalities of the time rose to the occasion, whether it meant making the most out of a relatively-abundant library (Isidore, Bede, the monks at St. Gall) or traveling to the Continent from the British Isles and braving the thick forests and their often-pagan human inhabitants or the politically-anarchic Gaul with its Christian culture in serious decline until Charlemagne. These hardy souls established monasteries, the beachheads for their evangelization and educating. They handed on to the next part of the Middle Ages the precious gift of a relatively well-rooted Christian educational culture and practice. The figures of the next few hundred years would build on the shoulders of these giants.

The Byzantines faced an entirely different set of circumstances, from the dispossession of much of their territories to a single political entity and national culture and a unique Church-state relationship. Even with these differences, much of the education followed the same lines. Despite the breakdown of the Roman Empire's ancient unity into the "two solitudes" of the Greek East and Latin West, enough similarities remained for cooperation and Greek inspiration of the Latin West, especially in later medieval centuries.

BIBLIOGRAPHY

Agapitos, Panagotiotis A. "Grammar, genre and patronage in the twelfth
century: A scientific paradigm and its implications," in *Jahrbücher
des Österreichischen Byzantinistik*, 64, 1–22 (Wien: Österreichische
Akademie der Wissenschaften, 2014).

Alcuin, *Life of Willibrord*. Translated by A. Grieve, in *Willibrord, Missionary in the Netherlands*. London, 1923. https://sourcebooks.fordham.
edu/basis/Alcuin-willbrord.asp.

Alibert, Dominique. La transmission des textes patristiques à l'époque
carolingienne. *Revue des sciences philosophiques et théologiques*. 91. 2007,
7–21. https://doi.org/10.3917/rspt.911.0007.

Ambrose of Milan. "Three Books on the Duties of the Clergy." In *The
Principal Works of St. Ambrose*. Translated by H. De Romestin. Grand
Rapids, Michigan: Wm. B. Eerdmans, 1885.

———. "Exposition of the Christian Faith." In *The Principal Works of St.
Ambrose*. Translated by H. De Romestin. Grand Rapids, Michigan:
Wm. B. Eerdmans, 1885.

———. "Concerning Virgins." In *The Principal Works of St. Ambrose*.
Translated by H. De Romestin. Grand Rapids, Michigan: Wm. B.
Eerdmans, 1885.

———. "On the Decease of his Brother Satyrus." In *The Principal Works
of St. Ambrose*. Translated by H. De Romestin. Grand Rapids, Michigan: Wm. B. Eerdmans, 1885.

Ancient Laws and Institutes of Ireland. Volume 3. Dublin: Alexander Thom
Publisher, 1873. https://archive.org/details/ancientlaws03hancuoft.

The Anglo Saxon Chronicle. Translation by James Ingram. London, 1823.
https://www.gutenberg.org/cache/epub/657/pg657-images.html
[Accessed July 10, 2024].

Anglo Saxon Riddles of the Exeter Book. Translated by Paull Franklin
Baum. 1963. https://en.wikisource.org/wiki/Anglo-Saxon_Riddles_
of_the_Exeter_Book/10.

Anonymous. *Life of Saint Fintán, alias Munnu, abbot of Tech Munnu*.
Translated by Roy Flechner. 2021. https://celt.ucc.ie//published/
T201046/index.html.

Anonymous. *Life of St. Declan of Ardmore*. Translated by P. Power.
London: Irish Texts Society, 1914. https://sourcebooks.fordham.edu/
basis/stdeclan.asp.

Anonymous. *Life of St. Féchín of Fore*. Translated by Whitley Stokes. In
Revue Celtique. Volume 12 1891, 318–353. https://celt.ucc.ie//published/
T201005/index.html.

Anonymous. *On the Life of St. Patrick*. Translated by Whitley Stokes. In *Lives of Saints from the Book of Lismore*. Oxford 1890. https://celt. ucc.ie/published/T201009/index.html.

Aristotle. *Rhetoric*. Translated by W. Rhys Roberts. Megaphone ebooks, 2008.

Assmann, Jan. "Cultural Memory and the Myth of the Axial Age." In *The Axial Age and its Consequences*, edited by Robert Bellah and Hans Joas. Harvard University Press, 2012.

Augustine. *On Order [De Ordine]*. Translated by Silvano Borruso. South Bend, Indiana: St. Augustine's Press, 2007.

Barrett, Graham. "God's Librarian: Isidore of Seville and His Literacy Agenda." In *A Companion to Isidore of Seville*, edited by Andrew Fear and Jamie Wood. Leiden: Brill, 2020.

Barthes, Roland. "L'ancienne rhétorique [Aide-mémoire] Aide-mémoire." In *Communications* 16, no. 1. 1970, 172–223. https://doi.org/10.3406/comm.1970.1236.

Bede. *Ecclesiastical History of the English Nation*. Translated by A.M. Sellar. London: George Bell and Sons, 1907.

———. *Historical Works*. Volume 2. Cambridge, Massachusetts: Harvard University Press, 1963.

Bellah, Robert and Hans Joas, editors. *The Axial Age and its Consequences*. Cambridge, Massachusetts: Harvard University Press, 2012.

Bellenger, Aidan. "A medieval novice's formation: reflection on a fifteenth-century manuscript at Downside Abbey." in *Medieval Monastic Education*, edited by George Ferzoco and Carolyn Muessig. London: Leicester University Press, 2000.

Benedict. *The Rule of St. Benedict*. Collegeville, Minnesota: The Liturgical Press, 1981. https://saintjohnsabbey.org/rule.

Benedict XVI. *Address of His Holiness Benedict XVI. Friday, 12 September 2008* (Rome: Editrice Libreria Vaticana, 2008). https://www.vatican. va/content/benedict-xvi/en/speeches/2008/september/documents/ hf_ben-xvi_spe_20080912_parigi-cultura.html.

Beyer de Ryke, Benoît. "Encyclopédisme." In *Dictionnaire du Moyen Age*, edited by Claude Gauvard *et al*. 475–477. Paris: Presses Universitaires de France, 2004.

Black, Robert. *Humanism and Education in Medieval and Renaissance Italy*. Cambridge: Cambridge University Press, 2001.

Boèce, *Institution Arithmetique*. Translated by Jean-Yves Guillaumin. Paris: Belles Lettres, 1995.

Boethius. "De Trinitate Proemium." In *The Theological Tractates*. Translated by H.F. Stewart. Cambridge, Massachusetts: Harvard University Press, 1968.

Bolgar, R.R. *The Classical Heritage and its Beneficiaries.* Cambridge: Cambridge University Press, 1973.

Bosch Rabell, Magdalena, and Baro Queralt, Xavier. "El Nacimiento de la Retórica Moderna a través de Cipriano Suarez (1524–1593)." In *Comprendre 20*, no.2 (2018). Pages 45–60.

Boulnois, Olivier. "Les États de la Raison: Formes et Fonctions de la Rationalité Médiévale." In *La raison au Moyen Âge*, edited by Dominique Poirel. Paris, Vrin, 2024.

Boynton, Susan. "Training for the liturgy as a form of monastic education." in *Medieval Monastic Education*, edited by George Ferzoco and Carolyn Muessig. London: Leicester University Press, 2000.

Braulio of Zaragoza. "Renotatio." In *Iberian Fathers, Volume 2: Braulio of Saragossa, Fructuosus of Braga*, translated by Claude W. Barlow. Catholic University of America, 1969.

Brown, George Hardin. *A Companion to Bede.* Woodbridge: The Boydell Press, 2009.

Brown, Nancy Marie. *The Abacus and the Cross.* New York: Basic Books, 2010.

Brumberg-Chaumont, Julie. " Raison et Logique au Moyen Âge." In *La raison au Moyen Âge*, edited by Dominique Poirel. Paris, Vrin, 2024.

Brunschwig, Jacques. *et al*, ed. *Le Savoir Grec.* Paris: Flammarion, 2011.

Burkholder, Peter J. "Introduction." In *Alcuin of York's "Propositiones ad Acuendos Juvenes."* https://www.math.muni.cz/~sisma/alcuin/anglicky1.pdf.

Cahill, Thomas. *How the Irish Saved Civilization.* London: Sceptre, 2018.

The Catechism of the Catholic Church. Citta del Vaticano: Libreria Editrice Vaticana, 1993. http://ccc.usccb.org/flipbooks/catechism/index.html.

Clark, J.M. *The Abbey of St Gall as a Centre of Literature and Art.* Cambridge: At the University Press, 1926.

Crialesi, Clelia V. "Les 'Raisons' Mathématiques." In *La raison au Moyen Âge*, edited by Dominique Poirel. Paris, Vrin, 2024.

Columbanus. *First Letter* in *Letters of Columbanus.* Translated by G.S.M. Walker. Dublin: Dublin Institute of Advanced Studies, 2008. https://celt.ucc.ie/published/T201054/index.html.

Comnena (Komnene), Anna. *The Alexiad*, edited and translated by Elizabeth A. Dawes. London: Routledge, Kegan, Paul, 1928. https://sourcebooks.fordham.edu/basis/AnnaComnena-Alexiad00.asp.

Contas, Nicholas. "Introduction," In Maximos the Confessor. *On Difficulties in Sacred Scripture: The Responses to Thalassios.* Translated by Maximos Constas. Washington, D.C.: The Catholic University of America Press, 2018.

Cummings, Brian. *The Literary Culture of the Reformation.* Oxford: Oxford University Press, 2007.

Da Costa, Ricardo. "Las definiciones de las siete artes liberales y mecánicos en la obra de Ramón Llull." In *Anales del Seminario de Historia de la Filosofía*. Volume 2. 2006.

De Bruyne, Edgar. *Etudes d'esthétique médiévale*. Volume 1. Paris: Albin Michel, 1998.

DeGregorario, Scott, editor. *The Cambridge Companion to Bede*. Cambridge: Cambridge University Press, 2010.

Einhard, *The Life of Charlemagne*. Translated by Samuel Epes Turner. Ann Arbor, Michigan: The University of Michigan Press, 1966.

Elfassi, Jacques. "Isidore of Seville and the Etymologies." In *A Companion to Isidore of Seville*, edited by Andrew Fear and Jamie Wood. Leiden: Brill, 2020.

"Enciclopedia." In *Enciclopedia Europea*. Volume IV. Milano: Garzanti, 1977, 496–497.

Fear, Andrew and Jamie Wood. *A Companion to Isidore of Seville*. Leiden: Brill, 2020.

———. "Introduction." In *A Companion to Isidore of Seville*, edited by Andrew Fear and Jamie Wood. Leiden: Brill, 2020.

Ferzoco, George and Carolyn Muessig, editors. *Medieval Monastic Education*, London: Leicester University Press, 2000.

Flusin, Bernard. "La culture écrite." In *Le monde byzantine I: L'Empire romain d'Orient (330–641)*. Paris Presses Universitaires de France, 2012, 257–280.

Flechner, Roy, and Sven Meeder, editors. *The Irish in Early Medieval Europe*. New York: Pagrave, 2016.

Fraga, Jose Carrededo. "Isidore of Seville as a Grammarian." In *A Companion to Isidore of Seville*, edited by Andrew Fear and Jamie Wood. Leiden: Brill, 2020.

García Juan, José Francisco. "La Biblia En 'De Institutione Clericorum' De Rabano Mauro." In *Estudios Bíblicos* 75. No. 2. 2017, 283–318.

Gem, S. Harvey. *An Anglo-Saxon Abbot: Aelfric of Eynsham*. Edinburgh: T & T. Clark, 1912.

Gilson, Etienne. *La philosophie au moyen age*. 2nd edition. Paris: Payot, 1986.

González Ochoa, César. *La música del universe*. México: Universidad Nacional Autónoma de México, 1994.

Graham, Hugh. *The Early Irish Monastic Schools*. Dublin: The Talbot Press, 1923.

———. "Irish Monks and the Transmission of Learning." In *The Catholic Historical Review*. Volume 11, No. 3. 1925, 431–442.

Grant, A.J. editor. *Early Lives of Charlemagne*. London: Alexander Moring, 1905.

Gregory of Nazianzen. *Oration 43. Funeral Oration on the Great S. Basil, Bishop of Cæsarea in Cappadocia*. New Advent, https://www.newadvent.org/fathers/310243.htm.

Gregory of Tours. *The History of the Franks*. Earnest Brehaut, 1916.

Gregory the Great. *The Book of Pastoral Rule*. Translated by George Democopoulos. Crestwood, NY: St. Vladimir's Seminary Press, 2007.

Guillaumin, Jean-Yves. "Introduction." In Boèce, *Institution Arithmetique*. Translated by Jean-Yves Guillaumin. Paris: Belles Lettres, 1995.

———. "Introduction." In Martianus Capella, *Les Noces de Philologie et de Mercure. Livre VII. L'Arithmetique*. Translated by Jean-Baptiste Guillaumin. Paris: Les Belles Lettres, 2003.

———. "Introduction." In Martianus Capella, *Les Noces de Philologie et de Mercure. Livre IX. L'Harmonie*. Translated by Jean-Baptiste Guillaumin. Paris: Les Belles Lettres, 2011.

Habiger Institute. *The Heart of Culture*. Providence, R.I.: Cluny, 2020.

Hadot, Ilsetraut. *Arts libéraux et philosophie dans la pensée antique*. Paris: Études Augustiniennes, 1984).

Henriet, Patrick. " Hagiographie et Raison." In *La raison au Moyen Âge*, edited by Dominique Poirel. Paris, Vrin, 2024.

Huneberc of Heidenheim. *The Hopoeporican of St. Willibald*. Translated by Canon W. R. Brownlow. London, 1895. https://sourcebooks.fordham.edu/basis/willibald.asp.

Hunter Blair, Peter. *The World of Bede*. Cambridge: Cambridge University Press, 2001.

Huyshe, Wentworth. *The Life of Saint Columba*. Dublin: The Educational Company of Ireland, 1922.

Ierodiakonou, Katerina and Dominic O'Meara. "Philosophies." In *The Oxford Handbook of Byzantine Studies*, edited Jeffreys, Elizabeth. Oxford: Oxford University Press, 2008.

Isidore of Seville. *The Etymologies of Isidore of Seville*, edited by Stephan A. Barney, et al, Cambridge: Cambridge University Press, 2006.

Jeffreys, Elizabeth, editor. *The Oxford Handbook of Byzantine Studies*. Oxford: Oxford University Press, 2008.

Jeffreys, Elizabeth. "Rhetoric." In *The Oxford Handbook of Byzantine Studies, edited* by Elizabeth Jeffreys. Oxford: Oxford University Press, 2008.

Jerome. *The Letters of St. Jerome*. Translated by W.H. Fremantle. Edinburgh: T&T Clark, 1892.

John of Damascus, *The Fount of Knowledge* in *Saint John of Damascus: Writings*. Translated by Frederic H. Chase. New York: Fathers of the Church, Inc., 1958.

John Scotus Eriugena, *Periphyseon*. Translated by John O'Meara. Montreal: Bellarmin, 1987.

Jordan, Alexandra Elizabeth. *The influence of Carolingian political initiatives and correctio in ninth-century Brittany and the march: a study of the hagiographical dossiers of saints Machutus, Maglorius and Melanius and their political and ecclesiastical contexts.* University of Durham, Durham E-thesis, 2021. https://etheses.dur.ac.uk/14177/1/Jordan_corrected_thesis000428058.pdf?DDD17+.

Kendall, Calvin B. "Bede and education." In *The Cambridge Companion to Bede*, edited by Scott DeGregorario. Cambridge: Cambridge University Press, 2010.

Kijewska, Agnieszka. "La Conception de la *Vera/Recta Ratio* dans le *Periphyseon de Jean Scot Erigene*, 25–38.

Kramer, Rutger. "'Ecce fabula!' Problem-solving by numbers in the Carolingian world: The case of the *Propositiones ad Acuendos Iuvena*." Austrian Academy of Sciences, 2017. Pp. 15–40. https://www.academia.edu/28403793/Ecce_fabula_Problem_Solving_by_Numbers_in_the_Carolingian_World_The_Case_of_the_Propositiones_ad_Acuendos_Iuvenes.

Lafontaine, Jacques *Isidore de Seville et la culture classique dans l'Espagne wisigothique*, deuxième edition. Paris: Études Augustiniennes, 1983.

Lauxtermann, Marc D. and Mark Whittow, editors. *Byzantium in the Eleventh Century*. London: Routledge, 2017.

Leclercq, Jean. *The Love of Learning and the Desire for God: A Study of Monastic Culture*. Catharine Misrahi, translator. New York: Fordham University Press, 1996.

Lemerle, Paul. *Le premier humanisme byzantine*. Paris: Presses Universitaires France, 1971.

Lemoine, Michel. "Les auteurs classiques dans l'enseignement médiéval : l'état de la question." *Histoire de l'éducation*, no. 74, 1997. Les Humanités classiques, 39–58.

Life of Burchard, Bishop of Worms. Translated by W.L. North. Hannover: Monumenta Germaniae Historica SS 4, 1841. https://sourcebooks.fordham.edu/source/1025burchard-vita.asp.

The Life of St. John the Almsgiver in *Three Byzantine Saints: Contemporary Biographies of St. Daniel the Stylite, St. Theodore of Sykeon and St. John the Almsgiver*. Translated by Elizabeth Dawes. London: 1948. https://sourcebooks.fordham.edu/basis/john-almsgiver.asp.

"Life of Brenainn." In *Lives of Saints from the Book of Lismore*. New York: AMS, 1890.

Long, Fredrick J. *Ancient Rhetoric and Paul's Apology*. Cambridge: Cambridge University Press, 2004.

Long, Micol. "Monastic Practices of Shared Reading as Means of Learning." In *The Annotated Book in the Early Middle Ages: Practices of*

Reading and Writing; Edited by M.J. Teeuwen and I. Van Renswoude. Utrecht Studies in Medieval Literacy. Turnhout: Brepols, 2017, 32–43.

Lopetegui Semperana, Guadalupe. "Teodulfo de Orleans y las Artes Liberales." In *VELEIA.* 2003, 459–476.

Love, Rosalind. "The World of Latin Learning." In *The Cambridge Companion to Bede,* edited by Scott DeGregorario. Cambridge: Cambridge University Press, 2010.

Lucrèce. *De rerum natura.* Translated by Olivier Sers. Paris: Les Belles Lettres, 2012.

Magdalino, Paul. "From 'encyclopedism' to 'humanism': the turning point of Basil II and the millennium." In *Byzantium in the Eleventh Century, edited* by Marc D. Lauxtermann and Mark Whittow. London: Routledge, 2017.

Marenbon, John. *Early Medieval Philosophy (480–1150).* London: Routledge, 2002.

Markopoulos, Athanasios. "In Search For 'Higher Education' In Byzantium." *Zbornik Radova Vizantoloskog Instituta.* 2013, 29–44.

Markopoulos, Athanasios. "Education." In *The Oxford Handbook of Byzantine Studies, edited* by Elizabeth Jeffreys. Oxford: Oxford University Press, 2008.

Marrou, Henri-Irénée. *Histoire de l'éducation dans l'Antiquité. 2. Le monde romain.* Paris: Seuil, 1948.

Martianus Capella. *Les Noces de Philologie et de Mercure. Livre VII. L'Arithmetique* Jean-Baptiste Guillaumin, translator. Paris: Les Belles Lettres, 2003.

———.*Les Noces de Philologie et de Mercure. Livre IX. L'Harmonie.* Jean-Baptiste Guillaumin, translator. Paris: Les Belles Lettres, 2011.

———.*The Marriage of Philology and Mercury.* Translated by William Harris Stahl, Richard Johnson, and E.L. Burge. New York: Columbia University Press, 1977.

Martin, Marie-Madeleine. *Immortal Latin.* Translated by Brian Welter. Waterloo: Arouca Press, 2021.

Maximos the Confessor. *On Difficulties in Sacred Scripture: The Responses to Thalassios.* Translated by Maximos Constas. Washington, D.C.: The Catholic University of America Press.

McKechnie, Paul. "St. Perpetua and Roman Education in A.D. 200." In *L'antiquité Classique.* Volume 63 (1994), 279–291.

McLuhan, Marshall. *The Classical Trivium: The Place of Thomas Nashe in the Learning of his Time,* Corte Madera, California: Gingko Press, 2006.

Meeder, Sven. "Irish Scholars and Carolingian Learning." In *The Irish in Early Medieval Europe,* eds. Roy Flechner and Sven Meeder. New York: Pagrave, 2016.

Miller, Timothy S. "Two Teaching Texts from the Twelfth Century Orphanotropheion," In *Byzantine Authors: Literary Activities and Preoccupations, edited* by John W. Nesbitt. Leiden: Brill, 2007.

Minois, Georges. *Charlemagne.* Paris: Perrin, 2010.

Mir, Gabriel Codina. *Aux Sources de la Pédagogie des Jésuites.* Roma: Institutum Historicum, 1968.

Moos, Peter I. "Le dialogue latin au Moyen Âge: l'exemple d'Evrard d'Ypres." In *Annales. Economies, sociétés, civilisations,* no. 4, (1989), 993–1028.

Moreau, M. Joseph. "L'essor de l'astronomie scientifique chez les Grecs." In *Revue d'histoire des sciences.* Tome 29, n°3. 1976, 193–212.

Muessig, Carolyn. "Learning and mentoring in the twelfth century: Hildegard of Bingen and Herrad of Landsberg." In *Medieval Monastic Education,* edited by George Ferzoco and Carolyn Muessig. London: Leicester University Press, 2000.

Mullett, Margaret and Roger Scott, editors. *Byzantium and the Classical Tradition.* Birmingham: Centre for Byzantine Studies, 1981.

Naas, Valérie. *Le projet encyclopédique de Pline l'Ancien.* Rome: École Française de Rome, 2002.

Nesbitt, John W. editor. *Byzantine Authors: Literary Activities and Preoccupations.* Leiden: Brill, 2007.

Newman, John Henry. *A Benedictine Education.* Providence: Cluny, 2020.

Notker the Stammerer, "Life of Charlemagne." In *Early Lives of Charlemagne,* editor A.J. Grant. London: Alexander Moring, 1905.

Ó Cronínín, Daíbhi. *Early Medieval Ireland.* London: Longman, 1995.

O'Meara, John. "Introduction." In *Periphyseon,* Translated by John O'Meara. Montreal: Bellarmin, 1987.

Ong, Walter J. *Ramus, Method, and the Decay of Dialogue.* Cambridge, Massachusetts: Harvard University Press, 1958.

Panti, Cecilia. "Pythagoras and the Quadrivium from late Antiquity to the Middle Ages." In *Brill's Companion to the Reception of Pythagoras and Pythagoreanism in the Middle Ages and Renaissance,* edited by Irene Caiazzo, Constantinos Macris, and Aurélien Robert, editors. Leiden: Brill, 2022.

Papaioannou, Stratis, editor. *The Oxford Handbook of Byzantine Literature.* Oxford: Oxford University Press, 2023.

Pellegrin, Pierre. "La nature et être." In *Le Savoir Grec,* edited by Jacques Brunschwig et al. Paris: Flammarion, 2011.

Pliny. *The Natural History of Pliny.* Volume 1. Translated by John Bostock and H.T. Riley. London: Taylor and Francis, 1855.

Poirel, Dominique, editor. *La raison au Moyen Âge.* Paris: Vrin, 2024.

Poirel, Dominique. " Introduction." In *La raison au Moyen Âge,* edited by Dominique Poirel. Paris, Vrin, 2024.

Pottakis, Ioannis A. "Socrates, Plato, Aristotle. Three Mentors in Ancient Greece." In *De l'Antiquite a nos jours: histoire et methodes de l'enseigne-ment*. Albi: Presses du Centre universitaire Champollion, 2007, 37–44.

Psellos, Michael. "The *Encomium* of His Mother." Translated by Jeffrey Walker. In *History of Rhetoric*. Volume 8. 2005. Pages 239–313. http://www.documentacatholicaomnia.eu/03d/1017-1078,_Michael_Psellos,_Encomium_of_His_Mother,_EN.pdf.

———. "Letter to Ioannes Xiphilinos." In *Psellos and the Patriarchs*. Translated by Anthony Kaldellis and Ioannis Polemis. Notre Dame, Indiana: University of Notre Dame Press, 2015.

———. "Letter to the Patriarch Kyr Michael Keroullarios." In *Psellos and the Patriarchs*. Translated by Anthony Kaldellis and Ioannis Polemis. Notre Dame, Indiana: University of Notre Dame Press, 2015.

———. *Psellos and the Patriarchs*. Translated by Anthony Kaldellis and Ioannis Polemis. Notre Dame, Indiana: University of Notre Dame Press, 2015.

———. *Synopsis of Rhetoric*. Translated by Jeffrey Walker. 2006. https://www.documentacatholicaomnia.eu/03d/1017-1078,_Michael_Psellos,_Synpsis_of_Rhetoric,_EN.pdf [Accessed July 16, 2024].

Rabanus Maurus. *On the Formation of Clergy*. Translated by Owen M. Phelan. Washington DC: The catholic University of America Press.

Rand, Edward Kennard. "The Classics in the Thirteenth Century." In *Speculum*. 1929, 249–270.

Riché, Pierre. *Ecoles et Enseignement dans le Haut Moyen Age*. Third Edition. Paris: Picard, 1999.

Riché, Pierre and Jacques Verger. *Maîtres et élèves au Moyen Age*. Paris: Pluriel, 2013.

Richer of Reims. *Histoire de Richer*. Tome deuxième. Translated by J. Gaudet. Paris: Jules Renouard, 1845.

Riehle, Alexander. "Rhetorical Practice." In *The Oxford Handbook of Byzantine Literature*, edited by Stratis Papaioannou, Oxford: Oxford University Press, 2023.

Rudolph of Fulda. *Life of Lioba*. Translated by Serenus Cressy. https://sourcebooks.fordham.edu/basis/leoba.asp.

Sandys, John Edwin. *A History of Classical Scholarship*. Cambridge: Cambridge University Press, 1903.

Spitz, Lewis W. "Saint Boniface." In *Concordia Theological Monthly*. Volume 25. 1954, 647–655.

Szabo, Arpad. *Les débuts des mathématiques grecques*. Translated by M. Federspiel. Paris: Vrin, 1977.

Tatakis, Basil. *Byzantine Philosophy*. Translated by Nicholas J. Moutafakis. Indianapolis: Hackett, 2003.

Taylor, Henry Osborn. *The Mediaeval Mind*. Volume 1. London: Macmillan and Co., 1911.

Treadgold, Warren. "The Macedonian Renaissance." In *Renaissances Before the Renaissance: Cultural Revivals of Late Antiquity and the Middle Ages*, edited by Warren Treadgold. Stanford University Press, Stanford, 1984, 75–98.

Vitruvius. *On Architecture*. Translated by Frank Granger. New York: Loeb, 1931.

Wallis, Faith. "Isidore of Seville and Science." In *A Companion to Isidore of Seville*, edited by Andrew Fear and Jamie Wood. Leiden: Brill, 2020.

———. "Bede and science." In *The Cambridge Companion to Bede*, edited by Scott DeGregorario. Cambridge: Cambridge University Press, 2010.

West, Andrew Fleming. *Alcuin and the Rise of the Christian Schools*. New York: Charles Scribner's Son, 1912.

Whitelock, Dorothy. "After Bede." In *A Companion to Bed*, edited by George Hardin Brown. Woodbridge: The Boydell Press, 2009.

Wildman, W.B., *Life of S. Ealdhelm*, London: Chapman and Hall, 1905.

Willibald. *The Life of St. Boniface*. Translated by George Washington Robinson. Cambridge, 1916. https://sourcebooks.fordham.edu/basis/willibald-boniface.asp.

Wolff, Catherine. *L'Education dans le monde romain*. Paris: Picard, 2015.

Wuellner, Bernard. *A Dictionary of Scholastic Philosophy*. Second Edition. Milwaukee: The Bruce Publishing Company, 1966.

www.ingramcontent.com/pod-product-compliance
Lightning Source LLC
Chambersburg PA
CBHW030910120626
46554CB00001B/95